*Glasnost' in Action*

## Also by Alec Nove

*Socialism, Economics, and Development*
*The Economics of Feasible Socialism*
*Political Economy and Soviet Socialism*
*The Soviet Economic System*
*Was Stalin Really Necessary?*
*Economic History of the USSR*
*Stalinism and After*
*Efficiency Criteria for Nationalized Industries*

# Glasnost' in Action
## Cultural Renaissance in Russia

ALEC NOVE

Boston
**UNWIN HYMAN**
London    Sydney    Wellington

**Unwin Hyman, Inc.**
8 Winchester Place, Winchester, Mass. 01890, USA

Published by the Academic Division of
**Unwin Hyman Ltd**
15/17 Broadwick Street, London W1V 1FP, UK

Allen & Unwin (Australia) Ltd,
8 Napier Street, North Sydney, NSW 2060, Australia

Allen & Unwin (New Zealand) Ltd in association with the
Port Nicholson Press Ltd,
Compusales Building, 75 Ghuznee Street, Wellington 1, New Zealand


First published in 1989

---

**Library of Congress Cataloging-in-Publication Data**

Nove, Alec.
  Glasnost in action: cultural renaissance in Russia/Alec Nove.
     p.    cm.
Includes index.
ISBN 0–04–445340–X.—ISBN 0–04–445440–6 (pbk.)
(1. Soviet Union—Intellectual life—20th century. 2. Soviet Union—
Politics and government—1982– . 3. Soviet Union—Economic
conditions—1976– . I. Title.
DK287.N67 1989
947.085′4—dc19                                                88–35300
                                                                  CIP

---

**British Library Cataloguing in Publication Data**

Nove, Alec, *1915–*
Glasnost' in action: cultural renaissance in Russia.
1. Soviet Union. Society
I. Title
947.085′4

ISBN 0-04-445340-X
ISBN 0-04-445440-6 (pbk.)

---

Typeset in 10 on 12 point Sabon by Computape (Pickering)
and printed in Great Britain by
The University Press, Cambridge

# Contents

# Preface

What is now happening in the Soviet Union is a real cultural renaissance, or revolution. This book represents an attempt to give to the nonspecialist reader some notion of what has happened in the Soviet cultural scene in recent years. By *cultural* I mean not only literature, but developments in history, law, the social sciences, the new frankness on issues such as nationalism, religion, women, corruption, and much else besides. The object is not to discuss the merits of this or that interpretation to be found in the Soviet publications, but to show what is discussed, contrasting it with past bans, taboos, and silences. For example, I note the wide-ranging debate on the nature of Stalinism, or on the role of the Party in society, but it is not in this book my task to criticise the debaters or to introduce my own views on these subjects.

Much of the new material now published is highly critical of the past and of the present. It may be thought that an assembly of such material is anti-Soviet propaganda. This is emphatically not so; it is not at all my purpose. Under Gorbachev previously hidden evils are exposed to view. That is good. It does not, of course, guarantee that they will be put right, but it is a precondition for any real attempt to put them right. For example, one welcomes the appearance of articles denouncing abuses of the legal system, or the many short-comings in medical services, in the same way one welcomes a correct diagnosis of a disease; action may then be taken to effect a cure. A cure may not be found, but that is another story.

Almost all the sources used are from periodicals, occasionally from newspapers. The *tolstyi zhurnal* ("fat periodical") has no equivalent in the Anglo-Saxon literary world today, but it should be recalled that many of Dickens's novels were serialized in the English equivalents, which then had a wide readership (e.g., *Strand Magazine* and *Blackwoods*). Books take a long time to publish, and what has already appeared in the periodicals may (or may not) appear later in book form. The periodicals are also vitally important as organs of opinion, expressing (whenever this is allowed) the ideas of various intellectual strata. Also, it has been the case for many decades that they have devoted space to challenging ideas on history, economics, the village, sociology, and politics, which did not find a welcome in the specialist professional journals. In the fifties and sixties a courageous editor, Alexander Tvardovsky, was able to make of *Novyi mir* the organ of the progressive intelligentsia, and it was a (reactionary) political act of importance that he was dismissed in 1970. Under Gorbachev these literary monthlies began a sort of competition with one another as to who could publish the previously unpublishable. Since 1985 *Novyi mir*, first under Karpov, then under Zalygin, resumed its former role, but was now joined by many other previously timid or undistinguished publications: *Znamya*, *Druzhba narodov*, *Oktyabr'*, and others. Even the provinces joined in. Though in general it is true that the provincial press is far more under the thumb of whoever is the local party secretary, the Moscow journals have a nationwide circulation and a very large and growing audience: *Novyi mir* alone sells 1,150,000 copies per issue.

The illustrated weekly *Ogonyok*, previously dull and conservative, has been transformed under its lively new editor, V. Korotich, and has published strikingly original and challenging material. So has the previously unreadable *Moscow News*, which, alongside its foreign-language editions, prints in Russian (about 400,000 copies, which are instantly snapped up) under the title *Moskovskie novosti*. Finally, in recent years the daily press from time to time devotes whole pages to some major issue or revelation: thus the most thorough exposure of the notorious "Leningrad affair" appeared, of all places, in *Komsomolskaya Pravda*. Then there is television and radio, at one time drearily conformist, now anything but. It is now possible, with the help of a satellite dish, to receive Moscow TV in Glasgow or London.

In fact, the problem is one of *embarras de richeses*. Far too many interesting materials now appear, far more than any one person can read even if he or she devotes his or her time to nothing else. Inevitably one relies on others who may notice something. The following is a perfectly authentic example, from which this manuscript has benefited:

**M. Dewhirst:** *Have you read the latest* Nauka i zhizn?
**A.N.:** *That's a popular science monthly. I don't read it.*
**M.D.:** *You should, though. Excellent article by Popov.*
**A.N.:** *Oh. Well, I will.*

A week later in Budapest:

**Hungarian colleague:** *Did you read Popov in* Nauka i zhizn?
**A.N.:** *Oh. Heard about it. Will do. We have it in the library.*

Next day, still in Budapest:

**Visiting Soviet economist:** Did *you read Popov* . . . ?

A week later, in Glasgow, A.N. reads Popov. Some might say that this is not a scientific way to conduct research. Agreed, but one does what one can.

So I take this opportunity to thank my Glasgow colleagues Martin Dewhirst, René Beerman, and Tanya Frisby for their help in drawing attention to the many things that I have missed. Also I benefited (in Chapter 6) from being able to refer to the remarkably complete *Encyclopaedia of Russian Literature from 1917* written in Germany by Wolfgang Kasak (it has been published in London in a Russian translation: *Entsiklopedicheski slovar' russkoi literatury s 1917 goda*, Overseas Publications Exchange, London, 1988). Finally, Elizabeth Hunter did the impossible in putting chaotic bits of paper into a typed manuscript, and Walter Joyce found obscure references. So many thanks to them. Note that, except where otherwise stated, all translations are by me.

*Glasnost' in Action*

# CHAPTER 1

# Introduction: What Was

To understand the scale of change, it is necessary to paint, however briefly, a picture of the status quo ante. This is no easy matter. Since Stalin's death the Soviet cultural scene has gone through one false spring, the Khrushchev "thaw", before shifting into the disappointingly grey period of Brezhnevite stagnation. However, we must not oversimplify. Under Brezhnev too there emerged some challenging and original material, while many matters now freely discussed remained taboo even at the height of Khrushchev's "liberal" period. And even under Stalin's despotism certain types of critical material could see the light of day.

Let us begin with the theory of "socialist realism", which emerged from the first writers' congress in 1934, and which dominated official doctrine for close to fifty years. In its original form it could be interpreted simply as realism (e.g., opposition to abstract art and symbolist poetry) combined with socialist commitment. However, it was linked with *partiinost'*, rendered variously as "Party-spirit" and "partisanship", and with what Lenin is alleged to have written in 1905 about "Party literature". It seems to me that Lenin (not for the first or last time) was misquoted: he did indeed insist on Party members producing literature of value to the Party, but he wrote this at a time when non-Party members (the vast majority, of course) were busy producing non-Party literature, which he neither wished nor was able to ban. There is another misunderstanding linked with Lenin. In conversation with the German communist Klara Zetkin, he is alleged to have said, "Literature should be understandable by the people" (*ponyatna narodu*), which was interpreted as meaning that it should be at a level at which people would understand it without difficulty. However, it seems that what he did say was that "literature should be understood by the people" (*ponyata narodom*), which implies that the people should raise their level of understanding, rather than that authors should lower themselves to the existing level. Applied to music, it would mean that Shostakovich could be allowed to write preludes and fugues, and not be criticised for not writing hummable tunes. Alas, in 1948 it was the narrower view that prevailed—and it is a sobering thought that the then secretary of the musicians' union, Khrennikov, a mediocrity who then attacked Shostakovich and Prokofiev for "formalism", should still be secretary of that union forty years on (no doubt now making "sincere" speeches about "perestroika"; such men are weathercocks with no views of their own). E. Ryazanov (*Moskovskie novosti*, 4 Sept. 1988) cites a good definition of "socialist realism": "It is an artistic style that tells the bosses what they want to hear in a form they can understand."

Under Stalin, "socialist realism" became further distorted because of the yawning gap between what was and what should be, between the official representation of reality and real life. It became necessary to be optimistic. Music had to be in a major key; in literature there was even a theory of *bezkonfliknost'*, of a homogeneous society without contradictions or serious conflicts. Real miseries and tragedies were not to be mentioned. Just as Stalin, in 1948, announced that Moscow had "abolished slums", at a time when overcrowding and neglect of the housing stock had reached an all-time high, so the peasants' misery had to be portrayed as prosperous happiness. Two examples of such "realism" will suffice. One was told me by a colleague who swears that he witnessed it himself. In Moscow in 1952 a film was shown, *Cavalier of the Golden Star*, in which well-dressed peasants were feasting at a well-stocked table. Sitting in front of him were two peasants. When the film ended, one of them asked: "Where is all this supposed to be?" The other peasant replied: "Dunno, probably somewhere in America."

But the *reductio ad absurdum* of "socialist realism" I saw myself. On my first visit to Russia (since my early childhood) in 1955, hotels and public buildings were still decorated with "Stalinist" pictures and statues. One painting, repeatedly copied by the hack-painters, showed Stalin in a napoleonic pose, with, in the background, *electric tractors*, which were powered by long cables attached to long-distance transmission lines (the sort which stretch from pylon to pylon). Not only were there no electric tractors (of this or any other kind), but at this period collective-farms were barred from obtaining electricity from the public grid!

Culture suffered acutely under Stalin from the arrests and killings of such admirable creative writers and theatre directors as Mandelshtam, Kharms, Babel, Pilnyak, Meyerhold, Tairov, Klyuev, Yasenski. Talented poets, for example Zabolotsky, survived years of prison and camp. The highly original poet Marina Tsvetayeva returned to Russia from Paris in 1937: her husband was shot, her daughter arrested, and she hanged herself. Anna Akhmatova, surely among the finest poets of the century, and Mikhail Zoshchenko, a uniquely gifted humorist, were denounced in 1946 in foul language by Zhdanov, and silenced. Akhmatova's husband and son were sent to the Gulag, though by some freak of fate Stalin had her evacuated from besieged Leningrad. Such great writers as Mikhail Bulgakov were almost totally censored (though Stalin reportedly saw his play *Days of the Turbins*, known here as *The White Guard*, fourteen times). He died in 1940 of natural causes. His masterpiece, *Master and Margarita*, first reached the public in 1967 under Brezhnev. Another great prose writer, Andrei Platonov, remained almost unknown; his major works stayed under wraps until the era of *glasnost'*. Great were the losses through self-censorship. Talented writers such as Konstantin Fedin reduced themselves to the level of Party hacks. They and their like were then to act as a barrier to originality and talent also after Stalin died.

It must be stressed that the general policy toward the arts reflected the tastes and prejudices of the official class, and since the official class which came into its own in Stalin's time was recruited predominantly from the ranks of ordinary people, they did reflect the ill-educated popular taste. Party intellectuals of an earlier generation—Lunacharsky, Bukharin, Trotsky—were far more tolerant of, and interested in, intellectual production and artistic originality. The taste of Stalin's cultural commissars was probably little different from that of provincial councillors in Britain or America. The difference was that these provincial councillors had neither the power nor the duty to interfere in artistic production. (One could add some thoughts about the taste of Hollywood cinema moguls, or television network bosses, but this takes us too far afield.) In the USSR, through a (distorted and vulgarized) "Marxism-Leninism" the political commissars led by Stalin claimed total control, refused to recognise cultural autonomy in any sphere, denounced art for art's sake. It is a question worth putting, and no attempt will be made to answer it: How far was this a straitjacket imposed by the despot on his unwilling subjects, or how much was due to the *trahison des clercs*, zealots, or time-servers rushing in to do what they believed was the despot's bidding, denouncing their more independent-minded colleagues?

Science and technology were also severely damaged. The tragic fate of the great geneticist Vavilov and the triumph of the ignorant charlatan Lysenko have been much written about. Less well known was the fate of such highly talented men as the aircraft designers Tupolev and Petylakov and the rocket specialist Korolev; they were all arrested in 1937, but then, on Beria's order, they were set to design aircraft in a special prison and so they survived. (This is described by a former fellow prisoner, L. Kerber, in *Moskovskie novosti*, 20 Nov. 1987.) There were some ignorant attacks on Einstein's theory as contrary to dialectical materialism, but physics was protected because even Stalin understood its potential. However, especially in the postwar years, the campaign against "kowtowing to the West" was accompanied by the condemnation of many Western scientific theories, the forced isolation of Soviet science, absurd declarations to the effect that Russians had invented everything from the steam engine to radio. (A whole category of Soviet jokes exist on this theme, under the general rubric of "Russia—motherland of elephants". One example: "Russian watches go faster than any other watches." In Stalin's time, this joke could cost the teller ten years.) This may be the place to mention two semicomic eipsodes, both relating to the *Great Soviet Encyclopaedia* and to the year 1953. The volume, containing a portrait and laudatory article on Beria, had appeared the previous year. When he was arrested, all subscribers (including Glasgow University Library) received a note to the effect that the pages concerned were to be cut out with scissors or a razor blade, and pages enclosed with the note substituted. These pages were devoted to the Bering Straits! The other instance related to a short entry on an eminent medical scientist named Zelenin. He was arrested just when the volume with the letter Z (seventh in the Russian alphabet) was already on press. A hasty substitution occurred: Zelenin was replaced by a short note on *Zelenaya lyagushka*, "green frog", thereby providing the only known instance of a professor actually turning into a frog. Readers will be glad to know that Zelenin was released, and the "green frog" disappeared from subsequent editions of the encyclopaedia!

Was there then no criticism in the Stalin era? There was, but it was limited in two basic ways. "Official" criticism presaged, or more often followed, the fall of the individual criticised or the demise of his or her policies. And criticism of specific deficiencies could and did appear: thus some shoes were of poor quality, some managers produced goods which were too heavy to fulfill a plan in tons, some bureaucrats behaved bureaucratically. Scapegoats abounded. But all this could never be seen as a criticism of the *system*, as distinct from the performance of specific, usually low-level executants.

Workers on the "artistic front" (they loved military terminology!) were supposed to act as "engineers of the human soul", to help the Party to remold Man—and to ensure his loyalty and obedience to the Party and to its one and only leader, the greatest genius of mankind, Joseph Vissarionovich, the father of his people, "the Lenin of today".

There was one odd exception. In the last months of Stalin's rule, Valentin Ovechkin was allowed to publish the first installment of *Rayonnye budni* (in *Novyi mir*, No. 9, 1952), wherein he generalized about rural Party secretaries who ignored peasant interests and requisitioned crops ruthlessly "for the needs of the state". We will have occasion to refer to Ovechkin in a more recent context. How did the then editor dare to publish him in 1952?

Stalin died in March 1953. There followed a "thaw", and one must note both the similarities and the contrasts with what happened after 1985. The first "swallow" that almost made a summer was an article by Pomerantsev in *Novyi mir* of December 1953, with the innocent-sounding title "On Sincerity in Literature". His suggestion that sincerity, and not just following the Party line, was a key requirement for artistic production caused a furor—and the dismissal of Tvardovsky, the editor! But better times were ahead. The state of the peasantry—and it was a sorry state indeed—led to a whole crop of critical sketches and stories: Ovechkin again, then Abramov, Yashin, Dorosh, and Mozhayev (see my "The Peasants in Soviet Literature", reprinted in *Was Stalin Really Necessary?*, Allen & Unwin, 1963). Since action was to be taken to remedy such notorious "minuses" as overcrowded housing, shoddy consumer goods, and the miserable conditions of the peasantry, these could be more freely commented upon. Dudintsev's *Not by Bread Alone* made a sensation, and was subject to attack, because it did touch, however obliquely, on the privileges associated with power and its abuse. Economics too awoke from its long enforced sleep. Stalin's last work was on economics (a recent article in *Pravda* referred to economics as "Stalin's last victim"). In 1955, a leading survivor-economist, V. Dyachenko, expressed himself as follows: "Until recently, dogmatism and scholasticism (*nachyotnichestvo*) showed itself quite openly in quotationism. Instead of independent and deep economic research, the authors of many works busied themselves with a selection of, and commentary on, quotations. Facts were selected and presented merely to illustrate and to confirm the assertions contained in the quotations. Matters went so far that the number of quotations was regarded as an indication of the author's erudition. An economist who found a quotation which had not been used many times in the works of other economists considered himself a creative researcher. After serious criticism of dogmatism and scholasticism in the Party press, quotationism diminished, but only on the surface. In many instances matters went no further than the omission of quotation marks, editorial redrafting of the quotations, but in essence things remained unchanged." He went on: "The elaboration of key problems of political economy is most backward. For many years not a single solid theoretical work in this field has been published." And, even more significantly: "Since the economic discussions of 1951, it has become customary in every work to refer to the objective character of economic laws of socialism, yet not a single work thoroughly examines in what the objective character of this or that law finds expression, how its requirement shows itself, in what respect and how breaches of these requirements can be identified" (*Voprosy ekonomiki*, No. 10, 1955).

This was before Khrushchev's so-called secret speech to the 20th Party Congress (February 1956), the contents of which (not published in the USSR) were read to hundreds of thousands, if not millions, at closed meetings throughout the country. The period 1955–56 also saw mass amnesties of political prisoners and exiles, and also some overdue social reforms: a minimum wage, improved pensions (previously the ordinary citizen's pensions were derisory; even after an average increase of 80% they remained small), elimination of tuition fees in secondary schools and in higher education, repeal of the law forbidding workers freely to change their jobs, and higher prices for peasant producers.

Against this background, literature recovered its voice. Erenburg's novel *The Thaw* caught the atmosphere. Since the present book centres on *glasnost'* of the Gorbachev period, there cannot be the space for a full view of the "Khrushchev thaw". I will confine myself to setting out the limits which, even at its height, it was impossible to transcend.

First, Stalin: as Khrushchev said, he was a good Party man until roughly 1934 (i.e., he was right to defeat various oppositions, and to collectivize the peasantry, and to launch the five-year plans), but then he turned to cruel repression against honest Party members and established a "cult of personality". Innocent victims named included the military (Tukhachevsky and his fellow generals), and such apparently loyal "Stalinists" as Eikhe, Postyshev and a number of secondary political figures were rehabilitated as well. Little was said about the countless "ordinary" victims, and in this respect the publication of Solzhenitsyn's *One Day in the Life of Ivan Deniso-*

*vich* constituted a sort of landmark, a high point of "permissiveness" in the 1960s, only because Khrushchev himself intervened. A number of major "cultural" victims were also rehabilitated and small editions appeared of works by Babel and Mandelshtam. However, no formal criticism was made of the infamous "Zhdanov" decrees which condemned Akhmatova and Zoshchenko—though selected works by these two authors did also appear. Hints about the circumstances of the Kirov murder and the so-called Leningrad affair (the killing in 1950 of Kuznetsov, Voznesensky, and many other Party leaders linked with Leningrad) were not followed by any explanation or analysis. The big show trials of "oppositionists" in the thirties were left untouched, the principal victims (Bukharin, Rykov, Kamenev) unrehabilitated. Trotsky remained an unperson. No serious history of the Party could be written. Such excellent "labour camp" memoirs as the two volumes by Evgeniya Ginsburg were published only abroad—though the author was not punished for this. Or to take another example: almost all the members of the wartime Jewish antifascist committee, arrested in 1948–49, were shot in 1952. Each of the families was informed in 1956 that this had been so, and also that their husbands and fathers had been innocent. But no public announcement, or any press reference whatever, was allowed.

Nonetheless, the atmosphere grew much less repressive. There was universal praise for Shostakovich; Stravinsky visited his native land and met Khrushchev. Soviet orchestras, soloists, choirs, athletes, and scientists were allowed to travel to the West—subject to many restrictions, to be sure. Western scholars and cultural figures visited Russia. All this did not happen without the odd snag, sometimes a comic one. Thus it appears that one Western scholar proposed the following research subject: "the struggle of the Ukrainian nationalists against the Bolsheviks, 1918–21". This was firmly rejected by the Soviet side, and the following was accepted instead: "the struggle of the Bolsheviks against the Ukrainian nationalists, 1918–21". Soviet scholars were usually sent as "delegations", under discipline. It is said that at one conference (of Africanists) two British scholars differed in their evaluation of the chief Soviet delegate's speech. Asked for his opinion on the session, the Soviet scholar replied: "We have done well. We have succeeded in splitting the British delegation."

These were all parts of a definitely "liberalizing" trend. Interestingly, the most "liberal" were the literary monthlies, notably *Novyi mir* under its courageous editor, Alexander Tvardovsky (reappointed in 1958). The specialist journals were much more cautious, more in the hands of timid orthodox editors. Thus the historian Burdzhalov got into trouble for his first-rate monograph on the revolution that overthrew the Tsar in 1917, which challenged established myths. Or, to take a very different example, the critique of official peasant policy, which included scarcely veiled criticisms of some "campaigns" waged by Khrushchev himself, appeared in the literary monthlies, while the agricultural journals remained dull and orthodox.

There were some setbacks, as when Khrushchev attacked abstract modern art, having been shown some examples at an avant-garde exhibition. He was intolerant of religion. He was also worried about the role of intellectuals in the Hungarian and Polish events of 1956, and sought to set limits on "labour camp" literature. It was during his period of rule that Pasternak was denounced for *Dr. Zhivago*. (It is a measure of the scale of change that his novel seems so innocent, so harmless, in today's context.) Khrushchev was an inconsistent, willful, well-meaning, unusual character. His fall led rapidly to a counterattack by the hard-liners. It must be stressed that at no time under Brezhnev was there a return to full-fledged "Stalinism". Nonetheless, many advanced "liberal" positions were lost, and many of the most active proponents of *glasnost'* today are those who had carried the torch of cultural liberty in the best years of Khrushchev.

The rot set in with the prosecution of Sinyavski and Daniel, in 1965, for sending works for publication in the West. Soon the doors were closing in the Institute of History: thus Nekrich's critical study *June 1941*, which showed Stalin's failure to heed warnings, was first published with the censor's approval, and then denounced as no longer permissible. (There were, however, a whole series of war memoirs by generals, some of which did cast some light on the early disasters.) In the same institute, Danilov and several talented colleagues were tackling the thorny subject of the history of collectivization. They were ordered to stop their work, and the newly appointed Party ideologist-"historian", S. P. Trapeznikov, came out with the anodyne official version: yes, there were some excesses, but all was basically done right. Rehabilitations ceased. Worse, biographical data even on the previously rehabilitated now ceased to indicate the fact that they had been arrested and shot. True, the date of death (above all, the fatal year 1937) suggested what their fate was, but presumably even in 1937 *someone* must have died of natural causes! Stalin was not put back on his pedestal, though—as a sort of compromise—a statue of the tyrant was put up by the Kremlin wall, in no conspicuous position, with oddly downcast eyes. And, alas, Tvardovsky was dismissed from the editorship of *Novyi mir* in 1970. The Czech events of 1968 strengthened the hard-liners' position. In the words of V. Lakshin, "The Prague spring affected our position in a most lamentable way" (*Znamya*, No. 8, 1988).

Obstacles mounted for those desiring to touch "awkward" themes. The KGB forced Solzhenitsyn into exile, and also made life difficult for many intellectuals who were by no means "dissidents". Two examples can be cited: neither the novelist Viktor Nekrasov nor that fine linguist and literary analyst Efim Etkind, both of whom ended up in Paris, was a political activist; even a moderately tolerant regime should have found room for them in the USSR. Those whom it considered misfits, as well as real dissidents, were often allowed or even forced to emigrate—which, though it lost Russia much talent, was certainly a more humane method than sending them to die in the Kolyma camp complex. A sizable part of original critical literature circulated in *samizdat*, or was published abroad (*Tamizdat*), without decisive action to suppress the authors. Though some arrests were made, the number of political prisoners remained a small fraction of what it had been under Stalin, and it is noteworthy that no one has been executed for an explicitly political reason since 1954 (when the victims were some of Beria's secret-police henchmen). The early seventies also saw a sizable Jewish emigration, and it is useful in this context to distinguish between "Russified" intellectuals who went abroad because conditions made it difficult for them to remain (two examples were the above-named Etkind and the balladeer Alexander Galich) and those who could say—as one did—"I did not emigrate from the Soviet Union, I emigrated from Russia"—that is, those who emigrated as Jews. Anyhow, Jewish questions, including that of emigration, were hardly ever referred to in the press or the media, save in the context of denunciations of "Zionism" and Israel.

But to return to the cultural scene under Brezhnev. It was by no means a desert. Some flowers did bloom. Novels and stories of value appeared, by Abramov, Rasputin, Shukshin, Tendryakov, Trifonov. For example, Trifonov was able to raise some awkward questions about the revolution and more recent times in novels published in the years 1976 and 1981. The excellent Kirghiz novelist Aitmatov's *I bolshe veka dlitsa den'*, which raised important issues of national traditions, memory, and religion, appeared in 1980. However, the limits were there, if not consistently applied. When a group of progressive writers prepared and circulated an uncensored almanac, *Metropol'*, this was strongly disapproved of, and some of the editors (for instance Aksyonov) emigrated, though others were able to continue writing and, like the poet-satirist Fazil Iskander, to re-emerge into prominence under *glasnost'*.

It is well known that many works published and films shown in the period of *glasnost'* were created—and put on the shelf—in the years of Brezhnev, or in some cases even earlier. Thus Vasili Grossman's great novel *Life and Fate* was completed in 1961, but the submission of the manuscript led not to publication but to the "arrest" of every copy (the author died at liberty, bemoaning what he believed to be the destruction of his magnum opus).

It might be important for the uninformed reader that I explain the motives of the censorship, exercised not only by the formal censoring body (*Glavlit*), but also by the editorial staffs. It is not by any means a purely *political* censorship as we might understand the word. Here are a few examples. Historians or novelists would be forbidden to criticise figures of the remote past: thus Kutuzov was to be a great general, Peter was definitely to be the Great. Of history since 1917 it is unnecessary to speak. Officials "graded" composers, authors, painters, into categories which became pedagogically fixed: "genius", "great", "outstanding", and so on. Even fictional characters achieved a sort of uncriticability: thus Tatiana in Pushkin's *Evgeni Onegin* was a Good Russian Woman. Nearer our own times, the novelist Anatoli Kuznetsov had problems describing the entry of the German army into Kiev in 1941. The problem was not the fact of that entry, which no one disputed, but a paragraph on the large size of German horses. This was thought by the censor to demean Russian horses! One poet was told that he could not in his poem start five consecutive lines with the same word. On being shown examples from nineteenth-century literature, the editor replied: "That's the classics". The balladeer-poet-singer Bulat Okudzhava has told that, when a collection of his poems was being prepared for the press, the publisher refused his suggestion for a title, *Poslednii trolleibus* ("The Last Trolleybus", one of his most popular songs) because it implied a minor key, it was sad, not uplifting; he substituted the title of another of the poems, "The Joyful Drummer". For the same reason his songs were for years not recorded. The same fate befell the exceptionally original poems and songs of Vladimir Vysotski. Unofficial tape recordings made these two (very different) talented men enormously popular all the same.

Efim Etkind has explained how he fell into disfavour in Leningrad for publishing a remark to the effect that the high quality of Russian translations of foreign poetry was due in part to the fact that poets had had difficulty in getting their own original work published. Or to take a completely different example: a book about the critically minded intellectual Chaadaev could only be published in 1987, though Chaadaev wrote in the reign of Nicholas I. The reason: he was critical also of *Russia*'s contribution to civilization.

Nationalism of any kind was seen as a highly sensitive issue. True, examples of *Russian* nationalism did appear, but in its more extreme manifestations it was felt to be dangerous in a multinational state. The line insisted upon was that the USSR had basically solved the national question. Any non-Russian nationalisms were severely discouraged.

So, to repeat, while the scene was not wholly bleak, and repression was neither massive nor bloody, the arts did suffer a decline. We heard less of "socialist realism", even less of anything to do with "engineers of the human soul". It was more a question of avoiding raising or touching awkward questions, of care not to step out of line, the line being defined by cultural bureaucrats characterised by mediocrity and often by just plain ignorance. Their obstructionism and obscurantism drove such lively intellects as the theatre director Lyubimov to fury—and into voluntary exile. Typical of the grey timidity which characterised the period was the fact that when Khrushchev died, no obituary could be published. The big questions concerning Russia's past could not be asked. Khrushchev in a careless moment had spoken of overtaking America economically in the seventies, and introducing the first elements of "full communism" by 1980. This was now to be forgotten, and instead the existing situation was labeled "developed (or mature) socialism".

Which brings me to the state of the social sciences. Again, a full account cannot be attempted here, but a few remarks must be made. Sociology, long almost a dirty word, began to revive under Khrushchev's rule, meeting resistance from those ideologists who maintained that Marxism-Leninism had said it all. Nonetheless, this left room for applied sociology, and efforts were made to create institutes for this purpose. But this proved too much for the political censors: a genuine study of the real contradictions of the real Soviet society was too hot a potato. Instead, it was asserted that Soviet society was united, cohesive, monolithic. The heretical would-be sociologists were scattered by a purge of that discipline in 1972. Political science never got off the ground as such. Since nature abhors a vacuum, some of what we call political science found expression in the Institute of State and Law, and some appeared under the name of philosophy, and both these disciplines sought to block the emergence of a separate political science discipline, to defend their "territory". Nor was the time yet ripe for any serious inquiry into the nature of Soviet "elections" or the real (as distinct from the formal) functioning of Soviets at all levels.

Statistics, a victim of Stalinism, revived in 1956, with the first publication of a statistical annual since 1938. The volume of data increased, though with some gaps and regrettable lack of clear definitions and critical comment. However, in the mid-seventies figures began to disappear; such as for the production of grain, exports of nonferrous metals, imports of oil, and infant mortality. Output and price indices were of dubious reliability, but few were allowed to say so. Defence expenditure under Brezhnev must have risen sharply, as efforts were made to catch up to the United States, but official expenditure figures remained (incredibly) modest. Economists complained about the inadequacy of their statistical "ration".

Economics, however, did move ahead. Already in the late fifties, with the vigorous advocacy of Nemchinov, the talented economists Kantorovich and Novozhilov put forward new ideas on programming techniques and approaches to optimal planning and the prices appropriate to it, repelling the counterattacks of dogmatists armed with a (misunderstood) labour theory of value. Publicity was given to the moderate reforming ideas of Liberman. A mathematical-economics institute was set up. Critical material multiplied: on waste-inducing success indicators (e.g., plans in tons or in roubles of turnover, which actually penalised economy in metal or in costs), irrational investment choices, lack of stimulus for quality or the satisfaction of user needs, shortages, queues. A few bold spirits raised the question of market-type reforms, for example G. Lisichkin, in his pamphlet *Plan i rynok* ("Plan and Market"), published in 1966. While he and his like were thrust aside (sent away on harmless little jobs), the ills of the economy continued to insist upon being given consideration. The Novosibirsk branch of the Academy published a bright and critical journal, known by its initial letters as *EKO*, and its editor, Aganbegyan, did useful work in giving publicity to radical ideas. The outline was forming of an alternative to the centralised planning system inherited from Stalin—and little changed in its essentials. Perhaps a useful way of showing which "reform" ideas were already current is to refer to my article, written in 1977, titled "The Economic Problems of Brezhnev's Successors" (*Journal of International Affairs*, Fall/Winter 1978). I presented it in the guise of a report by a team of reforming economists. A comparison between this article and the reform programme actually adopted in 1987 shows a great many similarities. This was not due to any especial perspicacity on my part; I simply summarised the known (and published) opinions of the would-be reformers. Thus, to take one example, the need for prices to reflect not only effort (cost) but also result (use-value, demand) was forthrightly expressed by Novozhilov and also by Petrakov and other progressive economists. However, the forces of inertia were far too strong and no action was taken. (Indeed, prices have yet to be reformed at the time of writing these words, in the second half of 1988.) The woes of agriculture were often the subject of press comment, but the chosen remedies, essentially bureaucratic in nature, led to waste of investment resources on a massive scale, while the USSR turned into the world's largest importer of grain.

What was lacking under Brezhnev's rule was the possibility of deep-going *systemic* analysis, to prepare a necessary *systemic* change. While a great many specific ills were repeatedly placed before the public eye, the centralised planning system as such was presented as basically good, socialist in its nature, subject only to "further perfecting". Of corruption in high places not a word could be uttered in the press. The "honour of the uniform" took priority. Low-level victims were denounced, but—to take a well-known example—while the corrupt Georgian Party secretary, Mzhavanadze, was dismissed, the reasons were never made public. Privilege of officialdom, and its abuses, was firmly on the list of taboo subjects. So were accidents. When a plane carrying the football team Pakhtakor (Tashkent) crashed and the entire team was killed (in 1979), the only way the incident found its way into the press was in a brief note to the effect that Pakhtakor's next match was "postponed", with no reason given.

In 1984 Andropov succeeded Brezhnev. He had the reputation of being a more literate man, with some cultural interests. Whether this was so or not, disease struck him down before he could have any impact. Chernenko was a nonentity. So we reach Gorbachev, whose election by his colleagues takes some explaining. We know from speeches by Ligachev and Patiashvili at the 19th Party Conference that it was a close-run thing.

# CHAPTER 2

# Stalin and Stalinism

The Gorbachev period began disappointingly for historians. Asked about "Stalinism" in 1985 by the correspondent of the Paris *Humanité*, Gorbachev replied to the effect that there was no such thing, the very term was the invention of enemies. But such an attitude, perhaps rendered necessary by the political balance of the time, did not last. Not only did Gorbachev express himself more vigorously about the crimes of Stalin in his 70th anniversary speech (November 1987), but *glasnost'* really did mean that others could be much more open and forthright, and get published with no ill effects for themselves or their editors. I will cite here a few of the general analyses of Stalinism and the character and aims of Stalin himself, leaving specific episodes—e.g., those related to the terror, or of peasant policy—to later chapters.

Instead of the compulsory quasi-silence on Stalin which characterised the Brezhnev years, few journals or newspapers are published now without the issue of Stalinism featuring in some way or other. To cover the entire ground is an impossible task. I shall confine myself to some of the more striking examples.

One of these is the novel *Deti Arbata* (*Children of the Arbat'*) by Anatoli Rybakov, serialized in *Druzhba narodov* (Nos. 3, 4, and 5, 1987). It has been noted that its hero, Pankratov, has a personal history similar to Rybakov himself, including a period in prison and exile in the thirties, though released in time to serve in the Red Army in the war. Stalin appears in the novel repeatedly, and the author has him soliloquising, thereby presenting an interpretation of what was passing through the despot's mind in the crucial year 1934, in which the novel is set. The 17th Party Congress ("the congress of victors") had just been held, Stalin appeared to be victorious; as he himself put it in his speech to the Congress, "At this congress there is nothing to prove and, it seems, no one to fight. Everyone sees that the Party line has triumphed."

So was this a time to relax or to forgive, as Kirov apparently desired? Not at all.

All his enemies, past, present and future, must be destroyed and will be destroyed. The only socialist country in the world can survive only if it is unshakeably stable within, . . . The state must be mighty in case of war, it must also be mighty in seeking peace, it must be feared.

To convert in the shortest possible period a peasant country into an industrial power requires countless material and human sacrifices. The people must accept them. But this cannot be achieved by enthusiasm alone. The people must be compelled to make sacrifices. For this there must be a mighty state-power, inspiring fear in the people. This fear must be maintained by all and any means, and the theory of the unextinguished class struggle provides great help in this. If as a result a few million people perish, history will forgive comrade Stalin for this. If he leaves the state defenceless, causes it to perish, history will never forgive him. A great aim requires great energy, great energy on the part of a backward people can be generated only by great cruelty [zhestokostyu]. All great rulers were cruel.

. . . Until the leader achieves full power he must persuade, give people the impression that they are his voluntary allies, that he is formulating and expressing their own ideas. Trotsky did not understand this, as he also failed to understand the significance of the apparatus. . . .

. . . The apparatus must be preserved and strengthened, but one must kill in it the very conception of independence, constantly change the personnel, not allow the cementing of mutual connections. A constantly changing apparatus has no independent political force, but remains a mighty instrument in the hands of the leader, of a mighty ruler. This apparatus, as an instrument of power, must inspire fear in the people, but it must itself tremble before the leader.

Has he such an apparatus? No, he has not. . . . He could not change the composition of the central committee even in HIS triumphal Seventeenth Congress. . . . This apparatus has served its purpose and in the present form it is not needed, what is needed is another apparat, that does not argue, for which there is but one law: HIS will. The present apparatus is obsolete rubbish [khlam], but these old cadres are mutually supportive and interrelated and will not leave of their own volition. They will have to be *removed*. But they will therefore be injured, forever hidden potential deadly enemies, ready at any time to join whoever will oppose him. They will have to be exterminated. Some among them have served well in the past. . . . Now their past services are harmful to the party's cause. They consider themselves participants in deciding the country's fate. Therefore they must be replaced. To replace means to exterminate. . . .

Now it is necessary to create a new, a special power apparatus and to exterminate the old one. The extermination process must be begun with those who actually did speak against HIM, with Zinoviev and Kamanev, they are the most vulnerable . . . they have already confessed their errors, they will confess to anything now. And no one will dare defend them, not even Kirov.

So we have Stalin, sure of the need for a despotism with himself as despot, sure also of the need to have a new brand of servitor, wholly devoted to him. Anyone else, whether ex-oppositionist or conditional supporter, would have to be not only removed but exterminated. The logic is simple: anyone who has been demoted or sacked has a grievance, and is thus a potential oppositionist. So he must not be allowed to live. It is strongly hinted in the novel that Kirov's murder was arranged by the Kremlin. One of the characters in Shatrov's play (of which more in a moment), addressing Stalin, says: "I thought that Kirov had been killed on Yagoda's orders to ingratiate himself with you [*chtoby vam ugodit'*], but now I believe you were responsible", to which Stalin replies tersely: "What did you say!?" (The question is still left open.)

In *Druzhba narodov* Nos. 9, 10, and 11, 1988, Anatoli Rybakov continues the story he began in *Deti Arbata*. This time Stalin is shown preparing and directing the Moscow trials. The novel quotes extensively from records and memoirs (without attribution and with many "inserts" based on the author's imagination—this is a novel, not a history). Again there are Stalin soliloquies.

Lenin guessed the hour which history presented to a real leader to seize power. But he did so as a great revolutionary of a Western type, whom history gave the opportunity in the east. He saw and utilized the weakness of the then-existing state, but did not know the reasons. The reasons for this weakness were due to the fact that the Russian people, though capable of occasional large-scale rebellion, is accustomed to be ruled. The power of Kevonsky was weak, was based on illusions about a parliamentary republic, it had to collapse. . . . The *muzhik* with his common sense himself wishes to be kept under firm control. Lenin understood that dictatorship requires a unified power [*edinovlastiya*] but did not understand that it also needed unified thought [*edinomysliya*]. . . . In fact the terror is not only a means of suppressing dissent [*inakomysliya*], it is above all a means of imposing unanimity of thought, flowing from universal *fear*. Only thus can the people be governed, in its own interest.

He will carry out "the cadre revolution"—liquidate physically the old party cadres. In so doing, he will "inoculate the people not only with the habit of total obedience, but develop indifference to victims, destroy bourgeois superstitions about morals and morality".

Interrogators began in 1936 to beat up their victims, though torture as such was not authorized until later. Yezhov's rise and the decline of Yagoda are linked to the difficulties of preparing the first of the show trials—that of Zinoviev and Kamenev. A senior interrogator is quoted as telling a colleague that "if anyone hesitates, doubts, feels unable to fight the Trotsky-Bukharin bands, let him openly and honestly say so. . . . You understand the meaning of these words? Each who 'honestly admits' his inability to conduct the investigation will be instantly arrested as a sympathizer with the accused", this line being attributed to Yezhov. Among the accused was one Nelidov, grandson of the (tsarist) Ambassador to France, who firmly refuses to give false evidence. Beria—then still in Tbilisi—reports to Stalin that he had shot the first secretary of the Armenian party in his office during a bitter argument. Stalin is shown to be well aware of Beria's "qualities", but supported and promoted him.

Zinoviev and Kamenev, the latter especially, are presented as human beings in a tragic situation. They and others were told that their lives and that of their relatives would be spared; in other cases their wives and children were shown to them in prison. Kamenev was told that only by his confession could he save his family, and that even his twelve year old son could be shot under the decree adopted in 1935 for such purposes. He and Zinoviev were also made to suffer a sort of torture when the radiators in their cells were put on full heat in high summer ("Zinoviev was an asthmatic and suffered terribly"). Stalin finally makes a formal promise that they and their families would be spared, but Rybakov ends with a list of wives and children (including Kamenev's two sons and both his first and second wives) who were shot all the same. Most of the Trotskyists who had refused to confess were shot also. Stalin justifies all this in his own eyes by reference to "the interests of the party and the state", and thinks that Lenin and Marx, great men though they were, suffered from "bourgeois prejudices" about morality and conscience.

Several writers emphasise how false is the view that Stalin "did not know" about the crimes being committed in his name. He did, all the evidence shows this. This, of course, does not exclude the possibility, even the likelihood, of things getting out of hand, of harmless individuals being swept up in the process of denunciation and "plan-fulfillment for extirpating enemies of the people". Stalin's personal responsibility has also been stressed, in his more recent speeches, by Gorbachev himself.

*Druzhba narodov* (No. 11, 1988) printed a long story by the

Belorussian writer Ales Adamovich (who, two months before, had made a remarkable pacifist speech at an international conference at Barcelona, which I attended). Before imagining Stalin's thoughts on his last day on earth, he cites four sayings. One, by Dzerzhinsky in 1926, expressed the fear that "the country will find its dictator, grave-digger of the revolution, however red the feathers decorating his costume". Another is by V. Shulgin, made in 1920 when he was with the Whites: "He [a future dictator] will definitely be Red in his power of will, and definitely White in the tasks he will set himself. He will be a bolshevik in terms of energy and a nationalist in his convictions. Yes, a difficult combination. . . . All that is now going on, all the horror in Russia today, these are just the hard and dreadful birth-pangs, the birth-pangs of an autocrat: It is no easy matter to give birth to an autocrat, an all-Russian autocrat . . .'. Then he cites Plekhanov: "Revolution could give rise to a political monster, similar to the ancient Chinese or Peruvian empires, i.e., to a renewed Tsarist despotism with a communist lining". Finally, this is from Dostoyevsky's draft of *Devils*: "The people will not want it", to which the seminarist replies: "Set the people aside" [*Ustranit' narod!*].

He, like Rybakov, has Stalin soliloquising. "Stalin returned to state-power its stability, reliability, authority. The Romanovs really were self-destroyed, not in 1917 or 1918 but much earlier, by eliminating the fundamental basis of autocratic power, serfdom in the village". Some called Stalin "Chingiz-khan with a telephone". Trotsky had said that he would be shot when the Germans got to within 100 kilometres of Moscow, but they got to within thirty kilometres—so who was shot? ". . . The people want a saint. The little-god tsar was taken away from them, so they began to make a saint of Mironych [Kirov]; well, a dead saint is even holier. So everything is in order." He recalls (in Adamovich's imagination) how Kirov rejected the offer made to him by a delegate at the Seventeenth Congress in 1934, how he had "only three votes, not three hundred" cast against him at the election for the central committee, and how Kaganovich falsified the result to conceal the numbers who voted against Stalin. He quotes the (widely believed) denunciation of Stalin to his face by his wife, Nadezhda Alliluyeva: "You are a beast, a beast. . . . I really thought you did not know that children swell with hunger in your *kolkhozy*". And when she stormed out on her way to commit suicide, "she was accompanied by Molotov's cunning Jewess-wife". Stalin in this version of his life recalls his role, under the pseudonym Fikus, as an informer for the tsarist *Okhrana*. Then Svetlana is quoted as saying: "Papa, is it true what I heard . . . that you ordered children to be shot, children of enemies of the people?" Poskrebyshev, his secretary, used to tell how he took part in the killing of the Tsar's family in Ekaterinburg.

Stalin is "cited" thinking about hanging the doctors in Red Square, and compelling the "obstinate" Erenburg and Marshak to sign that letter about the forced migration of all Jews. He bitterly resents the fact that his alienated eldest son, Yakov, and his daughter sought to marry Jews, and Stalin is suspicious of Molotov and others because they too had Jewish wives. He also noted that his devoted assistant, Poskrebyshev, came to beg for the release of *his* (arrested) wife, whereas Kalinin and Molotov did not feel able to do so in respect of theirs'. He imagines his son Yakov (who died in a German prisoner-of-war camp) visiting him and reproaching him for the 1941 disaster. Why did he kill 40,000 officers? Was this the "Tsaritsyn syndrome?" (In 1919 he had many prisoners, including officers, drowned in the Volga.) And what of the peasants, of innumerable other victims? "One death is tragic, a million deaths— that's statistics", replied Stalin. He thinks of the Ukrainians, who "arranged death from hunger for themselves" (*ustroili podykha-lovku*) in 1933, who welcomed the Germans, and who despite their numbers, ought to be deported. In a powerful scene, Adamovich imagines a knock at the door: the dying Stalin is visited by his ever-present familiar, Fear. ("I never needed a special pass, I have always been closest to you . . . you are behind barbed wire yourself, as if a prisoner on a life sentence. You are buried alive here . . . and now at last *you* must die"). Stalin imagines himself taken to prison, to a trial. He asks: is it trial by *troika* (of the NKVD)? The reply: "No, *troitsa*" (the Trinity).

Adamovich is giving his publication fee to the fund to build a monument to the victims of Stalinist terror.

Could Stalin do it all by himself? Is there not a wider circle of responsibility, and where does it end? Did not millions weep when he died? Did not millions willingly inform on their neighbours? Does this link up with the "servile" strand in Russian social history, with its tradition of autocracy? Did no one try to stop him? What happened to those who did? Was there an alternative, in terms of policy and of personalities, to Stalin's seizure of full power, which several authors have characterised as a coup d'état (*perevorot*), indeed, a "counterrevolutionary" one? The argument rages in the USSR, and on these issues Western Sovietologists are also far from being of one mind. In Stalin's own time, he was presented to the Soviet people as "the Lenin of today", implying that he was good, whereas Western anti-Soviet scholars were also inclined to present

Stalin as the continuator of Lenin's work—so that Lenin was bad, since he engendered Stalin. Even this sort of heresy, unthinkable a few years ago, has occasionally surfaced in the media. Thus Shatrov (in his play *Dal'she, dal'she dal'she*) has Lenin apologising by hindsight to the Soviet people for his part in raising up Stalin. Selyunin goes further: Stalinism is shown to be related to specific elements of Russia's past, and to utopian elements in Marxism, stressing in particular the role of forced labour. This point seems so important that it is worth dwelling on in greater detail (see *Novyi mir*, No. 5, 1988).

Selyunin's argument can be summarized as follows. First is its "Russian" part. Ivan the Terrible destroyed the feudal aristocracy, greatly strengthening the role of the service gentry, who were directly interested in enserfing the peasantry. Both Ivan and Peter are seen by some historians as positive figures, builders of the Russian state, but Selyunin (here echoing the emigré Alexander Yanov) sees them as enslavers of the people, with Peter as the creator of manufacturing establishments staffed by slave labour, producing to the orders of the state. He might have cited the poet Maximilian Voloshin: "Peter the Great was the first Bolshevik". It is not for nothing that Stalin saw in Ivan and Peter his two great predecessors.

Now to utopia. Selyunin begins with Thomas More, who did see that in such a society there would be a problem in motivating labour. So there had to be supervisors ("syphogrants") whose task it was to see that everyone worked properly. (The same problem appears in a work by Tendryakov, whose utopia is Campanella's "Empire of the Sun", but more of that later.) He turns to Engels, who saw no reason to pay people differently in a socialist society. Marx did, but only in the first stage, when unequal work earned unequal pay; but this, in Marx's words, "preserves bourgeois right", and so, remarked Selyunin, "it is clear that so unnatural a thing could only be tolerated for a short time".

After noting the excesses of the Jacobins in seeking to suppress markets and speculation, he then went on—for what must be the first time in living memory—to criticise Lenin himself, his fanatical opposition to "petty-bourgeois speculators" who should be "shot on the spot". He collects several of Lenin's more extreme sayings on the war-communism period, which he summarizes as follows: "If commodity production and the market with which it is associated will not be eliminated, then the October revolution will, so to speak, lower itself to bourgeois levels." State organs must replace, suppress, commodity production. Selyunin's essential point relates to the relationship of imposed egalitarianism and forced labour. Once

material incentives (therefore inequality) are excluded, what alternative is there to direction of labour, and to some twentieth-century
version of Thomas More's supervisors? There is also a relationship,
spelt out explicitly by Selyunin, between freedom to sell one's labour
and the products of that labour, and human freedom in general. He
praises the Stolypin reforms, which sought to break up the old
village commune, and deplores the effect of the revolution, which
largely destroyed the Stolypin reforms and returned most of the land
to "communal" control. Selyunin does not assert that markets are
by themselves a guarantee of freedom: we should all be aware of
Hitler's Germany and Pinochet's Chile. But efforts to abolish the
consequences of human inequality have disastrous effects, on
productivity and on liberty. To quote Selyunin: "The rights of the
individual are the obverse side of pitiless economic freedom. Conversely, with total state ownership of the means of production there
arises the temptation to expropriate the individual personality, its
physical and mental powers, to organize work in accordance with a
single plan." He quotes the decree setting up the Cheka, the
grandparent of the KGB, issued within weeks of Lenin's accession to
power. Yes, he agrees, the revolution had to defend itself against its
enemies. But he cites an early speech by the Cheka's founder,
Dzerzhinsky, to the effect that, among its functions, it was to enforce
labour discipline, punish backsliders, setting up "concentration
camps" for this purpose. Trotsky was to make some notorious
remarks about forced labour and socialism, in connection with his
ideas of 1920–21 on "militarization of labour". As we shall see,
some commentators have deduced from this that Stalin's excesses
were basically Trotskyist, even that, in the words of F. Belov, "Stalin
was the most consistent Trotskyist".

Selyunin then moves on to the administrative or functional logic
of marketless planning, the inevitably vast number of decisions to be
taken, bureaucratic offices and officials required to take them, and
the need for a supreme boss to sort out the demarcational and power
disputes among the functionaries: "Call him Emperor, dictator, the
father of the people [Stalin] or anything else, his role in the
administrative structure remains unchanged." The despotic iron fist
falls heavily upon ordinary citizens. "In our concern for Sergei
Mironovich [Kirov] and Nikolai Ivanovich [Bukharin], we must not
forget Ivan Denisovich" (the humble hero of Solzhenitsyn's tale).

Another original and influential writer on this theme has been
Gavriil Popov, especially in his contribution to the popular science
monthly *Nauka i zhizn* (No. 4, 1987). There, summarizing the
economic-political essence of Stalinism, he speaks of the "Adminis-

trative system" of hierarchical subordination, which enforced the wishes of the supreme despot. For it to function, several features had to coexist: first, the despot himself; second, "the subsystem of fear", i.e., the terror, "Beria" (not necessarily with the odious personal characteristics of the real Beria—it has been confirmed that he not only tortured prisoners personally but had his minions kidnap young girls for his pleasure—but *fear* was an essential part of the system); third, the tasks to be performed, the priorities the despot imposed, had to be such as could be handled by centralised administrative orders; fourth, and most important, there had to be devoted executants, loyal to Stalin but also willing to work desperately hard for the cause. Popov's article takes the form of a review of a book written many years ago by Alexander Bek, titled *Novoye naznacheniye*, which finally was printed in 1986.

In this novel the fictional hero is one Onisimov, but he was modeled after a real Stalinist captain of industry, Tevosyan. In another review-article, this time of Daniil Granin's novel *Zubr* ("the auroch", symbolic of rough-hewn independence of spirit), Popov argues that Stalinism needed a few such *Zubr* characters too, even though their existence seemed inconsistent with its nature; the conformist and timid would fail to advance vital scientific-industrial and military tasks. A number fell by the wayside all the same, but Popov cites the example of Kapitsa, great scientist and former pupil of Rutherford in Cambridge, whom Stalin protected from Beria's vengeance because he was needed. The contrast is made with the equally great scientist, the geneticist Vavilov, who had nothing immediately applicable to give to Soviet agriculture, with which he could counter the false promises of the charlatan Lysenko; so Vavilov, unlike Kapitsa, died in prison.

The Stalinist system was incapable of producing or reproducing either the "Onisimov-Tevosyans" or the "Zubrs". One came to it from the generation formed by the revolution, the other from the scientific community. Popov makes the point that their successors were likely to be far less bold and able, far more conformist and corruptible (Onisimov actually punished any subordinates who abused privileges, and never himself acted for personal gain). Furthermore, Beria and the subsystem of terror are no more, there is no supreme despot, and, finally, the nature of the tasks to be performed has become far more complex, far less manageable by straight orders from above. So Stalinism is obsolete, it must go.

But *was* it rational for its time? This brings us back to the issue of alternatives. In 1961 I wrote an article that later was also the title of a book: "Was Stalin Really Necessary?" So it is with great interest that I note the debate on this theme which, for the first time, has broken out openly in the Soviet Union.

Among the "debaters" are Selyunin, Gefter, and Klyamkin, the last two writing in *Rabochii klass i sovremennyi mir* (No. 1, 1988) and *Novyi mir* (No. 11, 1987). Others, too, have touched on this theme. But here, as elsewhere in this book, the point is to acquaint the reader with the range and depth of discussion which char- acterises *glasnost'*, rather than to list all interesting works (no one person could even have read them!) or to express my own interpreta- tion of the issues which are now so freely discussed.

The discussion involves inroads into the philosophy of history. Was what happened inevitable? One recalls E. H. Carr's crack: "No historian ever says anything is inevitable until after it happens." But Carr himself tended (in my view) to err on the side of too much determinism. The Soviet protagonists do not quote Carr, but are engaged in a related debate. It is a widely held view, in and out of the Soviet Union, that a Stalin-type despot was necessary, to build a powerful state equipped with a heavy industrial base in the shortest possible time, and that, while he certainly committed crimes and many innocents suffered, this was what the situation required. If collectivization of agriculture, with all its excesses and negative effects, was an integral part of the "Administrative system", then, since just such a system was needed, even this was justified. More will be said on this theme when we reach the discussion of collectivization and the peasantry, but this sort of argument is put forward by Klyamkin, who also sets Stalinism very much into its Russian-historical context: Russia was not Europe, and European Marxists such as Kautsky were quite unable to understand what was going on. The Bukharin alternative was (in Klyamkin's view) impracticable. Even Trotsky's "leftism", which was still within New Economic Policy (NEP), did not envisage the Stalinist policy, which was, therefore, by Trotsky's standards, "ultra-left". This view is not shared by others; the statement that Stalin adopted the Trotsky- Preobrazhensky policy after defeating them politically recurs several times in the published discussions.

Roy Medvedev (author of *Let History Judge*, an expose of Stalinism published so far only in the West) has at last been allowed to join in the published arguments (in *Sobesednik*, No. 18, Apr. 1988). He takes a view similar to Selyunin's and Gefter's: there are always alternatives, some more likely than others, some finely balanced, and in such circumstances it matters greatly who is (or what forces are) in control of the state. Medvedev points out that in, say, 1927 the policy actually adopted in 1929–30 seemed very improbable. (He adds that, seen from the viewpoint of 1985, the present scale of *glasnost'* and *perestroika* did not seem the most likely outcome.) It is, insist these writers, the duty of historians to examine missed opportunities, roads which were not in fact taken, and not to assume that they were impracticable simply because another road was chosen.

However, Medvedev points out, decisions, once taken, have some inescapable consequences. Thus, once Stalin used requisitioning as a solution to the grain-procurement crisis of 1927–28, this shook to its foundations the "vulnerable equilibrium" of NEP society, and the peasants' reaction then compelled a repetition of requisitioning, and this in turn led to the notion of (compulsory) collectivization, and "to open war with the peasantry". He clearly does not agree with Klyamkin: the excessive tempos of the first five-year plan, the tragedies associated with collectivization, led to very severe losses, disproportions, hunger. Far less painful alternatives, he insists, existed and would have been consistent with rapid industrialization. In his view, the terror against the Party was explicable by the fact that Stalin realized in 1934 (at the 17th Party Congress) that "in the Party the forces are ripening which would be capable of acting against him", that "in 1933–34 a secret opposition was forming against Stalin". Medvedev's conclusion: "From the standpoint of iron will and cruelty, Stalin was unique. As an executioner of his own people and a tyrant, he had hardly any equals in history". Roy Medvedev's views, as expressed in *Let History Judge* and other publications, are not new to us in the West. The point is that they now at last openly appear in Russia, with an editorial introductory note regretting the nonappearance in Russia (so far) of *Let History Judge*. It is soon to appear.

Gefter introduces into the discussion the interesting notion that Stalin deliberately chose policies and strategies that rendered him necessary. "Stalin was not absolutely necessary in 1924—but his necessity increased from year to year, he built the need for himself, and in doing so he gave the policy processes those features that made him all the more necessary. Look at his political behaviour, his language, his approach to state policy! His whole method of increasing tensions, in order that, in emergency situations, to strengthen the need for himself, to emerge from every such situation still more irreplaceable." Waging a war against a large part of his own people, eliminating alternative policies and the advocates of such policies, dealing in the methods and language of campaigns, fronts, bridgeheads, creating the atmosphere of a beleaguered fortress menaced by spies and saboteurs, all were part of the act. Not only (argues Gefter) were there alternatives, but Stalin saw them and consciously rejected them. In 1934 a policy of relaxation was certainly possible, and, as already mentioned, was apparently advocated by Kirov and many others who had supported Stalin in earlier factional struggles. Gefter speaks of the possibility of a sort of "antifascist democratization" in 1934–36, of which two potential milestones were the Seventh Congress of the Comintern (the Popular Front strategy) and the new constitution. Gefter speaks of a "sort of *glasnost'* period" which followed the Kirov assassination, with "criticism of high officials", and some relaxation, especially in peasant policy, giving rise in some quarters to hope. "Stalin had a choice, he could have become the leader of a process of normalization." Stalin, says Gefter, rejected such ideas because they would have undermined his own necessity: he launched the Terror instead. Then there were the first postwar years. The country had suffered terribly, and everyone, from the intellectuals to the peasants, hoped for a less repressive regime. Instead, they had the tightening of the screws in 1946–47. To cite Gefter: "The war years, especially 1941 and 1942, ... saw a kind of spontaneous de-Stalinization" (the same point was made by another writer on "the Leningrad affair", as we shall see). Then came victory, glory for Stalin, but Stalin felt a danger: "Did he see in the young men in military coats without rank badges [i.e., demobilized officers] a species of future decembrists, or was he again fearful of becoming unnecessary . . . ? Anyhow . . . he again revived the mechanism of 'permanent civil war', which, in my view, was the most significant personal contribution to what we call 'Stalinism'." ("Decembrists" were officers who had seen Paris after Napoleon's defeat, and who conspired against Nicholas I in 1825.) Thus, there developed the still-to-be described postwar tragedy: the fragmentation of a generation. "After such faith in each other, the country once again was teeming with 'traitors'. True, the scale of human losses was smaller than in the thirties, but how do we count the losses suffered by human souls, the moral effects and their long-term consequences?"

Gefter also discusses the causes of the failure to oppose Stalin effectively. Involved here were the ambiguities of NEP. "Was Lenin, was the Party, was Russia, was left-wing thought, ready to accept its complexity. . . . What was to happen next?" Lenin's own thought contained, in Gefter's view, alternative roads, a choice between spontaneous historical development (along NEP lines) and "seeking to make permanent the monopoly of power, whose credo was— might at any cost". Lenin thought that "out of NEP-Russia will come a socialist Russia". But "we have the right to ask: was he not wrong? Were NEP and the Russia of the NEP years mutually consistent?" Stalin was able to use "the iron law of class war" to combat the notion of tolerating "cooperative farmers" and cultural freedom. His potential and real opponents were defeated by their own uncertainties, confusions, revolutionary phraseology, and commitment to Party unity. His opponents seemed unable to appreciate what was happening until much too late. The 17th Party Congress (1934) he regards as "dreadful", because no one mentioned the millions of victims, the cost. All (including the ex-oppositionists) spoke only of glorious successes. Even Bukharin, in his (now published) "letter" he dictated to his wife on the eve of his arrest, said that he had had no disagreements with the party line (i.e., Stalin's policies) "for seven years", i.e., since 1930! (This last point is mine.)

In the end, Stalin "caused so much blood to flow, he is linked with blood so closely in all his actions, that it destroys all rational explanation, both of him as a person and of us, of our history". Gefter does not fail to tackle the question of his popularity, "the secret of the closeness to him of millions, both of educated and the semiliterate". Nor does Selyunin, who speaks of "sentimental memories of the past, a longing for a Boss [*Khozyain*] and order", these being real attitudes still today. One can quote the title of Gefter's article: "Stalin Died Yesterday". His system outlived him.

A challenging and subtly argued piece by M. Kapustin was recently published in *Oktyabr'* (No. 5, 1988). He too believes that there was a "Bukharinist" alternative: "The socialism of the Stalinist period bore semi-feudal and in some areas even feudal characteristics", with vassals, fiefs, and personal loyalty. The "de-Stalinizers" of the 1950s avoided attacking the essential—the Administrative system, authoritarianism, bureaucracy. "They, like others in past centuries, secretly hoped just to replace an 'evil' tsar with a 'good' one." A. Burganov, in *Druzhba narodov* (No. 6, 1988), under the title of "History—A Severe Mother", tackles the issue of "why Stalinism", in an article which is to a considerable extent a reply to Klyamkin, stressing human and material losses, the huge cost of Stalin's despotism, disagreeing with Klyamkin's view of collectivization (of which more in due course).

In *Literaturnaya gazeta* (9 Dec. 1987), Volkogonov discusses "the Stalin phenomenon", and while he condemns Stalin's cruelty and excesses, he sees no alternative to Stalin on personal grounds: the others lacked essential qualities, so that "the alternative of other leaders was hardly a possible one".

This is disputed in one of the best and most profound of the

articles on this whole theme, by O. Latsis in *Znamya* (No. 6, 1988).
Latsis also criticises Klyamkin. "There was another road. But then
why did it remain only a possibility?" To answer this question, he
examines with care the Party and its leadership. He emphasises the
thinness of the stratum of the old Bolsheviks (by 1922 only 2% of
Party members had joined the Party before 1917). As Lenin had duly
noted, much depended on this thin layer dominating the Party and
the (overwhelmingly peasant) country. Latsis then examines in
detail the dilution of the Party by the recruitment of hundreds of
thousands in 1924 and subsequent years, and the defeats by Stalin of
all his real and potential opponents. Until the end of 1927 Stalin
took a cautious line, wholly within the logic of NEP, strongly
opposing adventurism and speed-up of growth, rejecting coercion
with regard to the peasantry, opposing "those comrades who think
that it is possible and necessary to deal with the *kulak* by administrative measures through the GPU [political police]". He defeated the
left opposition with genuine support in the Party, the more so
because of the inconsistencies and clumsiness of Zinoviev and
Kamenev, which he amply documents, and Trotsky's lack of organizational base and support. But then how was he able to carry the
bulk of the Party with him, against Bukharin, when *he* (Stalin)
turned left, and blatantly contradicted his own previous arguments
for caution? Latsis traces step by step the policy changes, in the
adoption of ambitious investment plans, in forcing collectivization,
and does this in a very critical spirit. Nonetheless, an important role
is attributed to "the honourable enthusiasm of the builders of
socialism", such as Ordzhonikidze, and "to widespread economic
illiteracy". Also he notes, and documents, the lack of understanding
of law and legality: Krylenko, the then commissar for justice, was
repeatedly heckled at the 15th Party Congress when he spoke mildly
of observing legal norms.

He then turns to the situation in the country and the party after
the defeats of all the oppositions and deviations, and also after the
hunger and overstrain of the first five-year plan period. Stalin
realized that many Party members were ready for change by 1934.
"Therefore he could not allow the majority of the delegates [to the
17th Party Congress] to live until the next congress." There
remained the "second-echelon old Bolsheviks, who had replaced the
defeated rivals: Kirov, Ordzhonikidze, Rudzutak, Postyshev, Eikhe,
Tukhachevsky—any of them could become dangerous one day.
Maybe they do not yet know this, so it is necessary to act quickly,
before they do. They must be removed, together with the stratum
whose ideas they might be prepared to express." This helps to

explain the scale and nature of the purges, insofar as they affected the Party. However, millions of ordinary people were also affected, and here Latsis examines "the class nature of Stalin's policy"; Stalin sought effective control over the net product ("newly created value"), and so had to turn also on the workers and peasants. (Latsis is not clear precisely what *class* Stalin was representing; it could hardly be "the bureaucracy" when he killed so high a proportion of the bureaucrats!) "Usurping not only the rights of the Party but also the rights of workers and peasants, Stalin had to extend his measures of suppression beyond the Party leaders. He could not arrest all the workers and peasants, though the system of Gulag did represent a large-scale experiment in creating a special kind of 'working class', but objectively everyone represented a danger for Stalin, as he acted against the basic interests of both workers and peasants."

And yet there was real enthusiasm among millions, especially of youth, at any rate up to 1937, as is reflected (Latsis notes) in the literature of the time. Up until then, the immediate superiors of the masses were still the products of the revolution, devoted to the job, not yet corrupted. So in 1929 "Stalin won organisationally, but not yet socially or psychologically". For this the Terror would be needed.

Nevertheless, Latsis sees it as fundamentally wrong to regard "the cult of Stalin as merely the effect of terror and fear. . . . The paradox of the 'socialist' cult lies in the fact that it drew its strength from the proletarian revolution and its broad democratic social base." Yes, the excesses of the cult disgusted some, but there was "a favourable soil for the growth of the cult in the consciousness of an immature working class and of the youth generally". It is hard for the present generation to appreciate how "among the people there was both hatred and reverence towards the Leader and Teacher. Quite frequently, faced with this incomprehensible fact, people simply deny the fact. Some do not believe in the sincerity of the reverence—it was all falsehood and fear. Others doubt Stalin's evildoing. Yet in real life there was both." He ends: "The cult of personality is not a necessary attribute of socialism in general. But it seems that it was an attribute of early socialism, relying on an immature working class, and particularly in countries without an age-old democratic culture." The cult was organized not only from above, there was a tendency to create it from below; many wished to look up to a leader.

In *Literaturnaya Rossiya* (19 Aug. 1988), Lev Fink noted that when Stalin died Tvardovsky wrote a poem in his praise, though his father had been deported as a *kulak*. Olga Berggolts wrote a poem

too on that occasion, expressing sorrow and love. Yet her husband
had been done to death in prison, and she herself was imprisoned
and, while pregnant, beaten up by her interrogator so that she lost
the child.

When Stalin died, noted Alexei Adzhubei in his very interesting
memoirs (*Znamya*, No. 6, 1988), there was a "widespread feeling of
vulnerability, a sort of bereavement. For most people the name of
Stalin was linked with the place of our country in the world arenas,
with assurance that difficulties, obstacles, disasters would be overcome. 'He can do everything, he will find the one correct solution';
that was how people thought, that is how this personality was
regarded—higher than God, closer than father and mother,
unique." Clearly, this was not just a matter of a combination of
terror and propaganda. It reflected some sort of inner need.
However, as is stressed by a number of writers, this has become
totally alien to the generation of the 1980s, though many institutions, procedures, and habits of mind, are still left over from Stalin's
time (to quote Gefter again, "Stalin died *yesterday*"). So an honest
examination of the past, in all its complexity, is seen as a precondition for necessary societal change; it is a sort of exorcism.

There was published in *Druzhba narodov* (No. 3, 1988) a letter
written by an old Comintern activist, "Ernst Henry" (real name S.
Rostovsky), to Ilya Erenburg on the occasion of the appearance, 25
years before, of Erenburg's memoirs. Henry criticised Erenburg for
being insufficiently critical of Stalin, for seeing positive as well as
negative sides in his record. Unusually, he was particularly sharp
about Stalin's role in splitting the working-class movement and
helping Hitler to power with the slogan of "social fascism", treating
social-democrats as the main enemy. He then destroyed a large part
of the Red Army on the eve of war, demoralized Western communists by ordering them to cease antifascist propaganda following the
Nazi-Soviet pact. He was not, as Erenburg had suggested, a sort of
twentieth-century Machiavelli or Borgia, since this would be to
overstate his cleverness. He was fooled by Hitler; he ignored the
warning given, at great personal risk, by the German ambassador
Schulenburg. Stalin did not save Russia; following his disastrous
errors he was saved by the people. Interviewed by the journal, Henry
(still alive) said that Erenburg did not reply.

The cult affected everything. Boris Yampolsky (in *Znamya*, Nos.
2 and 3, 1988) wrote: "Stalin did not sleep, and ministers did not
sleep, nor did their deputies, their assistants, their researchers, their
secretaries, their stenographers, nor did chief accountants, chief
geologists, chief steel-makers, technologists, messengers, buffet

staff, cyclists, medical auxiliaries, telephonists on special lines, guards, and then in all the vast country Party *obkom* secretaries would not sleep, or the commanders of military districts, factory directors, supervisors—the whole country converted its day, its life, to fit in with the organism of a sleepless generalissimo."

On the painful issue of historical responsibility, *Pravda International* (No. 8, 1988) quotes *Sovetskaya kultura*, where Sergei Mikoyan, who married Kuznetsov's daughter and was the son of Anastas Mikoyan, wrote to the effect that his father's participation in Stalin's crimes was "unforgivable".

While the connection between Lenin and Stalin remains very sensitive, in a remarkable interview M. Shatrov (*Ogonyok*, No. 45, 1988) does at least tackle the issue by saying that quite a few people have written to the press to raise such a question: "There was not only *Stalinshchina* but also *Leninshchina*" [the *-shchina* is a suffix with a negative connotation], that Stalin was after all a follower of Lenin, that the real "catastrophe" was the October revolution itself. The canonization of Lenin (wrote Shatrov) and the oversimplified morality tale contained in the "Short course" (Stalinist official history) have done much harm. Far more research is needed as to the deeper roots of the October revolution: was it a peoples' movement or a conspiracy? What were the causes of the Provisional government's failure, and the history of relations with the SRs and the Mensheviks? What were the hopes for world revolution? What connection can be seen between "October" and "Thermidor"? Shatrov praises Solzhenitsyn's role in denouncing Stalinism, his *One Day in the Life of Ivan Denisovich*, *First Circle*, *Matryona's Home*, and *Cancer Ward*, but cannot accept the anti-Lenin pages of *The Gulag Archipelago* and *Lenin in Zurich* and Solzhenitsyn's basic hostility to the October Revolution in these and more recent works. However, the way to deal with his arguments is "by the pen", by deeper and truer analyses of the basic causes of Stalinism. He proposes a long-running, high-level seminar with the participation of foreign scholars. Was Stalin "inevitable"? What and who supported him? Speaking of himself, Shatrov states that his father was shot in 1937 (though he was at first told that he had died in a camp in 1944; such lies were apparently frequent), that his mother was arrested, and that the family was related to Alexei Rykov. Failure of *perestroika* today would open the door to black reaction, chauvinism, and anti-Semitism. He quoted from a letter that drew attention to black-shirted storm troopers who support *Pamyat'* in Leningrad.

A different view found expression in an article by V. Kozhinov in *Nash sovremennik* (No. 4, 1988) built around a criticism of

Rybakov's *Deti Arbata*, which he accuses of numerous inaccuracies and, above all, of not understanding that the "cult", the making of Stalin a divine being, had its deep roots. Kirov made his contribution to this. Also Shatrov, like other intellectuals, stressed the special horror of 1937. Yet many more died in 1933, but they were not intellectuals but peasants. Far more had died in 1918–22, and only a fraction had been killed in the Civil War. Lenin had spoken of the bloody birth-pangs of a new society, so 1937 should be set within a "chain reaction" of which the horrors of the Civil War period were a very bloody beginning. Kozhinov decries the attempt (by Rybakov and others) to find a basis for Stalinism in "Asiatic" features of Russian history. Ivan the Terrible was much less bloody than Henry VIII. Peter was a "Europeanizer". In the nineteenth century the death penalty was used far more sparingly in Russia than in the West. Even the victims of tsarist repression in 1906–10 represented only a tenth of the victims of the repression of the Paris commune in May 1871. So there was no strictly Russian precedent (he claims) for what happened in 1918–22, 1933, or 1937–38. (Kozhinov also selected a range of mainly Jewish names among those responsible for Gulag, collectivization, the reconstruction of Moscow, and even for Lysenko.)

The debate continues.

Western scholars will be joining the debate. Stephen Cohen has been quoted on Bukharin, and *Moskovskie novosti* (21 Aug. 1988) recently printed an interview with Robert Tucker, of Princeton, on Stalin and Stalinism.

In *Neva* (No. 10, 1988) a remarkable article by V. Chalikova is devoted to the young man, Dmitri Yurasov, who shook the audience at a lecture in April 1987 when he queried the lecturer's assertion that there are no statistics as to the number of victims of Stalinist repression. He had collected data in various archives in which he worked and accumulated a vast card index. He referred then to "the largest total he was able to see", a total of *sixteen million* (arrested and also those "administratively exiled"). His card indexes cover over 128,000 individual cases. He had seen files that showed the Tukhachevsky case was already being prepared in 1936 (i.e., military victims were being forced to implicate him). Among those shot in Orel in October 1941 he noted a number of wives and children of executed generals (Yegorov, Kork, Uborevich, and Gamarnik). He noted also the names of those old Bolsheviks who, despite tortures, refused to confess or implicate others: Uglanov, Preobrazhensky, Shlyapnikov, and Smilga. (This, in the circumstances, is indeed a roll of honour.) Chalikova's article refers to the alleged meeting of

Trotsky's son and one of the accused in a show trial at the Hotel Bristol in Copenhagen: the problem with that "confession" was that the hotel had been burnt down previously. Chalikova went on to cite with evident approval Robert Conquest's *Great Terror*, and Solzhenitsyn's *The Gulag Archipelago*. She also cited Arthur Koestler's *Darkness at Noon*. She went on: "A decisive question for our memory and our consciences is the number of innocent people who perished, who lie in a bottomless mass grave of a size unknown in our history". She also quotes Vasili Grossman's still unpublished *Vsyo techyot* in connection with the excessive grain procurements which led to the famine of 1933: "We did not see such a terrible decree under the Tsars, the Tartars, or the Germans. This decree condemned the peasants of the Ukraine, the Don, the Kuban' to death from hunger, all, including small children." She continued: if in the period 1930–50 there were on average eight–twelve million prisoners, then, taking the lower figure and the modest death rate of 16 percent a year, this would mean twelve million dead in fourteen years. To which she would add "kulaks," victims of famine and others, which would bring the total deaths to twenty million. Stalin, she said, really absorbed the "new morality" (what I called "revolutionary immorality"), whereas men like Bukharin and Kamenev still had scruples. Kamenev bargained for his son's life, agreed to accuse himself of monstrous crimes, and Stalin killed his son all the same.

Turning to Trotsky, she attributes to him the words "In the interests of the proletariat one has to rob the peasantry", but also attributes to him genuine ideological beliefs and a contempt for the trappings of power, which is why he did not oppose Stalin's rise. He (Chalikova said) was an oppositionist by nature, "and he could no more govern the state than his semi-literate would-be-revolutionary admirers. . . ." There were and are states of the Stalinist type, but a "Trotskyist" state never was or could be. However, "in countries not yet cured of crazy utopianism there are still neo-Trotskyist movements and parties, and not only in the seething countries of Latin America but in respectable England too". Stalin himself was not "right" or "left", "his real ideal was oriental despotism". Some assert that "Stalin's politbureau was Jewish, though there was only one, Kaganovich", or that "it was all due to Marxism, though the clean-out of those who knew and loved Marx was one of the aims of the Terror". Others claim that "the repressions were a terror within the party, although data presented by academician A. Sakharov show that among those who perished the proportion of party to nonparty was at least 1:10". Chalikova refers to arrest plan

"norms" imposed from above with occasional "monstrous excesses
such as the disgraceful exiling of Crimean Tartars, Chechens,
Ingushes, Kalmucks, the cynically anti-Semitic 'doctors' plot', or the
fantastically barbarous 'Leningrad affair'." She ends: "Stalinism is
our misfortune and our weakness. It is inseparable from badly baked
bread, from sticky-dirty trays in dining halls, from drunken vomit,
from stinking public toilets, from the production of statistics instead
of real goods, from clever slimy speeches and slavish silences, from
the gaping void between word and deed".

All this upsets some people, high and low. In the next chapter I
will be citing at length the attack on all this revisionism by Nina
Andreyeva and the powerful counterattack by Yuri Afanasyev.
Indeed, this and the next chapter should be read together, since
Stalinism and Soviet history (and historiography) are inseparably
linked.

This (incomplete) survey of discussions in progress is surely
evidence of two things. First, the ideas now publicly debated go very
far beyond the limits of what could be said in Khrushchev's time.
(Indeed, as Kapustin reminds his readers, Khrushchev also went out
of his way to make positive references to Stalin's role, including his
defeat of Trotsky-and-Bukharin oppositions.) Second, most of the
fundamental issues involved in trying to understand the phenomenon of Stalinism, which previously could appear only abroad or in
*samizdat*, can now be discussed in the openly available Soviet media.
The observant reader may have noted that there is in the above pages
not a a single quotation from a historical journal. There is a reason
for this. The Institute of History and its publications were, until the
beginning of 1988, in the hands of the dogmatists. A new editorial
board has been appointed, and the situation is in the process of
changing. Historians have been given the job of rewriting the history
of the Party, to fill in "blank pages", and have been given access to
archives. We shall learn much more soon.

No sooner had these words been written than a major article on
Stalinism appeared in the previously dull journal *Voprosy istorii
KPSS* (No. 8, 1988). In the article, G. Borgyugov and V. Kozlov
discuss intelligently the "Bukharinist" alternative and the reasons
for Stalin's elimination of NEP. They ask: "Where is the dividing
line between historical necessity and subjective arbitrariness?" The
same two authors have discussed Stalin's methods and motives at
length in *Pravda* (3 Oct. 1988). On "1937", they expressed the view
that "the bacchanalia of repression can be seen as the criminal
attempt of Stalin finally to assert his personal dictatorship, parasitiz-
ing on genuinely-existing contradictions between the 'apparatus'

and the masses, between local and central interests, seeking to resolve them once and for all by enforcing blind obedience and suppressing any independence". Stalin was "able to create a highly specific sort of administrative system. A 'normally' functioning administrative system, while formally exalting the leader (as it was, for instance, with Brezhnev) in fact subordinates him to it. This kind of system lacks dynamism and leads to stagnation. Stalin, however, aimed at dynamism. . . . To goad and whip the administrative system he needed to keep the apparatus under constant pressure not only from the top but from below. . . . It is evident that the process of annihilating the cadres got out of control, and the number of victims substantially exceeded the level which, if one can so express it, was needed by Stalin personally." As Latsis did, these authors stress the lack of maturity of a largely ex-peasant working class. "In a certain sense one can say that Stalin and his conceptions of socialism grew out of the backward, residual and obsolete attitudes. Not only he built up the image of the leader among the masses; the mass of new workers also built up the image of the leader." Stalin himself while on his way to supreme power was quite ruthless in adopting or changing policies that suited the power-manoeuvre of the moment.

The Latsis view has been challenged by A. Tsipko, in four articles in *Nauka i zhizn* (beginning with No. 11, 1988). The dilution of party membership in the twenties he sees as irrelevant. "Stalinism is above all the tragedy of the Bolshevik old guard, its pain, its historical guilt. . . . It was precisely the old guard that, already in Lenin's lifetime, voluntarily handed over to Stalin the vast power created by the revolution. . . . The deep contradictions of the task undertaken by us in 1917 have still not received thoughtful and responsible analysis". Tsipko attributes much blame to messianic and anti-market strands in the ideas of Marxism and of the Russian radical intelligentsia and to the widespread contempt and the negative attitude of the "petty-bourgeois" peasantry. This intellectual time bomb must surely cause an orthodox counterattack. (As I send this to the press, one has duly appeared, from G. Smirnov in *Pravda*, 1 March 1989.)

*Moskovskie novosti* (4 Sept. 1988) has announced the formation of a committee (unofficial) on the erection of a monument to the victims of Stalinist repressions, organized by this paper together with *Literaturnaya gazeta* and *Ogonyok*. Among the proposed members, along with D. Likhachev, Rybakov, and Shatrov, are Sakharov and also Solzhenitsyn—though it is said that he declined the invitation.

*Novoe Vremya* (No. 40, 1988) reported an unusual event. Following the appearance of a denunciation of Stalin's crimes by Ales Adamovich in *Sovietskaya kultura*, a pensioner from Kharkov named Ivan Shekhovtsev sued the author for defamation of Stalin's character, and the case was heard, with witnesses, before a court in Moscow.

# CHAPTER 3

# The Rehabilitation of History—
# Or the History of Rehabilitation

Soon after Gorbachev's election as general secretary, it was being pointed out that Soviet history was in a very unsatisfactory state: there was Lenin, there is Gorbachev, and in between hardly anyone. Nothing could be said about the actors in the controversies of the twenties, Stalin's name was mentioned only infrequently, Khrushchev's not at all. The "blank pages" needed to be filled. In the previous chapter we examined Stalin and Stalinism. What of the other actors?

Mikhail Shatrov had been writing historical plays for decades. One, *Bolsheviki*, was played in the small *Sovremennik* theatre, in a production by Oleg Efremov, who was subsequently to become head of the Moscow Arts Theatre. I saw this play in 1969; it was set in 1918, at the time Lenin was wounded in an assassination attempt. It was necessary then to keep the "unpersons" off the stage, but many were mentioned. Thus, "Stalin is at Tsaritsyn, Bukharin and Rykov are visiting a factory, and Trotsky is at the war-front". Shatrov had other plays, too. In 1985, the theatre put on *Tak pobedim (Thus We Will Win)*, which showed Lenin in serious argument with serious opponents. But Shatrov's most striking reconstructions, which he had written years earlier, were staged in 1987–88. One was *Brestski mir* (on the Brest-Litovsk treaty, in 1918); the other, the already-mentioned *Dal'she, dal'she, dal'she (On, On, and On)*. These plays were published in *Novyi mir* (No. 3, 1987) and *Znamya* (No. 1, 1988), respectively.

Well ahead of the professional historians, Shatrov put on stage the real protagonists in the debate over whether or not to sign the Brest-Litovsk treaty. Bukharin and Dzerzhinsky were against Lenin on this issue, arguing passionately for a revolutionary war. Trotsky was shown as he actually had been: aware that one cannot fight with no army, hopeful that it might be possible not to sign, hesitating between a promise to Lenin to sign and the fact that at that time there was a majority against signature on the central committee. The point was that Shatrov, for the first time since perhaps 1927, actually put before the public the real Trotsky; the script had him arguing his real case in a reasonable and human way (though he was wrong). This contrasts with the crude attack, under the heading of "Yudushka" (Judas), which had appeared in *Sovetskaya Rossiya*. Such crudities have not been repeated. *Brestski mir* was also shown on Soviet television, to an audience of millions.

*Dal'she, dal'she, dal'she* is set on the eve of the October revolution, but the characters all have the benefit of hindsight; on stage there are flash-forwards (not flashbacks). The characters include Kerensky, Kornilov, Martov, Dan, Plekhanov, Spiridonova (the leader of the Left SRs), and all the principal Bolsheviks, including, of course, Trotsky. Stalin is shown to be in agreement with Trotsky, and not with Lenin, on the issue of the date of the uprising, which the former wished to coincide with a favourable vote on the Congress of Soviets. But, much more important, each character presents him- or herself to the audience. Thus Spiridonova tells how she was repeatedly arrested, and finally was shot in Orel prison in 1941, just before the invading Germans arrived, "together with the Bolshevik Rakovsky". Trotsky lists his various functions in and after the revolution, that he was in opposition and expelled, and falsely accused. "I never had any contact with any intelligence agents," he says. However, after a pause, he adds that he was visited in Mexico by a man who said his name was Jackson, but who was really Mercader, who killed him with an ice-axe. (This was the first time, to my knowledge, that this was ever published in the USSR.) On stage Stalin interrupts him with the words: "Proletarian justice".

When Bukharin makes his autobiographical speech to the audience, he quotes from his (1938) letter to posterity and informs them that he was shot. Stalin interjects: "But Nikolai, I let you go to the West in 1936, why did you return?" Plekhanov is able to question whether what was built in the USSR could be called socialism at all. And, as already mentioned, Lenin (again by hindsight) apologises to the people for not devising adequate barriers to Stalin and Stalinism, and enters into arguments with Stalin over the latter's policies. This is not the only instance in which Lenin is presented as in the wrong, as having something to apologise for. Rosa Luxemburg also

makes an appearance, and presents on stage her criticism of Bolshevik repression of opposition, which she made in her well-known
letter from (a German) prison in 1918. However, the bulk of the
historical and critical material claims to be in line with Lenin's
ideas.

Znamya (No. 5, 1988) recently devoted 18 pages to letters from
readers, most of them praising Shatrov's play; a few thought it was
outrageous, and their letters too were printed.

Several authors have put forward a positive view of NEP, a
mixed economy, as the right road. For example, Nikolai Shmelev
(Novyi mir, No. 6, 1987), notes that Marx and Engels had only the
vaguest notion what a socialist economy might be like, and so
(before 1917) had Lenin, who during the war-communism period
"seems himself to have come to believe that orders from above are
the basic methods of a socialist economy". However, he learned
from bitter experience. "Many still consider that NEP had been
just a manoeuvre, just a temporary retreat. There was indeed a
retreat: Soviet power gave some leeway to private enterprise in
towns. But the basic and relevant significance of NEP lies elsewhere. For the first time there was formulated the basics of a
scientific and realistic approach to the tasks of socialist economic
construction": full economic accounting, genuine cooperatives,
real convertible currency, a price system, various kinds of real
cooperatives. It was a disaster to have abandoned it. It was argued
that this was because of the danger of fascism and war, but this is
false: the decisive steps were being taken in 1927–28, when Hitler
was still on the sidelines.

A similar pro-NEP line is taken by Nuikin (Novyi mir, Nos. 1
and 2, 1988): "We are paying today the cost of having abandoned
NEP." Such quotations can be extended. The authors link their
arguments with a denunciation of the excesses of despotic and
undemocratic centralization, and with advocacy of market-type
reforms today. Nuikin also speaks of "the catastrophe of collectivization", and is one of those who regards Stalin's accession to
supreme power in 1928–29 as a coup d'état.

Why, then, was NEP abandoned? We have already cited the
subtle and complex view of Gefter, which stressed not only its
remarkable economic results but also the political-ideological
ambivalence of the Party's attitudes toward the very phenomenon
of NEP. Were the majority of the members willing to tolerate this
mixed economy, dominated necessarily by an independent
peasantry, as a long-term perspective? It is in this context that one
must see both the reaction of the Stalin group to the economic diffi-

culties of 1927–28 and the willingness of Party members to accept the drastic "left turn" Stalin made.

Klyamkin, in *Novyi mir* (No. 11, 1987), titled his article "What Road Leads to the Temple?" These words come from the final scene of the well-known film *Repentance*: an old woman asks if a road leads to the temple, and on being told that it does not, replies: "Then why this road, if it does not lead to the temple?" Klyamkin has much to say about alternative roads, but he begins by stressing the importance of facing up to the past. Under Khrushchev it had become impossible to get anything published about Stalin which was not negative. Afterwards, it became impossible to write anything at all about Khrushchev. People felt that "the road did not lead to the temple", but for them history was a sort of blank, they felt themselves to be "without a past". Or they sought spiritual sustenance among nineteenth-century thinkers, including Dostoevsky and Slavophils, with apparently little attention paid to "Westernizers". Was there at any time a "Westernizing" road? For centuries Russia was trying to catch up to the more developed West, "especially in the area which ensures independence, that of armaments". There was but one instrument available, "that of autocracy, which acted in the only way it then could. It replied to the challenge of Europe by enserfing the peasantry, which for the West was a remote or recent past. From the serfs the state pumped out the material and human resources needed for the 'europeanization' of the army and of industry. In the West, the beginning of the industrial era was accompanied by the growth of freedom, in Russia—by the growth of slavery." (Interestingly, this last point is strongly made by V. Grossman in his *Vsyo techyot*, a work published so far only in the West, and he explicitly extends his argument to Lenin as well as Stalin.) The bourgeoisie remained weak well into the present century, while "in Russia the penetration of capitalism into the village, led to the rapid destruction of the patriarchal, communal way of life without its replacement by anything new, which in the end alienated the peasantry from the Asiatic-despotic government, which relied on it for support, without turning the peasant himself into an independent proprietor". The intelligentsia played a unique role, and Klyamkin quotes extensively from the critique of the radical intelligentsia contained in the famous collection *Vekhi* (*Milestones*), published in 1909. His essential point is that, though Russia was seeking to catch up to the West, the road chosen and the methods used were unique. The feeling that this was so helps to explain the attraction of Dostoevsky today. It helps to explain, too, why the programmes of *Vekhi*, and indeed of liberals and moderates in 1900–17, were doomed, by their insistence on dressing Russia up in European clothes. "The people (and the radical portion of the intelligentsia) believed in the reality of the miracle of revolution, and did not believe in the reality of gradualism, considering this to be a miracle." The authors of *Vekhi* were concerned about this. Thus Gershenzon wrote at the time: "Given what we are, we not only cannot wish to merge with the people, we should fear the people more than we fear any executions by the powers-that-be, and we should bless that power, which with its bayonets and prisons is still able to protect us from the people's violent anger." (One recalls Herzen's quip, about the intellectuals' willingness to wear chains, for fear of what might happen if the people were unchained.)

After the revolution, a group of emigre intellectuals produced a volume entitled *Smena vekh* (*Changing Milestones*), on the "national" or Russian nature of Bolshevism. Klyamkin quotes from it at length. However, this group came to believe in the durability of NEP, which would (in their view) lead to a gradual democratization. Some mensheviks were equally hopeful. They all looked at things through "European spectacles". The road actually taken under Stalin in 1929 seemed to them impossible. In particular, collectivization had to lead to a peasant uprising. It did not. Why not? Because, although of course many peasants suffered acutely from this cruel policy ("were the meat in the grinder"), their attitudes were still conditioned by patriarchal-communal traditions. This view of Klyamkin has been criticised by other Soviet writers: there *were* a few uprisings, but the scattered villages were surely unable to stand up to the coercive powers of the state, once this state was firmly established (the peasant uprisings of 1920–21, e.g., that of Antonov in Tambov, were specific to the conditions of the time). We will return to this theme in discussing the literature on collectivization.

But to return to Klyamkin—he cites with approval Popov's article on the logic of Stalin's Administrative system, with its "subsystem of fear". But Popov did not discuss the foundations on which this system rested, its "sergeants and junior officers". Yes, the brutality of the sergeants *had* been noted, but too often the wrong question was asked: instead of "why", one had "who was to blame". Some writers even blamed Trotsky. Klyamkin devotes to Trotsky's ideas some very interesting pages. Partly he does this to show that Trotsky's views on militarization of labour in 1920 were shared by most Bolsheviks, including Lenin, and so could not be used to blame him for the brutalities of 1930, but partly it is to show that Trotsky himself was a left-oppositionist *within the assumptions of NEP*. So that it was not the case that Stalin simply took over the Trotsky-Preobrazhensky policy after their defeat (a view put forward by several Soviet critics of Stalin's "left turn"). Was there, then, a Trotsky "road"? This raises the question of "socialism in one country". By 1925 Stalin had adopted this slogan, and Trotsky had not. Trotsky favoured industrialization, developing productive forces by joining in the international division of labour, and waiting for revolutions in Western Europe, which would help to overcome the contradictions involved in trying to build socialism in a backward country. But (writes Klyamkin) "what if there were no such revolutions? Answers came there none." Industrialization, how? At the cost of the village? Without coercion, would this be possible? Was this a viable policy?

"Socialism in one country," argues Klyamkin, "was a slogan of survival, self-preservation, national defence. It was the slogan which combined the socialist idea with national independence."

"Yes," continued Klyamkin, "I know, I often heard: it was wrong to eliminate NEP, it was a gigantic error for which we are still paying. It is even a risky enterprise today to speak otherwise, one might be labeled antiprogressive, a defender of old-style administrative methods. Yet, once again: could NEP have been preserved? If you reply 'Yes', then please transfer yourselves into that time and explain how you would resolve the problems that arose in the second half of the twenties." He lists the very real contradictions. He agrees that there was at that moment no direct military threat to the USSR, but the creation of a defence industry was still vital and urgent. Bukharin too had no viable policy: "None of the political activists of that time who stood for NEP had convincing answers to the questions which then arose: 'how', 'at the cost of what'." Then he roundly asserts: "Those who then won were the strongest, and only they could have won, and no road-building project capable of competing with collectivization then existed. To admit this does not imply that we should condemn those who thought otherwise. Indeed today the position taken by many of them looks more attractive than that of the victors. The point is just that the correlation of historical forces was in favor of the latter, not the former." But, he stresses, none of the circumstances of the time are relevant to today's problems, and Klyamkin strongly backs reforms and *perestroika*.

His historical arguments have been vigorously criticised, along predictable lines: there *was* another road, we cannot assume that whatever happened had to happen, the damage done by, and the costs of, Stalinist industrialization and collectivization exceeded the benefits, and so on. We will return to the "peasant" aspect of the controversy later.

"In 1929, and even more in 1937, *we* did not commit errors, *they* committed crimes. Our error was to have failed to notice how they concentrated too much power in their hands." Collectivization was not "fated" (all this from Nuikin). The essential point, in the context of *glasnost'*, is not the validity or otherwise of Klyamkin's arguments, or of those who oppose him, but that a real, open debate is taking place, with no holds barred, no (or very few) blank spaces or taboos—though a critical examination of some of Lenin's thoughts is only just beginning.

In his second article, Nuikin cites a would-be reformer of today as saying: "We will not allow [a return to] NEP." Why not? Because of the vision of profiteering "fat-bellied Nepmen". Nuikin points out that in a mere three or four years NEP had enabled a ruined economy to recover. What was wrong with "harmony between personal and social interest, feeding the people, a healthy economy, soundly-based prices, a full-weight rouble?" Yes, there was some "foam", but the essentials were sound, and its abandonment was "a world-historical error". The centralized system set up under Stalin provided ample opportunities for corruption and waste. Quoting some examples from the experience of recent years, he attributes the "no-return-to-NEP" ideology to defence of special rights and privileges of officialdom. Meanwhile, they shout "stop thief!" and point the finger at old women who sell dill, or persecute private tomato growers. Many officials took bribes to tolerate illegal enterprise of various kinds, or diverted supplies for their own needs.

So the debate has a direct link with today, though, to repeat, Klyamkin supports reform; it is a defensible position to argue both that the Administrative system of the thirties was necessary as a replacement of NEP and that the system has now totally outlived its usefulness and needs to be replaced via radical reform.

A major obstacle to the writing of Soviet history had been the nonrehabilitation of the principal victims of the show-trials and of Trotsky. Trotsky, of course, was never tried, but we have already seen that his ideas can be cited and criticised in a reasonable way. A whole page of *Pravda* (9 Sept. 1988) was recently devoted to Trotsky, this being another extract from (General) D. Volkogonov's book (*Triumph and Tragedy*). In this extract he tries to explain Stalin's hatred for the man, and for the first time the details of Trotsky's murder are set out; Volkogonov speculates that the murder could have been organized by Beria, and states that certainly Stalin wished Trotsky dead, but also that there seems no likelihood

of the true story emerging "in the near future". The picture
Volkogonov draws of Trotsky's character and policies is certainly
not a favourable one, but he does mention the fact that for several
years Trotsky's name was second only to Lenin's in popularity, and
that he did serve the revolution. A serious study of Trotsky's ideas
and policies is yet to come.

Preobrazhensky's article on "primitive socialist accumulation"
was reprinted in full in *Voprosy ekonomiki* (No. 9, 1988), together
with Bukharin's reply. *Ekonomika i matematicheskie metody* (No.
6, 1988) printed a critical article on Preobrazhensky's ideas by N.
Petrakov. Interestingly, he cites extensively the criticisms made at
the time by L. Yurovsky and V. Novozhilov (the former was arrested
in 1930 and was indeed a brilliant monetary economist; the latter
survived to be awarded a Lenin prize in 1965). In the same issue, A.
Belykh analyses the evolution of Bukharin's economic ideas, from
the time he attended Böhm-Baweck's lectures in Vienna, and
Western authors quoted included Stephen Cohen and Pekka Sutela.
Much was also made of the influence of Bogdanov and the relationship of Bukharin's ideas with those of Feldman.

The formal rehabilitation of Bukharin, Rykov, Rakovsky, and
others was announced in January 1988, after a deliberately elaborate legal procedure. This was followed in August 1988 with a
similar decision concerning Zinoviev, Kamenev, and others: they
were falsely accused, the trials were lies. Then there was another
important "rehabilitation", of the victims of another false trial, of
an alleged but nonexistent "working-peasant party", led by Chayanov, Kondratiev, Chelintsev, and Makarov, a trial which took place
in 1930. These men were tried because of their ideas on agriculture
and the peasants (Kondratiev was much better known in the West
for his "long-wave" theory of trade cycles). There were other trials
too, which led to prison and death for many theoreticians and
planners who distinguished themselves during the NEP period:
Bazarov, Yurovsky, Groman, Ginzburg, and others. These have not
yet been formally rehabilitated, though one suspects they soon will
be. (Yurovsky has had several favourable mentions.) The ground
has been at least partially cleared for a reassessment of the politics
and economics of the twenties.

We have seen that Klyamkin rejects the "Bukharin" alternative
almost without argument. Others plainly disagree, and inevitably
the discussion about "an alternative road" turns on Bukharin and
his group. However, there are obstacles, and these are not censorship obstacles. Bukharin has featured in several journals as a good
man, a favourite of the party, as Lenin said. Gorbachev praised him

in his anniversary speech, insofar as he fought Trotskyism, but distanced himself from Bukharin "the Right oppositionist". *Pravda* reprinted an article by Bukharin which it had published in 1925, about Lenin, and *Kommunist* (No. 2, 1988) published his "Political Testament of Lenin", a speech he made in January 1929, which can be taken to show that Bukharin was cautiously citing Lenin's ideas in defence of NEP, which was not yet openly under attack. When Stalin turned left in 1928 (leaving Bukharin to the "right" of him), their disagreement was behind closed doors, and Bukharin never spoke or wrote anything to explain his own viewpoint (his reference at the Politbureau to "military-feudal exploitation of the peasantry" was not published). A partial exception was his "Notes of an Economist" (printed in full in *E.K.O.*, No. 8, 1988), but the main criticism was disguised as an attack on Trotsky's alleged industrialization excesses, though cognoscenti could recognise at the time that this plea for a balanced plan was in fact a critique of the "plan-maximum" which Stalin had by then adopted. In his message, which, on the eve of his arrest, he asked his young wife to memorise, he claimed that for seven years he had no disagreements with the Party line. This message was published in *Ogonyok* and was featured also in Shatrov's play. But while it certainly has an effect on today's reader as a painful human document, what it denounces is not Stalin or any of Stalin's policies, but police terror—even while explicitly justifying terror used against genuine enemies of the revolution.

It is quite another matter with Chayanov. A series of articles praised him as a fine and original economist (and also an imaginative writer: his futurist novel, *The Journey of My Brother Alexis to a Peasant Utopia*, was set in 1984!). Chayanov's works are well known to Western students of peasant smallholdings, and he also had much to say about (genuine!) agricultural cooperatives. Eight volumes of his works were edited in Paris in 1967. They are to be edited and published in Moscow very shortly. Since questions regarding peasants and cooperatives, including family cultivation, are now high on the agenda, the reformers have seized upon Chayanov as highly relevant to their cause. An example of this is the article by V. Nikonov in *Voprosy ekonomiki* (No. 2, 1988). Presenting Chayanov as "the ideologist of the working peasant family enterprise", he stressed that he also devised and developed ideas on different forms of agricultural cooperatives. "His ideas now have a new birth. They are particularly relevant today, when there is such a broad development of nontraditional forms of organization of agricultural production and cooperatives." The history of cooperatives in the twenties has much to teach. However, when "command and administrative methods predominated there was a clear trend toward limiting cooperatives and ignoring their principles". The forcible implantation of *kolkhozy* was wrong. "Life showed that Chayanov was right." The peasant became alienated from the soil. "Here lie the origins of inefficiency, difficulties and stagnation in agriculture."

*Sotsialisticheskaya industriya* published an article praising Kondratiev, a fine and original economist, unjustly sentenced. An article on Kondratiev by L. Pnyasheva in *Druzhba narodov* (No. 7, 1988), informs us that some prison manuscripts have been found (which should be published soon), and also of the fact that Kondratiev was shot in 1938 on the very day he was due to be released from his eight-year sentence. An article extolling the virtues of Kondratiev appeared also in *Mirovaya ekonomika i mezhdunarodnye otnosheniya* (No. 9, 1988), which also reprinted an article by him. A volume of his collected works is announced for publication in 1989. Earlier several publications seized upon the hundredth anniversary of the birth of the great geneticist Vavilov to print articles in his praise, declaring him to be a "martyr to science", victim of the Stalinist system and of the charlatan Lysenko. Details were printed of his arrest and his end: he perished in the death cell of a prison in Saratov; the document showing that his death sentence had been commuted to life imprisonment never reached the prison. (See, for instance, *Literaturnaya Rossiya*, 20 Nov. 1987, and *Ogonyok*, No. 47, 1987.)

It used to be said by Western critics that no adequate history of the Soviet Union in the twenties, or indeed for any other period, could be written because it would involve admitting the fraudulent nature of the public trials and the rehabilitation of many victims. This cannot be said today. There are indeed some trials not yet declared fraudulent, some major academic figures and planners not (yet) formally cleared, but this is surely only a matter of time. No one now takes at their face value such trials as that of the "mensheviks" and of the "Industrial party" (*Prompartiya*), and no one censors positive references to the victims. Emigré sources too can be used, as for example when O. Latsis cited N. Valentinov's memoirs, published in America, about his time in the Supreme Council of the National Economy in the twenties (he spoke positively there of Dzerzhinsky's role in that Council). More certainly needs to be published about the Kirov murder and some rumoured attempts at or after the 17th Party Congress to clip Stalin's wings. However, these are not forbidden territories, and we may soon see historians penetrating them, especially as more archives are being opened.

The next historical theme to be tackled is the Nazi-Soviet pact. In previous years this pact was seen as logical and necessary, though there had been some criticism of the inadequate use made of the time that was gained to prepare for war. But now Colonel-General D. Volkogonov has written a book entitled *Triumph and Tragedy*, in which the years 1939–41 are fully examined. Extracts have been published in *Pravda* (20 June 1988). It is interesting and instructive to compare this work with that which got Nekrich into trouble when it was published in 1965, and with a pro-Stalin novel-documentary by Ivan Stadnyuk, *Voina (War)*, published in the seventies. All agree, of course, that Stalin had hoped to post-pone war, was ready to negotiate and forbade military precautions in the hope of avoiding "provocation", also that warnings had been received from many sources and disregarded. Volkogonov in this respect says nothing new, but says it well and clearly. He deplores the TASS declaration, published on 14 June 1941, to the effect that rumours of a German attack are false. It made sense to try to put out feelers, but to do this publicly could only have a "demobilizing" effect on the Soviet public and the military. True, Stalin did move several armies closer to the Western frontiers, but this was too little and too late. (This did not prevent an emigré author, "Suvorov", from asserting that Stalin was planning an immediate offensive! For this there is no evidence.)

Volkogonov is the first, to my knowledge, to publish in the Soviet Union a critique of "the treaty of friendship and frontiers between the USSR and Germany of 28 September 1939". Accepting the need for the nonaggression pact signed the previous month, this was unnecessary and confusing. "Friendship" with fascism? "It is hard to explain such a 'sliding' of Stalin and Molotov . . . into a de facto denial of all their previous antifascist ideological declarations." He went on: "Once again the sharp arrows of criticism were directed not at the fascists but at the social-democrats as 'allies of the militarists'." No wonder (he continued) Hitler was able to announce in the Reichstag that "he could agree with every word uttered . . . by Commissar of foreign affairs Molotov". The bound-ary agreement was reached easily, to the joy of Moscow, yet it should have caused suspicion: the Germans clearly regarded the agreed-upon frontiers as temporary. The *Pravda* article is illus-trated with a photograph of a smiling Stalin shaking hands with Ribbentrop. Similar views were expressed by A. Yakushevsky (*Voprosy istorii KPSS*, No. 8, 1988). He referred also to the handing over to the Nazis of a number of German communists held in Soviet prisons.

Volkogonov also casts some new light on the preparations and plans which were made. The general staff (Shaposhinikov, Vasilevsky) wished to concentrate the main defensive forces in the centre, but Stalin overruled them, and the largest number of Soviet divisions were placed to the south, covering the Ukraine. No attempt could be made to prepare "a strategic defense operation", and when one such was suggested during tactical exercises Stalin sarcastically remarked: "Why cultivate such attitudes? Are you planning a retreat?"

The following represents something not previously known, at least to Soviet readers. "At the beginning of 1941, when the flow of reports about German concentrations in Poland increased substantially, Stalin wrote a letter to Hitler, asking about German intentions. Hitler replied with a personal and 'confidential' note [*doveritel'noe*, which suggests also both 'personal' and 'sincere']. In this letter the Führer wrote that indeed there are military units in Poland, but, in the assurance that this information will not be repeated by Stalin, he can state that this troop concentration in Poland is not directed at the Soviet Union, as he intends strictly to adhere to the (Nazi-Soviet) pact, which he promises to do on his word of honour as head of state." Stalin (as Zhukov confirmed) believed the story that this was to keep the troops out of range of British planes!

Volkogonov says that it is hard to blame the generals for failing to press their point of view, given recent events, i.e., the drastic purge of the military. He cites some critical remarks by Vasilevsky about gaps in plans and in deployment, but regrets that they first saw the light in 1978 and not in 1940. Stalin's domination, his excessive self-confidence and obstinacy, cost the country very dearly. So did the losses in trained officers, losses which gave Hitler confidence in a successful attack, losses inflicted by Stalin in 1937 and after (for details of the military purge the reader is referred to the chapter on the Terror).

It is noteworthy that even the "Stalinist" book by Stadnyuk, while finding all possible excuses for Stalin's error about the timing of the German attack, does refer to the damage done by the paralysing effect of Stalin's authority. Stadnyuk cites what seem to be authentic details of the court-martial of the hapless commander of the central front, D. Pavlov. The front collapsed because elementary precautions were not taken, and they were not taken because, in the last resort, Pavlov was more frightened of his reponsibility to the Kremlin than he was of the enemy.

We are promised more research on the war itself, since the official story and the memoirs of many generals are incomplete. There is the role of Stalin as "generalissimus". There is much more to be said about the years of disaster. How can one explain the speedy collapse of the northwest front, which allowed the Germans to reach the outskirts of Leningrad so quickly? There are still too few details of the collapse of the southern front in 1942, and of the several futile offensives south and east of Leningrad. Above all, there are still no figures as to Soviet losses. Vague totals such as "20 million" include civilians. *Moskovskie novosti* (30 Aug. 1987) published the total number of Soviet prisoners of war, 5.7 million, of which 4 million perished and many who returned were "rewarded" with Soviet labour camps. How many were killed in action, how many wounded? We should soon know, though one suspects that records are incomplete. Similarly, the silence on the shooting of Polish officers at Katyn and elsewhere will surely soon be broken—there is a joint Soviet-Polish historical commission at work. Now that the Soviets have published the number of *Soviet* officer purge victims—40,000!—it is politically acceptable, surely, to admit that the executioners also shot many Poles. As we shall see, public statements have been made about mass deportations from the Baltic states, which relate to the same period, i.e., the first half of 1941. So gradually the number of blank pages diminishes.

The above lines were already written when *Voprosy istorii* (No. 9, 1988) published an article by B. Sokolov on war losses, citing new calculations. The Soviet forces through the whole war mobilised 30.6 million. The army at the outbreak of war numbered 5.9 million. Some 8.5 million men were killed, and 2.5 million died of wounds. There were 5.8 million who became prisoners of war ("up to May 1944"), of whom this source claims 3.3 million died in captivity. Throughout the war the ratio of Soviet troops killed to those of Germans and their allies was 3.7:1. Losses of equipment were in similar proportions. Some 100,000 men were lost in the Soviet assault on Berlin. Attacks regardless of cost were all too frequent.

On the cover of *Voyenno-istoricheski zhurnal* (No. 10, 1988) there appear these words: "classification 'secret' removed". The issue does indeed explore previously blank or half-hidden pages: there is a list of generals who were on the active list in 1940 with names of those shot in 1941 (several, such as Shtern and Smushkevich, were shot just before the war, others, e.g., the commander and staff of the central front, after the initial disasters), those who were released from prison and given commands, and a long list of those generals captured by the Germans and what happened to them. (Some died in captivity; others were shot by the Soviets after the war, and so on.) Other articles examine the breakdown of communications between armies and divisions in June 1941, and also the virtues (and negative characteristics too) of Marshal Zhukov. Evidently we are due for a large amount of new information, which will interest military historians.

Konstatin Simonov, whose war novels (especially the first, *Zhivye i mertvye* [*The Quick and the Dead*] gave a realistic picture of early disasters, found difficulty for many years in securing permission to publish his war diaries. Of unusual interest was the long-delayed publication by *Znamya* (No. 5, 1988) of a record of his interviews with leading military men, who said to him things they were not allowed to publish in their memoirs while they (and Simonov) were alive. One episode was cited by Admiral Isakov. Just before the war, at a meeting of the Military Council, the then commander of the Air Force, Rychagov, in reply to questions about air crashes, suddenly remarked: "Crashes are frequent because you compel us to fly in coffins." Stalin calmly remarked: "You should not have said that." A week later Rychagov was arrested and was never heard from again.

Rokossovsky told Isakov of how, after the disgraceful collapse (in 1942) of the Soviet armies in the Crimea (Kerch), he was present when the commander, Kozlov, went to see Stalin to try to justify himself. He blamed Mekhlis, the sinister political commissar ("member of the Military Council") who interfered constantly— which was in fact the case. Stalin replied: "You were the commander. Why did you not inform us by telephone that he did not allow you to command? . . . You clearly feared Mekhlis more than you feared the Germans." Kozlov exclaimed: "You do not know comrade Mekhlis"; to which Stalin replied: "That is not really so, comrade Kozlov, I do know comrade Mekhlis." (Indeed he did, and demoted him for his part in the "Kerch catastrophe".)

Isakov himself recalls the terrible shock to Stalin of the German attack, the shock being explicable "by the scale of his responsibility and by the fact that Stalin, accustomed to total obedience and absolute power, had collided with a force which at that moment was stronger than him".

In a long interview with Marshal A. Vasilevsky, Simonov quotes his very sharp remarks about the inefficient conduct of the Finnish war in 1939–40, when Stalin rejected Shaposhnikov's military advice and the first Soviet attacks were repulsed with heavy losses. "The Finnish war was for us a major disgrace and created a deeply unfavourable impression abroad about our army." The damage done by the military purge was immense. "You say that without 1937 there would not have been the defeats of 1941. I say more. Without 1937 there might well not have been a war in 1941. Hitler's decision to start the war in 1941 was greatly influenced by his estimate of the consequence of the massacre of military cadres. . . . I myself [i.e., Vasilevsky] saw that in 1939 in the Leningrad military district there were divisions commanded by captains, since all their superior officers had been arrested."

Stalin as generalissimo could be "intolerably rude and unjust". Vasilevsky had much to suffer from this. But there were other episodes: thus when one army commander, Volsky, wrote to Stalin on the eve of the Stalingrad operation that he feared it would fail, Stalin ordered Vasilevsky (who was Volsky's superior at the front), to fly to Moscow; Stalin questioned him about the prospects of success and about Volsky. When Vasilevsky expressed confidence in that commander's abilities, Stalin telephoned him and said he was confident that he would cope successfully with his task—which he did. Vasilevsky expressed negative feelings about Eremenko, whose generalship (he said) was inferior to his qualities as a bootlicker and flatterer. He had kind words about Khrushchev, who, though a member of the Politbureau, never tried to contact Stalin over Vasilevsky's head.

Other and more painful matters are also receiving an airing. B. Shaposhnikov (*not* the general, who died in 1942) wrote in *Literaturnaya gazeta* (22 June 1988) on "the price of victory", mentioning not only the huge losses due to frontal attacks, bayonet charges, and even on one occasion (in the Kerch disaster) a cavalry charge against tanks, but also the truly vicious disciplinary methods, including shooting not only for desertion and cowardice, but even for allegedly being the first to lie on the ground under fire during a futile attack on an enemy position. General Gorbatov (himself released from prison in 1941) referred in *Ogonyok* (No. 20, 1988) to "100,000 casualties" sustained in storming Berlin in April 1945, although there was no military necessity for this. In one of his posthumously published stories, V. Tendryakov described (in *Novyi mir*, No. 3, 1988) the execution of two soldiers. The painful subject of returned prisoners of war is tackled, too, in *Moskovskie novosti*, by Shaposhnikov in the above-cited article, and also in a detailed account of partisans in Karelia (*Znamya*, No. 5, 1988), in which the author (D. Gusarov) cites the cases of escaped prisoners of war making their way back to the Soviet lines, and then being treated with great suspicion, imprisoned, sent to Siberia, and in three instances shot as alleged spies. As we shall see, Shalamov's belatedly published "Kolyma tales" refer at length to repatriated prisoners of war ending up in these most dreadful of camp areas.

Gaps are being filled also for the first postwar years. The turn to repression in 1946 has already been noted. Details have been published, as we shall see, of the literary purge associated with the name of Zhdanov. In his memoirs, Simonov (in *Znamya*, No. 4, 1988) enlarges our knowledge of Stalin's personal role in literary "politics", showing that Stalin actually read an astonishing number of new novels and had a direct hand in the award and nonaward of "Stalin prizes". Simonov provides some fascinating details. For example, Simonov himself wrote a book about the postwar ruins of Smolensk, entitled *Dym otechestva* (*The Smoke of the Motherland*). Simonov liked it. Zhdanov liked it. A central committee cultural official, Ryurikov, wrote a favourable review. Stalin read the review, read the book, and issued instructions to Zhdanov, saying it was bad. So Ryurikov's review was cut, and a hostile one written on Zhdanov's instructions. Simonov cites, in his memoirs, many instances where Stalin had full knowledge of books (or films) under review, and judged them by a mixture of political and literary criteria. Simonov also has some fascinating remarks as to Stalin's (positive) view of Ivan the Terrible, and his approval of the first and disapproval of the second part of Eisenstein's film. Simonov also has comments on the excesses of the so-called struggle against kowtowing to the West. He notes that Stalin himself criticised the lack of "conflicts" in Soviet novels and plays. Then, after Zhdanov's death, there followed the bloody purge of the Leningrad Party, now at last given publicity and an explanation (Khrushchev had hinted that Malenkov had been involved in the "Leningrad affair", but gave no details). We will return to this "affair" when discussing the Terror. The anti-Semitic policies of these years have also had public exposure for the first time (see Chapter 5).

Some hitherto unknown or unpublished details of the politics of Stalin's last year have emerged in the Simonov memoirs. Simonov, apart from attending "literary" meetings called by Stalin, was an alternate member of the Central Committee elected by the 19th Party Congress (October 1952). It is, of course, known that at this Congress Stalin said little, the keynote speech being by Malenkov. It is also known that the Politbureau was renamed "Presidium", that it was enlarged to 25 members, and that this was intended to lessen the influence of the surviving old guard. A major purge seemed to be in preparation, and the "doctors' plot", discovered in January 1953, was in some way part of its preparation—all to be interrupted by the despot's death in March 1953. (Interestingly, Simonov speculates as to whether Beria had a hand in hastening Stalin's end, since he, too, felt threatened.)

After the 19th Congress, there was a plenum of the Central Committee, presumably at the very end of 1952 (Simonov gives no date). Stalin made a long speech, which included a sharp criticism of Molotov and Mikoyan; they were too weak to face up to the dangers of the world as and when old age incapacitated him, Stalin. He was particularly hard on Molotov. Molotov and Mikoyan tried to excuse themselves. Stalin clearly intended, in Simonov's view, to ensure that Molotov should not succeed him. Stalin said that he (Stalin) was too old to control the Party secretariat, that someone else should do it. Simonov wrote that Malenkov, in the chair, looked desperate, and was much relieved when from the body of the hall came shouts urging Stalin not to resign the general secretaryship. Malenkov must have thought that this was a test, and that, as the chairman, he might lose his head (literally) if Stalin's "request" were granted.

Stalin proposed that within the Presidium of 25 there should be a "bureau", and the membership of this inner inner group did not include Molotov and Mikoyan (it consisted of Malenkov, Beria, Kaganovich, Bulganin, Khrushchev, Voroshilov, Saburov, and Pervukhin, plus, of course, Stalin himself). So, in effect, as Simonov notes, Stalin reconstituted the Politbureau within the so-called Presidium, omitting two of his oldest and formerly most trusted minions. Interestingly, as soon as he died the "Presidium" was sharply reduced in size (i.e., it was again the Politbureau in all but name; that came later), and consisted of the above plus Molotov and Mikoyan.

Simonov listened to the speeches at Stalin's funeral (by Malenkov, Beria, and Molotov) and was struck by the lack of human warmth in the expressed attitude to the dead despot. In particular, Malenkov and Beria suggested "an attitude of men who had come to power and were pleased about it"; Molotov did sometimes sound as if he felt a personal loss, and this despite the crude attack on him by Stalin at the last Central Committee plenum.

In view of the number of citations from Simonov, it is worth mentioning that the old and respected writer, Veniamin Kaverin, in an interview with *Literaturnaya gazeta* (15 June 1988), deplored the publication of Simonov's memoirs, because Simonov had distinguished himself for so many years as one prepared to write anything to order.

Both Simonov and Adzhubei (Khrushchev's son-in-law, whose memoirs were printed in *Znamya*, Nos. 6 and 7, 1988) have some interesting remarks about the manoeuvres that followed Stalin's death. It was Beria who proposed Malenkov as premier, and apparently (to cite Simonov) was willing to have Khrushchev as the senior of the Party secretaries, considering him of secondary importance, "never until his own fall understanding his personality". It was apparently intended that power be exercised primarily through the Council of Ministers, into which went all the leaders—except Khrushchev, who devoted himself to Party affairs.

Several sources, including those cited here, assert that Beria was aiming at supreme power for himself, and that he regarded Malenkov as an ally. Adzhubei quotes Khrushchev as evidence that Beria did not conceal his joy at Stalin's death even when the despot lay dying. It was Khrushchev who took the initiative in organizing the plot to remove Beria. "I told Bulganin," said Khrushchev, "that once Beria achieves power he will exterminate us all." Khrushchev is also cited in a quite admirable article by Fedor Burlatsky (*Literaturnaya gazeta*, 24 Feb. 1988), conversing at Stalin's deathbed with Mikoyan. The latter said: "Beria is off to Moscow to seize power." Khrushchev replied: "While this bastard is around, none of us can feel safe." Khrushchev feared Malenkov's reaction, and praised "Georgi" for supporting action against his friend and associate. Because Beria could move internal security troops, it was important that Marshal Zhukov returned to Moscow to become deputy head of the Ministry of Defence (under Bulganin), and General Moskalenko, commanding the Moscow garrison, also played a part in Beria's arrest, at a meeting of the Party Presidium. Adzhubei mentions that Khrushchev had also won over a senior secret-police official, I. Serov, who "gave firm support" to the anti-Beria group. Adzhubei denies that Beria was shot without trial. There was, as the papers said, a special court, presided over by Marshal I. Konev, which sat for several months. There are volumes of as-yet unpublished evidence. Beria and six of his principal collaborators were sentenced to death in December 1953. Before being shot, Beria wrote a letter to Khrushchev begging for mercy.

This is not a history of the USSR, but an account of how *glasnost'* filled in the blank pages of that history. One such blank page was the very existence of Khrushchev. Now he can be discussed, and in a thoroughly sensible way. In the old days it was all black and white: a political or intellectual figure tended to be presented (if not relegated to unperson status) as all good or all bad. This is no longer the case. Khrushchev's record received balanced and sympathetic attention in the already-cited article by Burlatsky, who had been employed for a time as an assistant in his office. As he stated at the beginning of his article, a brief positive reference to Khrushchev in Gorbachev's speech on the occasion of the 70th anniversary of the revolution helped to remove "the twenty-year taboo" on the very mention of his name. This, along with the Adzhubei memoirs, is the principal way in which this remarkable man's achievements and errors have been presented to the Soviet reader. (It must be stressed that these are mass-circulation publications: *Znamya* has a circulation of half a million, *Novyi mir* double that, and *Literaturnaya gazeta*'s circulation is close to 4 million.)

To cite Burlatsky: "How is it that after Stalin it was Khrushchev who acquired the leading position? Surely Stalin had done everything to 'cleanse' the Party from any real or imagined opponents. . . . So only the most faithful, the most reliable, remained alive. How is it that Stalin failed to observe in Khrushchev the grave-digger of his cult?" Burlatsky notes in this connection Stalin's actions against Molotov and Mikoyan, taken in his last months of life, but he did not act against Khrushchev.

He cites Machiavelli (Burlatsky has written a book about Machiavelli!): "Brutus would have become Caesar if he could have pretended to be a fool." Khrushchev was able to pretend to be "a tame man without ambitions", willing to dance the gopak at Stalin's villa, a "reliable executant of the will of others". But his frustrations boiled over once Stalin died. "He came to power not by accident, yet also by accident." He did represent the widespread attitudes of those who desired relaxation, the end of repression, some democratization. But accident played its role: "If Malenkov had reached an understanding with Beria, if the Stalinist old guard had combined in 1953 and not in 1957, then Khrushchev could not have become leader."

How, he asks, did Khrushchev have the courage and daring to make his "secret speech" denouncing Stalin to the 20th Party Congress (February 1956), when "he knew that the vast majority of the delegates would be against such revelations"? Burlatsky writes: "This was one of the rare occasions in history, when the political leader gambled with his own personal power and even his life in the name of higher social objectives." None of the other post-Stalin leaders would have dared to speak thus. Burlatsky frequently heard Khrushchev speak of his attitude toward Stalin. "He was deeply wounded by Stalinism. Several elements coexisted: a mystical fear of Stalin, who could destroy anyone for just one false step, look or gesture; and horror at the shedding of innocent blood. Also there was the feeling of personal guilt, and the accumulation of decades of (unexpressed) protest." Yet, according to Burlatsky, when the Italian communist leader Palmiro Togliatti sought to find "the roots of the cult of personality in the system", Khrushchev rejected this approach. He undoubtedly wished the people to live better, but was far from clear about the means of achieving this. His own willful enthusiasm led to the coexistence of highly desirable reforms and excessive campaigning, as in the campaign to sow maize (*kukuruza*) everywhere. He ignored the effect of his campaign against the Stalin cult on other socialist countries. This campaign was in fact only partial, since "many in the party knew of his own role in the Ukraine and in the Moscow Party organization. Since he did not tell the whole truth about himself, he could not tell the whole truth about the others." So his denunciations were incomplete, unbalanced. "Khrushchev carefully avoided the period of collectivization, since he was personally involved in the excesses of that period."

He tried to amend the Party statutes to ensure "rotation of cadres", but here he was forced to retreat. His proposal (now repeated by Gorbachev) that no one should hold top positions for more than two periods met with strong objections. It is worth quoting in this connection the remark of Adzhubei, explaining the "evil-intentioned silence" about Khrushchev after his fall: "He could not be forgiven by that administrative bureaucratic system which he dared to trouble. It was this system which demonstrated its strength and warned any future contender: do not touch us."

Burlatsky confirms Western reports about the 1957 crisis. The majority of the Politbureau voted for Khrushchev's removal, but his appeal to the Central Committee succeeded, with substantial help from Marshal Zhukov, who "uttered a historical phrase to their face: the Army is against this decision, and no tank will move without my order". In the last analysis "this phrase cost him his political career", since Khrushchev removed him soon after, "for fear of a strong man".

Alas, Khrushchev was too ready to rely on unreliable flatterers, such as Podgorny. He was persuaded to attack the creative intelligentsia, on modern art and over Pasternak's *Zhivago*, though at times he supported them. Adzhubei noted these contradictions too: thus Dudintsev's *Not by Bread Alone* annoyed him, "even though it described the very same negative phenomena that Khrushchev was criticising". He was oversanguine about "overtaking America" and moving toward communism, reflecting (according to Burlatsky) genuine optimism and enthusiasm. His reorganizations were excessive, the division of the Party was foolish and did him great political

harm, and so could have been suggested to him by those who wished
to discredit him.

Adzhubei also regretfully noted (in *Moskovskie novosti*, 15 May
1988) Khrushchev's support for Lysenko, despite efforts by the
great physicist Kurchatov, and by his own son, to persuade him to be
tolerant of genetics, while his daughter Rada said: "You will see,
you will be ashamed of yourself." "Khrushchev could not wait.
Fruit-flies and similar clever researches in his view simply diverted
attention from the immediate need for more grain. Impatience
predisposes to hope for miracles," and Lysenko "fed" these hopes.

Burlatsky has other acute observations. Thus "the people, who
accepted [Ivan] the Terrible and condemned Boris Godunov, could
not accept, after Stalin, a leader lacking in mystical magic, earthy
and sinful, liable to error and confusion". The following phrase was
attributed to Sholokhov at the height of the "thaw". Referring to
Stalin, he said: "Yes, certainly there was a cult, but there was also a
personality." The tragic events in Hungary in 1956 were a blow to
reformers. So was Khrushchev's own "light-hearted carelessness"
(*bespechnost'*) in matters of theory and political strategy. "Khrush-
chevism as a concept of socialist renewal never materialised. . . .
Khrushchev walked on two legs, one of which boldly marched into a
new epoch, the other was totally stuck in the mud of the past." His
reforms relied on "traditional administrative methods", i.e., on the
very apparatus which real reforms would adversely affect. And "the
people were silent", or critical. "How many times did I hear: in what
respects is Khrushchev better than Stalin? At least in Stalin's time
there was order, bureaucrats were imprisoned and prices were cut."
So when, in 1964, he was removed, "maybe a majority of society as
a whole heaved a sigh of relief". Khrushchev was a victim of his own
nature, and not only of his environment. "Haste, thoughtless speed,
emotionalism, were essential features." Burlatsky ends with remarks
which Churchill made to Khrushchev, warning him to introduce
reforms with care and circumspection. "It is not easy to cross a
precipice in two jumps." Nor can it be done, concludes Burlatsky,
"when you do not know where you are jumping to".

Khrushchev's role was discussed also in the pages of *Moskovskie
novosti*. In No. 18 (1988), Levada and Sheinis blamed him for "not
fully carrying through anything that he began", thus dooming his
reforms to failure. In No. 33 (July 1988), G. Fedorov agreed that
he was often inconsistent, but some of his reforms were real: "the
abolition of punishment without trial by the so-called *troiki* and
'special councils', pension reform (before pensions were so miserably small that they were symbolic)"; housing; peasant policy

("before Khrushchev the peasants were subject to unbelievable exactions and taxes and led a miserable existence"). With all his defects, Khrushchev in general acted in the interests of the country and its people. "He performed a heroic deed, risking not only his political career but his life, when he boldly decided to 'dethrone' Stalin and to rehabilitate millions of innocents, alive and dead. Remember that he acted wholly surrounded by Stalinists. In the upper echelons of authority at that time, unlike ours, there was no one else but. Furthermore, Khrushchev himself was part of Stalin's entourage, so that Khrushchev had first to overcome the Stalinist in himself, which he tried to do, and then only to combat other Stalinists, creating the conditions without which today's renewal would have no possibilities, cadres or tradition. He was a real leader, an ice-breaker."

In the second part of his memoirs (*Znamya*, No. 7, 1988) Adzhubei also has some remarks about Khrushchev's "secret speech" at the 20th Party Congress. When he announced his decision to make it, Molotov, Malenkov, and Voroshilov objected. He suggested that Molotov should speak about Stalin, adding that he, Khrushchev, would then speak after him. Molotov refused. Khrushchev boldly took serious political risks. Adzhubei refers also to Kirov's murder, the suspicious circumstances surrounding it (his bodyguard was killed in an arranged traffic accident, and those who arranged it were shot in their turn); he treats the murder "as the most dreadful secret, not yet fully clarified". About the 17th Party Congress (in 1934), he is sure that Stalin's action in subsequently killing the majority of the delegates was linked with the fact that hundreds did not vote for him in the secret ballot, even though he was applauded with apparent unanimity ("How could he trust people; they applaud and they hate!").

Adzhubei goes on: "How can one understand Molotov, with his exceptional faith in all that was Stalin, when he tolerated the arrest and imprisonment of his own wife? Did he believe in [her] guilt and calmly wait for Beria to report on it? And how could M. I. Kalinin feel, whose wife spent many years in penal servitude and he could do nothing to help her?" In 1936 a courageous Latvian communist, Jan Kalnberzin, was sent to Latvia to work as organizer of the illegal party. He was arrested in Latvia, and released in 1940 when the Soviets took over. But in 1937 his wife was arrested and died in prison; his three children were sent to orphanages. With great effort he found his children, and one of his daughters, who was a classmate of Adzhubei's, said that her father told her: "I did not ask about your mother, there was no point. They also said nothing. Do not blame me. I do not even know where she is buried." The great rocket specialist Korolev was arrested and sent to Kolyma before being employed, as a prisoner, in a secret research establishment. He told how he survived by luck; his group missed their sailing, and the ship, as he later discovered, foundered and its passengers drowned.

Adzhubei mentions another obscure historical episode. The commander of the Second Cavalry in the civil war was F. K. Mironov; when *Izvestiya* was preparing to publish an article about him (he was killed in prison in 1921 in mysterious circumstances) there was an immediate protest from Budyonny, who also protested about a piece on another Red cavalryman, Dumenko. This confirms stories published abroad about Budyonny's unseemly behaviour; he had taken an active part in the trial of Tukhachevsky and other generals in 1937.

Adzhubei sheds a little light on the plot which removed Khrushchev in 1964, rumours of which (he says) did reach Khrushchev when he took a short holiday, but, as Mikoyan remarked at the time, "Khrushchev forgot that under socialism too there can be a struggle for power." He emphasises the role of Suslov, also as the *éminence grise* of Brezhnev. Adzhubei expresses his "astonishment at the 'technology' of leadership change: in fact neither the party nor the country heard any arguments, no serious reasons 'pro' or 'con'. No discussions, no passionate speeches, no information; in April it was 'hurrah', in October it was 'away with him'. We never were able to discover what Nikita Sergeyevich wanted to say, if indeed he wanted to say anything, and yet it was not only his personal fate that was decided. . . . I and many of my comrades felt deep shame when, by the same methods . . . Chernenko was selected as general secretary." He also states that first Kirilenko and then Pelshe forbade Khrushchev to write his memoirs, that he had heart attacks after talking to these former "comrades" of his.

In *Ogonyok* (No. 33, 1988), G. Fedorov describes the elaborate precautions taken by the authorities to prevent the public from attending Khrushchev's funeral, and cites a short speech made by a woman released from a long and horrible imprisonment, who said she spoke "on behalf of millions who perished in prisons and camps, to whom you, Nikita Sergeyevich, gave back their good name, on behalf of their relatives and friends and of the hundreds of thousands that you freed . . . , receive our gratitude and deep respect". To avoid any subsequent gatherings, the Novodevichy cemetery was thereupon closed to the public.

*Ogonyok* has been printing in instalments the memoirs of Khrushchev's son, Sergei. In No. 43, 1988, he describes in detail the way in which Khrushchev was ousted from power in October 1964, noting the particular hostility to him of Shelest and Shelepin. These and other publications (e.g., those by Simonov, Adzhubei, and Burlatsky, quoted above) open many doors and windows on real political manoeuvres, plots and counter-plots that have been almost totally hidden from view for nearly sixty years.

In *Druzhba narodov* (No. 11, 1988), Anatoli Strelyany discusses Khrushchev, under the title of "The Last Romantic", a vivid account of his virtues, his vices, and his fall. Nikolai Cherkashin analyzes the previously secret explosion in Sevastopol which sank the former Italian battleship *Giulio Cesare*, which the Soviets had rechristened *Novorossiisk*, in 1955.

Clearly, there is now no barrier to a genuinely full discussion of Khrushchev's internal policies. Nothing has yet appeared about his foreign policy, but no doubt it will come.

The debate meanwhile has swung back to a reexamination of Soviet history as a whole. At about the same time Latsis was contributing his challenging ideas to *Znamya* (see Chapter 2), Yuri Afanasyev was sending his historical interpretation to *Literaturnaya Rossiya*. Meanwhile the "conservatives", in such journals as *Nash sovremennik*, were seeking to defend what they believe to have been a glorious past against besmirchment; Stalin did kill innocent people, yes, but . . . This view found its most eloquent expression in a "letter to the editor" (full page, in five columns) by Nina Andreyeva (a chemist who teaches in a Leningrad technological institute), published by *Sovetskaya Rossiya* on 13 March 1988. This daily is described as "the organ of the Central Committee of the CPSU, the Supreme Soviet and the Council of Ministers of the RSFSR" (i.e., of the Russian federation). This produced a full-page counterblast in *Pravda* (5 Apr. 1988), itself the organ of the central committee of the CPSU, a rare example of "socialist pluralism", a sure reflection of difference of view in the upper strata of the hierarchy. However, *Pravda* also printed (on 25 June 1988) a counterattack directed at Yuri Afanasyev's interpretation of history, under the title of "Voprosy istoriku" ("Questions to the Historian"), though, as we shall see, it also printed Afanasyev's hard-hitting reply.

Let us begin with Andreyeva, whose letter caused such a stir. She is typical of many. Thus, both *Ogonyok*, in its correspondence columns, and *Znamya*, in its collection of readers' reactions to Shatrov's play (which it had published and which is discussed in Chapter 3) printed a number of letters protesting the revisionist views of Stalin and of Soviet history. Bestuzhev-Lada (in *Nedelya*,

No. 15, 1988) devoted a whole article to letters from readers who protested at his criticisms of Stalinism. Thus, Andreyeva represents a significant current of opinion, and this is why the *Pravda* editors, or their political masters, thought it necessary to reply—the more so as they understood, and specifically stated, that Andreyeva and those who think like her were also attacking *perestroika*. Nothing can better illustrate the contemporary political significance of the writing and rewriting of history. And not only of Soviet history. We have already noted that views on such long-dead monarchs as Ivan the Terrible matter in terms of today.

So to Andreyeva; her kind of views are also held by influential professional historians, whom Afanasyev was combating. She complains that Soviet history is presented as consisting of mass repressions, "'terrorism', 'politically supine people', 'spiritual slavery', 'total fear', 'coercion by louts [*khamy*] in power'", and this causes ideological confusion among students. She resents "political anecdotes, lack of respect even for Lenin, who, in Shatrov's play *Brestski mir* "goes down on his knee before Trotsky" (!?). Shatrov, in his *Dal'she, dal'she, dal'she* falsifies history, "departs from the canons of socialist realism", ignores the objective laws of history and overemphasises the subjective factor, accuses Stalin of the murder of Kirov and Trotsky, "without troubling himself with providing proof". His views remind her of Boris Souvarine's book on Stalin, published in the West in 1935. Rybakov's *Deti Arbata* also uses emigré sources. Yes, there were indeed repressions and innocent victims, she readily admits and deplores this, but "common sense emphatically protests against painting the contradictory events in one (black) colour, as some press organs are doing". Stalin's personality, she says, greatly impressed Churchill, and she quotes his praise of him ("he inherited a Russia with a wooden plough, and left it with atomic weapons" and so on). Stalin played a great role in the war. Yes, his were grim times, but "personal modesty, even asceticism, were nothing to be ashamed of then, and potential soviet millionaires were scared to penetrate backstairs offices and trade centres". Youth were not consumer-oriented, were devoted "to Labour and Defence", were not subjected to imported "mass culture". Attacks on Stalin and on "the cult of personality" extend also to "collectivization, industrialization, the cultural revolution, which brought our country up to great-power status". Novels and films wrongly present the heroic period of socialist construction as "a tragedy of the peoples".

She expresses the view that "these attacks on the state of the dictatorship of the proletariat and on the then leaders of our country

have not only political, ideological and moral causes, but also their
social basis. . . . Along with Western professional anticommunists,
who long ago adopted the pseudodemocratic slogan of 'anti-
Stalinism', there still live the descendants of classes which were
overthrown by the October revolution, who have not all forgotten
the material and social losses suffered by their ancestors. Here one
could also place the spiritual descendants of Dan, Martov and
other Russian social-democrats, the spiritual followers of Trotsky or
of Yagoda [!?], descendants of Nepmen, *basmachi* [Turkestan rebels
of the twenties], and *kulaks*, offended by socialism. Peter the Great
is still considered great, since under him Russia became a great
European power, and his personal traits do not matter any more."

Some now deny that "peaceful coexistence is none other than a
form of class war in the international arena", the class view and the
class war are seen as obsolete. Andreyeva cites with approval the
view of a Leningrad writer to the effect that two "ideological towers
exist" which each in their own way are seeking to "overcome the
socialism built in our country", that they "have in common only
attacks on socialist values", though they claim to be for *perestroika*.
One presents itself as "neoliberal intellectual socialism, with an
emphasis on individual values, technocratic idols, praise for the
'democratic charms of today's capitalism', defence of animal rights
[?], the inheritance of intelligence [??]". They are particularly guilty,
in her view, of falsifying the past history of socialism in the USSR;
"whence this passion for denigrating the authority and dignity of the
leaders of the world's first socialist country?" The "neoliberals" are
guilty too of "cosmopolitanism". Here Andreyeva wanders onto the
thin ice of barely concealed anti-Semitism. "I once heard that after
the revolution there came to see Trotsky at the Petrograd soviet a
delegation of merchants and factory-owners, to see him 'as a Jew' to
complain about oppression by the Red guards; Trotsky replied that
he was 'not a Jew but an internationalist', thereby greatly puzzling
the petitioners." According to Andreyeva, Trotsky believed in the
backwardness and uncultural nature of the Russians. Today, too,
any reference to the national pride of the Great-Russians attracts
accusations of great-power chauvinism. She then at once goes on to
attack the "refuseniks" and the emigrés, who betray their country
after having benefited from Soviet education, some of whom, if their
services are not well paid in the "free world", now try to return.
Marx and Engels called some nations, at certain stages of their
history, "counterrevolutionary", "and I underline: not classes, or
strata, but nations". They did at times "give harsh characteristics to
whole nations, including Russians, Poles and those nationalities to

which they themselves belonged". (In the context, this can only be read as a roundabout way of calling the Jews a "counterrevolutionary nation".)

Finally, Andreyeva gets to the other "ideological tower", which clearly upsets her less than do the "neoliberals": these she calls "guardians and traditionalists which wish to overcome socialism by moving backwards in time, to the social forms of prerevolutionary Russia, especially the peasant commune [*obshchina*]". They have, in her eyes, merits: they fight corruption, take up ecological causes and the preservation of ancient monuments, they dislike "mass culture" and consumerism. However, they are wrong in seeing collectivization in an exclusively negative light, they accept uncritically religious-mystical philosophers, they do not see the revolutionary role of the working class. Then she returns to the attack on those who believe in "separation of powers", "parliamentary regime", and "free trade unions", putting into question the leading role of the Party, introducing "non-socialist pluralism", weakening ideology. *Pravda*'s counterblast reflected the realization that her attack was directed at the rethinking of both history and Stalinism, and at the liberalizing aspects of *perestroika*, at the ideas not just of many in Gorbachev's entourage but of Gorbachev himself, though this is nowhere said openly in her article. Hence the vigour of the reply, which attacked *Sovetskaya Rossiya* for publishing a sort of antireform manifesto, thus going beyond the limits of tolerable Party discussion.

Now to Afanasyev's creed, which, as will be seen, tried *Pravda*'s patience from what could be called the opposite direction. Under the title of "*Perestroika* and Historical Knowledge" (*Literaturnaya Rossiya*, 17 June 1988), his essential points were as follows. First, "despite vast sacrifices, we did not achieve socialism in the form in which Lenin and Lenin's comrades envisaged it in the twenties". So one must ask: "why did we build so that we now have to restructure?" "If we turned off the road opened up by October, then why and in what circumstances?" This "touches the nerve of our society". The argument rages. Some see Stalinism as the "rational or even triumphant completion of the October revolution". Others discuss the existence and desirability of "the alternative whose incarnation was N. Bukharin". Afanasyev urges the abandonment of "our dogmatized historical materialism, which presents the whole path since October as a straight-line process, governed by a priori predetermined 'laws'". There were and are always some choices. *Perestroika* is itself a choice, "an alternative to Stalinism, stagnation, lawlessness as a system, corruption". One must welcome "the polyphony of voices, even if some are dissonant". There should be "open competiton between various ideas, to ensure free, democratic choice. . . . It is here that are combined history and politics, the past and the present." What forces blocked the reforms in the sixties, and why did Stalinism in modified form remain for decades after his death? "We enter into a kind of moral dialogue with those who lived in the thirties." Alas, historians have been backward in tackling such questions.

Referring to Marx's aphorism, *de omnibus dubitandum*, Afanasyev adds to this one from Danton: "Lack of trust is the highest quality in a citizen." Much is now questioned, for example, whether or not state property is genuinely social property. What about the view that we have "a definite sort of private property in the function, the job, the appointment"? Suppose the form in which socialism was achieved could be characterised by Marx's definition of "barracks socialism"? Are not Zaslavskaya, Karpinsky, and others right in saying that "in the thirties, with the Stalinist form of collectivization, the working peasant was alienated from property, that the peasants as a class were liquidated"? Freedom of wide-ranging search for the truth upsets some people, who want to stop it. Afanasyev cites here as an example Andreyeva's letter, "a real political manifesto against *perestroika*, based simultaneously on the falsification and dogmatization of history". Some adopt the subtler tactic of "half-truth": thus Trotsky is no longer presented as an agent of a foreign power, he did not join the Bolsheviks in 1917 to disrupt the Party, he was even a talented orator who did something for the revolution in 1917 and during the civil war. Yet in the end Trotsky, and also Zinoviev and Kamenev, are presented politically in the same Stalinist manner. Thus Kamenev's disagreement with Lenin over the October rising is highlighted, but the fact that Lenin nonetheless nominated him to be the first postrevolutionary chairman of VTsIK (the executive of the Soviets) is ignored. "The whole Stalinist version of the struggle against various deviations in the twenties is reproduced unchanged, there is no mention of the existence of the Stalinist anti-Party fraction." Collectivization too is presented as if in line with Lenin's ideas, instead of a distortion of Lenin's concepts, at the cost of millions of lives. These "peddlers of half-truths" take the line that on the one hand there were mass repressions and crimes, but on the other there were joy, enthusiasm, and records, and there should be "no blackening of our glorious past". Yes, replies Afanasyev, there were stakhanovite records, "but also the record number of killing one's fellow citizens, exceeded perhaps only by Pol Pot". This two-handed approach is unhelpful, and we need to get beyond blaming only Stalin for what occurred. Some are prepared to blame his psyche, and in this way "sacrifice Stalin in the name of preserving Stalinism", failing to ask the question: "How far was Stalin the creator and how far the product of the system which was consolidated when he was in power?" Khrushchev never got beyond blaming Stalin personally.

Turning to Soviet historians, Afanasyev notes their "helplessness" in the new situation. Two academicians even replied to a question from the chairman of the state education committee by saying that the history textbooks are almost satisfactory. Yet "in the history textbook for the 9th class [16-year-olds] there is not a single unfalsified page. The whole textbook is a lie. . . . The same is true of university textbooks, especially on Soviet history and the history of the CPSU. In the past decades we have barely moved conceptually beyond the Stalinist 'short course'. . . . I doubt if there is a country in the world with so falsified a history as ours." Historians alone are not to blame, when party officials like Trapeznikov (in Brezhnev's time) drove good historians out into the wilderness. As for Lenin, Afanasyev disagrees with the view that Lenin had a fully developed conception of socialism. No, he was in the process of working it out; "after all, he did not live under socialism, he could only imagine and think that out of NEP Russia would emerge a socialist Russia, hoped that this would occur, and elaborated the principles of such a transition". He then makes a very important point (also touched upon by Gefter): "Was there a NEP Russia? Yes, there was a New Economic Policy, but did Russia have time to become Nepist—that is an open question. . . . And Lenin would be seen as even more grandiose if shown to be a man seeking answers and not always finding them."

He then puts an even more fundamental question, "about the attitude to Marxism-Leninism." Dogmatic scholasticised ideology inherited from the thirties is now an obstacle to clear thought. We must "critically reconsider Marxism, return to its roots, shake off the domination of dogmatists". Real Marxism must criticise also itself. Marxists must conduct a free dialogue with other schools of thought, including Western Marxism, the followers of Gramsci and the Frankfurt school. Marx and Lenin believed that capitalism had already played out its historical role, but we now know that what Lenin called the imperialist stage was in fact an early stage of capitalism. No one could have foreseen the electronic, nuclear, laser, or computer revolutions. Also, Marx and Lenin believed in a speedy achievement of communism. This too proved mistaken. The "classics" did not foresee the long-term coexistence of capitalism and socialism. It is necessary, in looking at the Western world, "to free ourselves once and for all from stereotypes that demonize capitalism", while avoiding "the fetishization" and mythologizing of the West, which "stands on its head our official picture of ourselves". Non-Marxist ideas must be studied seriously. So should Western historical work on the Soviet Union. Three generations of Soviet historians have been brought up in ignorance of Western thought. "To criticise, which we have always been ready to do, it is first necessary to know, to study."

For Stalin and Brezhnev, history as such was not needed, except as a justification for unjust acts. "Our collective memory was gradually extinguished. . . . The result is the crisis of identity of our contemporary society. . . . We look in the mirror and cannot recognise ourselves. . . . And precisely in this vacuum is to be found a place for such chauvinist and anti-Semitic groups as the extremists of 'Pamyat'."

Afanasyev ends by expressing disagreement with the proposal to write a new official Party history, with a plea for open access to archives, including Party archives, now much more freely available.

Stirring stuff! *Pravda* did not (as was the case with Andreyeva) reply "editorially". It did print, within a week, a long article by Pobisk Kuznetsov, who accepts that there is much to agree with. However, he disagrees about the criticism of the "on the one hand—on the other hand" approach: after all, there *were* both enthusiasm and repression, achievements and tragedy. Also he is unhappy about not achieving the socialism imagined by Lenin. Yes, he agrees, we got a deformed system that now needs a *perestroika*, yet "we did not leave the road opened by October, . . . otherwise there would be no socialism in the world". Afanasyev raised the question Is our society socialist? and then failed to answer it. Kuznetsov cites Gorbachev's formulation, in his 70th anniversary speech, to dismiss the "Bukharinist" alternative envisaged by Afanasyev: "Was it possible in the conditions of the time to choose another course than that the party proposed?" He answers—no. As might be expected, Kuznetsov cannot accept the notion of private property in rank or position. "I do not think that the History-archives institute, which the author of the article directs, is considered by him as his private property." A new textbook on Party history is desirable, is being prepared. Not a very sharp rap on the knuckles.

Afanasyev replied in *Pravda* on 26 July 1988. Kuznetsov had written, "We were not able, and we did not know how" to build a nondeformed socialist society, "we were not fully consistent", and

Afanasyev counters with the following: "'We', 'we', that's great! 'We'—millions of prisoners led by Yagoda, Yezhov and Beria. 'We'—the enserfed, robbed and hapless peasantry destroyed as a class by Stalin and his cohorts. Let us remember that Stalin abolished NEP, converted (not alone, but at the head of a whole social stratum) the Party into a 'Teutonic knights order' [*mechenostsev*], tore up the union with the peasants, subjected the workers to barracks-discipline, suppressed or destroyed the intelligentsia, made blood and fear into the foundations of the state, since he could not be 'fully consistent' in applying Lenin's directions." Kuznetsov's argument would imply that this conversion of socialist ideas into "totalitarian and terrorist" ones was "historically predetermined".

Afanasyev referred again to Nina Andreyeva's letter to *Sovetskaya Rossiya*: the menace is not from her, but from "those who stood behind this modest chemistry teacher and turned her letter into a directive, which was at once utilized by 30 *obkomy* [provincial committees] of the CPSU". (An editorial footnote states that this allegation "did not find confirmation".) Afanasyev went on: "The idea of market socialism is one that we reached through our own painful history; or must we still say it is an invention of our enemies? What would Lenin say if in 1988 he saw ration cards, millions of Russians in distant towns [*glubinke*] dreaming of a ring of adulterated sausage, or how we are 'learning democracy' 35 years after the death of Stalin. . . . Did we have socialism or barracks-socialism, on the one hand half a barrel of honey and on the other half of tar."

An editorial comment disapproved of some of Afanasyev's formulations, but they printed his piece, though with three weeks' delay.

A few days later, I. Dedkov and O. Latsis joined the fray. They agreed with Afanasyev about the "inhuman stalinist system", but stated that "he leaves it unclear what our people had created in seventy years, if indeed anything. . . . Stalin and his circle monstrously deformed socialism so as to strengthen their power, created a pitiless mechanism for suppressing dissent. But they were compelled to ensure industrialization and the defence of the land of socialism. The people followed them, believing in the practical deeds and not knowing all the truth about the carefully concealed crimes." Despite everything, "socialism survived". The rest of their article argues sensibly for economic reform and against old-style dogmatic thinking.

It is also worth quoting an article by A. Burganov (*Moskovskie novosti*, 25 June 1988), in which he discusses another interesting question: Why did historians fail in their professional duty for so

long? He cites the reply of one scientist, asked why he defended
views he knew to be unscientific: "I am a soldier of the Party." Too
many historians acted thus. Some years ago Burganov himself was
criticised by a friend and colleague at a public gathering. When he
asked the critic whether he had at least read his work, he got the
reply: "What for? We have in the Party those whose job it is to read.
And I, you understand, must support the views of a central press
organ." When Burganov in 1963 published an article with the title
"October—A Genuine People's Revolution", he got a Party reprimand and the editor was dismissed. Why? Because "there still
dominated the Stalin conception that the revolution was solely
proletarian, and the use of the term 'people' in connection with
October was considered criminal". His own doctoral dissertation,
when it cited (without quotation marks) ideas actually drawn from
Marx and Lenin, drew such comments from official reviewers as
"SR", "menshevik", "bourgeois-falsifier". The university administration then decided to withdraw the dissertation, and placed it in
the library's *spetskhran* (closed section); the records of the defence
of the dissertation were removed and placed under lock and key in
the local Party secretary's safe!

Burganov concluded: in the bad old days, historians had the
excuse that the facts were hidden from them, i.e., *they could not be
historians*. But "now the situation is different. The truth, if not the
whole truth, is known." So "those historians who cannot give up
their previous position *do not wish to be historians*". There is a
difference.

As has already been noted, the bulk of the historical material has
so far come not in books, not even in articles in historical journals,
but in newspapers and literary periodicals. This will change. The
way has been cleared for the professionals, especially after much-
needed changes in the leadership of their own ranks. We know that a
new history of the Party, for use as a textbook, is in active
preparation, and we can await books and monographs on a wide
variety of hitherto taboo themes.

The June 1988 issue of *Voprosy istorii* shows a clear desire to
bring together the historians (under new management) and the
literary men. A discussion between them fills over a hundred pages.
Afanasyev repeats his claim that no country has ever had so falsified
a history as Russia, and this produces a riposte: bad, yes, but not *so*
bad. He mocks the teachers of the compulsory social science
(ideological) courses, calling them *popy marksistkogo prikhoda*
(priests of the Marxist parish) and the courses "disgusting" (*bezo-
braznye*). Astafyev, the novelist, considers that the official histories

of the war, especially the 12-volume edition, were a travesty, a disgrace, falsified in the extreme, unrecognisable by those who fought in the war. In 1941, he says, out of the 5 million soldiers originally deployed, 3 million were captured, or so he believes. When will the true figures about losses be published? What of such disgraceful episodes as the loss of three whole armies in the Crimea (the Kerch disaster) under attack from Manstein's two corps, which is passed over almost in silence? Volkogonov repeats the figure of 40,000 as the number of victims of the military purges of 1937–40. Lanshchikov cites a figure of 20 million as the demographic gap, i.e., what would have been the population in 1939 if it had been rising by 3 million a year from 1930. Ovcharenko raises the question of whether there was ever a "right-wing deviation" at the end of the twenties: Bukharin stayed in the position that Stalin had himself occupied in 1927. Students, he says, ask questions about the Shakhty and so-called *Prompartiya* trials, which were clearly phoney, and about the famine: "How could Kirov say [to the 17th Congress in 1934] 'The devil take it, one wants to live and live!', when there were millions had died the previous year and bodies were yet unburied." A very fair point!

Stadnyuk defends himself against the accusation that he was a neo-Stalinist, cites his early work on the famine (*Lyudi ne angely*), and his careful study of the records of the interrogation of Pavlov, the commander of the central group of armies who was shot in 1941 together with his staff. He had questioned witnesses, including a security officer who was there when Pavlov was arrested in Smolensk. Shatrov also speaks, defending himself against some accusations of inaccuracy: thus, he mentioned in his play that the conspirator Savinkov had offered Plekhanov the premiership of a government that would replace Lenin in 1918; the source (says Shatrov) was an article in *Izvestiya* by Plekhanov's widow, which stated that Plekhanov was asked if he would "form a government". Amabartsumov says that he understood the historians' difficulties in the "stagnation years", the literary men had them too, but when pressure was relaxed the literary men had substantial works in their desk drawers ready for publication; as for the historians, "What was in *their* desks?" Other remarks worth citing include one by B. Mitin to the effect that a history textbook in use in schools covered the seventeenth century without mentioning Tsar Alexei Mikhailovich, Patriarch Nikon, or Avvakum (!), and several urged the renaming of old towns (Tver, not Kulinin; Mariupol, not Zhdanov), and disputed such statements as "we" built prisons and "we" blew up the Christ the Saviour Cathedral: these things were done by order.

Chakovsky, attacked by name, defends his record as long-time editor of *Literaturnaya gazeta*: it did raise genuine problems in the "stagnation" years, one of the few that did. Fingers are pointed at the editors of *Molodaya gvardiya* and *Nash sovremennik* as conservative journals, who "defend our history from libels" and print attacks on Rybakov's *Deti Arbata*. Criticism is also directed at the Party historical journal, *Voprosy istorii KPSS*. Clearly sparks will continue to fly.

Blank spaces continue to be filled in as I write. Thus *Pravda* on 12 August 1988 devoted a whole page to the reconstruction of the so-called Georgian incident which so upset Lenin in 1922, involving a clash between Stalin and Ordzhonikidze on the one hand and the majority of the Georgian Party committee on the other. Reproducing the details of the conflict, and Lenin's reaction to it, *Pravda* also cites Lenin's letter to Trotsky, asking him to intervene on his behalf, as well as Trotsky's own note sent to members of the Politbureau in April 1923, which clearly show that on this issue Trotsky was with Lenin and against Stalin. The article does not fail to note that Stalin in due course had all the Georgian comrades who had disagreed with him shot during the Terror. *Voyenno-istoricheski zhurnal* (No. 7, 1988) describes in some detail the collapse of the Northwest front in 1941, with the loss of most of its troops and nearly all its equipment in the first two weeks of the war. More surprisingly, Falin, in *Moskovskie novosti* (21 Aug. 1988), questions the authenticity of the "secret protocols" to the Nazi-Soviet pact, even while these very protocols were being publicly discussed and denounced in Estonia. On some matters *glasnost'* has some way to go.

An interesting new departure is a book, published in 1987, by G. Yoffe, *Velikii Oktyabr i epilog tsarizma*, devoted to the fate of the tsar and his family. The author and the reviewer in *Novyi mir* (No. 7, 1988), P. Cherkasov, are clearly shocked by the massacre of the tsar's children and remaining servants: "four daughters and an incurably sick son. What was their guilt before the Russian people and the revolution?" The author pins the blame on the executive of the Ekaterinburg soviet, claiming that there is no evidence that instructions were issued from Moscow. Indeed, Moscow sent an emissary, one Yakovlev, about whom many legends have circulated; Yoffe presents evidence which suggests that Yakovlev, on instructions from Sverdlov, was attempting to get Nicholas and his family to Moscow, but met with obstruction from the Ekaterinburg soviet. Anyhow, the book and the review show that it is now possible to write a serious work on this difficult subject.

At long last the historical journals are becoming interesting. Thus

*Voprosy istorii* (No. 6, 1988) contains a long and well-documented article on Chou En-lai by S. Tikhvinsky, which also contains a criticism of Khrushchev's "precipitate" action in recalling Soviet technical advisers from China. In the next issue (No. 7) L. Shkarenkov discusses the role of Bukharin, reminding us (inter alia) of Bukharin's role in the Comintern, in which he played an important part in the ultra-left turn at its 6th Congress (1928), when Bukharin himself criticised the "right deviation" in the Comintern. Also in this issue is a throughly detailed and well-documented account of the Stalin-Tito rift and its consequences. And in *Voprosi istorii KPSS* No. 8, an article appeared titled "The 'Turn' of 1929 and the Bukharin Alternative". Also *Pravda* has been devoting full pages to a remarkably full and subtle discussion of the policy dilemmas which arose in the last years of NEP and of the harsh terror regime that followed (30 Sept. and 3 Oct. 1988), a debate that now has no (or very few) intellectual holds barred—except, of course, that the October revolution itself, and Lenin, must be approached with circumspection.

At long last something is being printed about the persecution of the church in the first postrevolutionary decade. In *Ogonyok* No. 50, 1988, in an interview with A. Nezhny, the chairman of the government's council on religious affairs, Kharchev, refers to the shooting in 1918 of Archbishop Vladimir of Kiev, and of the Metropolitan of Petrograd, Veniamin, in 1922 (i.e., in Lenin's time). The same interview has much to say about the Church's many vicissitudes, not only under Stalin but also under Khrushchev, under whom a great many churches were ordered closed. Kharchev even makes a parallel between the blowing up (in 1931) of the Cathedral of Christ the Saviour and the Chernobyl disaster. He also sharply criticises the obstructionist behaviour towards the church of local authorities still existing today.

# CHAPTER 4

# The Terror

There is little doubt that the largest number of victims of the brutalities of Stalinism and its policies were the peasants. So this chapter will begin with them.

In our survey of the rehabilitation of history we have had repeated occasion to refer to the traumatic experience of collectivization. Let us briefly examine what could and could not have been printed on this sensitive subject prior to *glasnost'*. Here too it would be misleading to assert that there was nothing. Soviet historians, and writers dealing with peasant themes, were well aware of the tragedies of the thirties, and were on occasion able to express themselves. The work on this period by Moshe Lewin (*The Peasants and Soviet Power*) and the relevant chapter in my own *Economic History of the USSR* were able to quote a number of Soviet scholars, who deserve credit for doing their best despite the obstacles placed in their way. The senior one was—and is—V. Danilov; the others were Moshkov, Vyltsan, Ivnitsky, and Bogdenko. I was told, on a visit to Moscow, that all five are now again engaged in work on a history of collectivization, interrupted by order from above in Brezhnev's time. However, even at the height of the Khrushchevian "thaw" it was compulsory to say that collectivization had been necessary, despite the crudeness and excesses with which it was accompanied, and indeed this was still Gorbachev's line in his anniversary speech—though *glasnost'* has meant that his words did not set limits to the researches and publications of academics or journalists.

The controversy over whether collectivization was necessary has already been mentioned. We have seen that Klyamkin, in *Novyi mir* (No. 11, 1987), answered with a regretful "Yes". He thought that most peasants were still in the grip of a patriarchal-communal approach, that collective farms had some connection in their minds with the traditional communes, that they did not rebel (as Western peasant-proprietors certainly would have done), and indeed that many poor peasants joined willingly in extirpating the *kulaks*, their richer fellow-villagers. He cited in support the recently published novel (written in 1930) by that fine writer Andrei Platonov, *Kotlovan (The Building-Site)*, which appeared in *Novyi mir* (No. 6, 1987). Platonov shows poor peasants driving out the *kulaks*. Klyamkin agrees, indeed stresses, that "in view of what happened afterwards they were dancing on their own graves", but that such things did happen. Collectivization did not weaken the regime, it strengthened the "Administrative system".

This is strongly disputed by several writers, for example, Roy Medvedev in *Sobesednik* (No. 18, 1988). There *were* some rebellions, all too easily crushed. In any case, most real *kulaks* had lost land and status already in 1918, argued Selyunin; those who were so called in 1930 were simply the sober, efficient, and energetic. The loss caused by their deportation was immense. The contribution to capital accumulation was reduced because of the fall in output and in livestock numbers. Better results, say several critics, could have been achieved with different policies. Yuri Afanasyev, in his powerful piece in *Literaturnaya Rossiya* (17 June 1988), calls collectivization "just about the biggest crime of the Stalin regime. . . . The organized hunger of 1932–33 carried away millions of lives." To which a reply in *Pravda* (25 June 1988, by P. Kuznetsov) countered by quoting Gorbachev's anniversary speech, in which he claimed that, though there were indeed cruel excesses, there was no other way. The essential point is that the argument continues, without any official attempt to limit it or to impose a "line". This sort of debate has gone on also among Western historians and critics. Those on the Soviet side, at long last, are in a position to join in.

This chapter will not be concerned with pursuing this point further. Its main object will be to highlight new material both about how collectivization was carried through and on the famine that followed it. That coercion had been used was not in itself news: after all, Stalin himself admitted it in his hypocritical "Dizzy with Success" (in March 1930), blaming these "excesses" on subordinates. Coercion was already present in Sholokhov's "Virgin Soil Upturned", written at the time. The harshness of the methods used figured in S. Zalygin's *Daleko ot Irtysha*. The famine, however, did not get a mention in the histories of the period, though some of the Danilov team (notably Moshkov) were able to include in their books references to excessive procurements causing grave food shortages in some areas. The earliest published exception to the taboo on mentioning actual famine was, rather surprisingly, Ivan Stadnyuk, already labeled Stalinist in connection with his later novel-documentary on the war. In his *Lyudi ne angely*, published in 1962, he spoke directly of starvation, due to excessive state exactions "which left the cultivators with no bread". V. Tendryakov, who will be cited at length, was able to make reference to deaths from famine in a novel published by *Moskva* (No. 3, 1968). There was also M. Alekseyev's novel *Drachuny*. These were, however, isolated exceptions.

Now both the historians and the literary men are free to speak the truth. Danilov is resuming his history of collectivization. In *Voprosy istorii* (No. 2, 1988), he tackled the hitherto totally taboo question: How many died in the famine of 1933? The fact that there were millions he takes for granted, and from his text can be deduced that in his view they numbered around 3 to 4 million, and also that the birthrate in these hard years had fallen sharply. His article is in the form of a polemic: Robert Conquest, in his "Harvest of Sorrow", made a much higher estimate, adding also large numbers of deported *kulaks*. Danilov cites a number of Western critics of Conquest (e.g., Davies, Getty). This is not the place to comment on the substance of the argument; the point is that, for the first time, there *is* an argument, about a matter which was almost totally taboo. Danilov also mentions another sensitive issue: whether the policies which caused the famine (i.e., grossly excessive procurements) were in some special sense anti-Ukrainian. No one doubts that Ukrainians suffered acutely, but was the campaign directed against recalcitrant peasants, many of whom were Ukrainians, or against Ukrainians, many of whom were recalcitrant peasants? Danilov, unlike Conquest, evidently prefers the first of the two formulations; I had taken a similar line in my review of Conquest's book for the *New Republic*. The question of "how many victims", and the reliability of the few published figures on the thirties, was raised also by M. Tolts in *Ogonyok* (No. 51, 1987), though without any definite estimate.

Documentary-novels vividly describing the coercion and the brutalities of compulsory collectivization have come from V. Belov (*Novyi mir*, No. 8, 1987) and B. Mozhayev (in *Don*, No. 3, 1987). Threats, deportations, excess taxes, arrests, all are there. The odd thing, however, is that both Belov and Mozhayev blame Trotsky. Mozhayev actually lists three villains: Trotsky, Kamenev, and Kaganovich. They shared only one common characteristic: all three were Jews. Trotsky and Kamenev have total alibis, being either out of the country or out of power in 1930. We have already cited Klyamkin's argument that Stalin's policy was much further "left" than Trotsky's. After the publication of Klyamkin's article, Belov returned to the charge in an article in *Pravda* (15 Apr. 1988): "In my opinion Trotsky's ideas triumphed after 1928. Unbearable taxes and levies, the destruction of cooperatives, the confiscation of their assets, and finally, repression, arrests, shootings. This is what Trotskyism meant for millions of peasant families! Historians do now speak of it. But historians have not calculated how many people perished. Or, if they have, they do not make the figure known. Repressions continued right until the Great Patriotic War—I have documents and facts. . . . In my view, the chief Trotskyist was Stalin, although some specialists pretend that he was anti-Trotskyist" (!). This is wrong, but is widely believed, if in less extreme form. However, in *Druzhba narodov* (No. 4, 1988), A. Turkov criticises both Belov and Mozhayev: "[Trotsky's] position at the time of full-scale collectivization could be judged from the way it was characterised by S. Ordzhonikidze at the 16th Party Congress in July 1930: . . . 'In agriculture', wrote Trotsky, 'stop further collectivization!' See, how left he is! (laughter). 'Stop dekulakization', demands Trotsky." Ordzhonikidze mocks him for not being really "left"! Once again, this is not the place to comment on the validity or otherwise of the protagonists' arguments, only to state that they can now be made openly.

Roy Medvedev stressed how Stalin had to manoeuvre, present the Politbureau with a *fait accompli*, to get sufficient support for his "war against the peasants". The more timorous members (e.g., Kalinin) were unwilling to risk a split, and left Bukharin, Rykov, and Tomsky in a minority. The "anti-*kulak*" drive removed millions of the most hardworking peasants. The measures were far harsher than in 1918–19, when real *kulaks* were actually engaged in armed struggle against Soviet power. At that time "no one thought of their deportation with their families, nor of physical elimination of thousands. In 1930–32 this is what was done, in order to support in some way the *kolkhozy* at the expense of the accumulations of the more prosperous peasants."

Sholokhov, the author of *Tikhii Don*, wrote a letter in June 1929—note the date, since this was before the mass collectivization campaign—which was published for the first time in *Moskovskie novosti* (12 July 1987) and included the following: "They press on the *kulak*, yet the middle peasant [*serednyak*] is already squashed. The poor are hungry. . . . One lad, a cossack who volunteered for the Red Army in 1919, served in it six years, a red commander, was for two years, to 1927, the chairman of the village soviet", sent a telegram to Kalinin in Moscow which read: "We are being devas-

tated more than what the Whites did to us in 1919." Sholokhov
continued: "In speaking with me he smiled bitterly: 'They took just
grain and horses, but our own (soviet) authority took every last
thing, even blankets from children.'" He ended by denouncing those
who "hypocritically, pharisee-like speak loudly of alliance with the
middle peasant while throttling him".

The crude and ruthless methods of "dekulakization" were commented on by G. Shmelev in *Oktyabr* (No. 2, 1988): dekulakization
"affected substantial strata of middle peasants. . . . At various
periods in the country as a whole 12 to 15% of the peasantry were
dekulakized. Clearly the object of this action was not the kulak but
the middle peasant", compelling them by threats to join the *kolkhoz*.

The whole process found its reflection in three stories, evidently
autobiographical, by the talented novelist V. Tendryakov (*Novyi
mir*, No. 3, 1988). The first story, set in 1929, relates to the
beginning of the process of "dekulakization". The narrator's father,
given the name of Tenkov, is a party official in a rural area. The
policy there is to force all *kulaks* to leave their homes and to
exchange them for the hovels of the poor. So the village is in chaos
and the cattle, coming back from the fields, are as confused as the
peasants as to where they are supposed to be. A poor peasant finds
himself in a "rich" house with a metal roof, and sells the metal to get
drunk, then staggers around the village shouting that he is the
"hegemon class". Another acquires horses and a house, and has to
be warned by Tenkov that dekulakization is in full swing and will hit
him if he is not careful. A prosperous peasant gives away his
property, to the deep suspicion of Tenkov (once a *kulak*, always a
*kulak*), and he announces that he has turned himself into a prop-
ertyless proletarian, "free like a bird, and birds neither sow nor
reap." The attitude of officialdom is well summarized in the reply
given to complaints that there were no soap, matches, or kerosene in
the village shop: "We are tearing up history by the roots, and you
moan about matches!" This is the stage prior to deportation and
death, which will follow not only for the so-called *kulaks*. At the end
of the story, Tendryakov adds a sort of documentary note: his two
sources are Churchill's war memoirs, in which Stalin holds up ten
fingers to designate the total number of peasant victims (including
the subsequent famine, of course), and also Roy Medvedev (then
only available in *samizdat*—Tendryakov died five years before the
publication of these stories). The latter cites an eyewitness, an old
Party member who witnessed in 1930 in Siberia the following scene:
"In winter, in bitter cold, he saw a large group of kulaks and their
families on horse-drawn carts on a 300-kilometre journey to a

distant part of the province. The children were crying out and
weeping from hunger. One of the peasants could no longer stand
the cries of his baby sucking the empty breast of its mother,
grabbed the baby from its mother's arms and smashed its head
against a tree."

Tendryakov's second story, entitled "Bread for a Dog", is set in
the summer of 1933. By the railway station there were bodies, some
just about alive, "in filthy louse-ridden rags", dying of hunger.
"They had somewhere about them a dirty piece of paper, certifying
that the holder, on the basis of such-and-such a decision, was exiled
with loss of legal rights and the confiscation of all his property." So
they had no work, nothing to eat. These were "dekulakized
peasants from near Tula, Voronezh, Kursk, Orel, from all over the
Ukraine". The Ukrainian word kurkul (a local form of kulak) came
with them. Some looked like live skeletons, others were swollen
from hunger. Some tried to eat the bark off trees. A militiaman was
there to ensure that the starving did not crawl into the station or
into the town. (The stationmaster, seeing this horror day by day,
could not stand it and committed suicide.) Tendryakov paints a
winter scene: "A woman in a neat and threadbare coat with a velvet
collar slipped, fell and spilt some milk she had been able to obtain
at the station. The milk ran into a frozen rut made by a horse's
hoof. The woman went on her knees before it, as if it were her
daughter's grave, stifled a sob, took a worn wooden spoon from her
pocket. She wept and spooned up the milk from the hoof-mark,
drank and wept, drank and wept, tidily, neatly."

As his father was a Party official, he had enough to eat, but the
sandwich he brought to school attracted much attention, from
fellow pupils and even from the teacher. None had eaten their fill.
"I lived in a proletarian country and I knew well that it was shameful to have had enough to eat. My father, as a responsible official,
had a responsible ration. My mother even could bake pies with
cabbage and chopped eggs!" He and other children soon got used
to the starving in the station square: some were nicknamed "skelet-
niks", and the swollen ones were "elephants", some sang mocking
songs about kurkuli skeletniki. He knew that these were "enemies,
about whom the great Gorky had said: 'if the enemy does not surrender he must be exterminated'. So these did not surrender."

He describes another scene. The local Party secretary
encountered on his path a ragged man dying of hunger, who said to
him: "Let's talk, chief. Are you scared of me?" A local committee-
man ordered him to be silent, but the secretary stopped and said:
"Talk. Ask. I shall answer."

"Before I die, tell me, what for? Can it really be because I had two horses?"

"Yes, because of that," came the calm and cold reply.

"You admit it, you beast!" . . .

"Would you give the workers bread-grains for pig-iron?"

"Could I eat your pig-iron with my porridge?"

"That's it, but the kolkhoz needs pig-iron, the kolkhoz is ready to feed the workers in exchange for iron. Did you want to join the kolkhoz? Honestly, now?"

"No."

"Why not?"

"Everyone is for his own freedom."

"It's not freedom that bothered you, but the horses. You wanted to keep the horses. You fed them, cared for them, and suddenly you are asked to give them up. You clung to your property. Not so?"

The dying man grew silent, blinked sorrowfully, and seemed almost ready to agree.

"So take the horses and stop at that. Why deprive me of life too?"

"But would you ever forgive us for confiscating them? Won't you sharpen a knife against us? Honestly, now."

"Who knows?"

"Well, we do not know either." . . .

Early every morning "Abram the coachman went round with his cart to collect the corpses from the street."

His father had told him that "there were villages where every inhabitant died of hunger—adults, old men, children, even babies. . . . About them one can hardly say: 'if the enemy does not surrender' . . . "

The son, conscience-stricken, tries to give food to the hungriest, but soon he is beset by too many, who cry out to him: "I'm finished lad, just a piece of bread to bite on before I die." In the end he gives some to a hungry dog, which is what gives this dreadful story its title. "It is not this moth-eaten dog I fed, I fed my own conscience."

Tendryakov ends by noting that at the height of the horrible famine, in February 1933, there gathered in Moscow the all-union conference of kolkhoz shock-workers. There Stalin uttered much-quoted words: "Make the kolkhozy Bolshevik, make the kolkhoz members prosperous." The author then cites "the most extreme of Western specialists" who claim that "in the Ukraine alone there died of hunger 6 million people". The cautious Roy Medvedev "used more objective data, probably 3 to 4 million in the country as a whole" (this is similar to Danilov's estimate, quoted above). A powerful article stressing Stalin's crimes, written by the sociologist

Bestuzhev-Lada (*Nedelya*, No. 15, 1988) refers to recent estimates of the real scale of deportations of so-called *kulaks*, involving "between an eighth and a sixth of the 25 million peasant households that then existed", deported with families, "often in goods wagons without food; a large number of old people and children perished; then endless heavy forced labour, of which many adults died. This all runs to millions. To which must be added millions to cover those who died of hunger in the villages."

Grain was exported in these years of hunger. And there is plenty of evidence to show that many *kolkhoz* members starved, in addition to so-called *kulaks*. The *kolkhoz* system was intended to impose the priority of state procurements, and in 1932–33, according to many works, the state was engaged in a battle with *kolkhozy* and their members, who tried to retain enough food for themselves to eat.

The horrors that accompanied the anti-*kulak* campaigns also figure in G. Shmelev's article in *Oktyabr'*, quoted earlier.

Tendryakov's third short story, in the same issue of *Novyi mir*, is set in 1937, in a village, where loudspeakers endlessly praise the great Stalin in song and verse. In this village there is a female half-wit, teased by the village youths. She claims at first to have a special relationship with Jesus Christ. But, under the influence of the radio, the half-wit "adopts" Stalin as her dearly beloved lord and master: "O great and merciful leader, I hear you, I come to you, your loving slave." The villagers are dismayed to hear such words from one with unwashed face, filthy hair, and incoherent speech. The local police official thinks that this claim to be a sort of bride of Stalin is altogether too much, and he arrests the girl. But then people say that, after all, "she praised comrade Stalin, not Trotsky". Someone reports the policeman, and his superiors declare that he is a "*provokator* who puts in jail people who express heartfelt love for comrade Stalin, Yosif Vissarionovich". The "provokator" is arrested and disappears. The madwoman is released. She soon tumbles to the fact that those whom she denounced as plotting against the beloved Stalin were arrested, since the authorities had to show their *bditel'nost'* ("vigilance", alertness to plots by the enemy). Panic seizes the villagers, they hide from her. Finally one man she is in the process of denouncing kills her. Asked why, he explains that to be sentenced just for murder would be preferable to being arrested under Article 58, i.e., as a counterrevolutionary!

Several other works tell of collectivization and "dekulakization", including Boris Chernyak's *Pakhari i mudretsy* (*Novyi mir*, No. 8, 1988). A letter from a peasant, in 1930: "In February, I was mobilised for forestry work. . . . In my absence the village soviet and the district plenipotentiary for some reason confiscated all my property, not to mention house and livestock, removed the seed and bread-grains which had been issued to me by the village soviet as a month's ration, removed even potatoes and cabbages. My family, consisting of my wife and little children, were thrown out, and into a house on the outskirts of the village with no glass in the windows. When, after 20 days, I returned from work, not knowing anything about what had happened, I found in my house . . . two good-for-nothings, both well and truly drunk. I went to where my family was and saw a tragic picture—weeping children, hungry, in twenty degrees of frost. Two days later I was arrested. . . . I was a *serednyak*" (middle peasant, not a *kulak*).

In the same issue of *Novyi mir*, Ksenia Myalo seeks the roots of the destruction of old rural Russia, stressing that it was not just a matter of one despotic man: it is wrong to forget the "hatred which even in the early twenties was directed to the peasants' traditional way of life" in all its aspects. "The year of the great turn was not due to a single decision, it was prepared by vigorous ideological work in previous years." This particularly affected proletarian youth in the *rabfaki* (workers' education institutions), who played a very active role in the liquidation of the *kulaks* as a class. Myalo blames left-wing intelligentsia, but adds that "no one of the leaders after Lenin had any affection for the village, often seeing in it the basis and expression of hateful 'old backward Russia'". (She could have included Lenin in these strictures!) She blames not only Trotsky but also Bukharin, citing his vicious attack on the peasant poet Yesenin, and noting also his view of the peasant as an object of policy, who must be "led" and "changed". In 1929 Bukharin addressed the conference of the godless, and supported the "struggle with religion", which took the form of destroying or closing thousands of village churches. In another article in the same issue, A. Latynina reminds us that "the destruction of churches and cultural monuments was the natural consequence of the belief in the world-historical mission of the proletariat".

We shall be returning to 1937, which is widely regarded as the most dreadful year of the Terror. However, this may well be because a high proportion of the victims in that year were Party officials, intellectuals, and officers. One would guess that the peasant victims of 1930–33 outnumbered them substantially. And several writers have reminded us that conditions for those who remained in the villages were often little better, if better at all, than for those imprisoned or in labour camps.

Let us now turn to the *political terror*. It is appropriate to begin
with the case of Ryutin. Party histories published in the West have
long noted that this man had attempted, already in 1930, to form a
group opposed to Stalin and his policies, that Stalin demanded his
execution, but that the Politbureau by a majority refused to allow
this. The taboo against killing one's own errant comrades was still
too strong. In the USSR the matter was left as one more historical
blank spot, until 26 June 1988, when *Moskovskie novosti*
published, under the heading "*Nakonets!*" ("at last!"), the facts of
the case, by Lev Razgon. Ryutin had supported Stalin against the left
opposition, in his capacity as secretary of one of Moscow's Party
districts, but he supported Bukharin when Stalin turned left in
1928–29, along with the Moscow Party secretary Uglanov. They
were all dismissed. Some recanted. But Ryutin, together with such
men as Slepkov and Maretsky, drafted what became known as "the
Ryutin group programme", of 200 pages, analyzing critically the
policies of Stalin, "who, motivated by considerations of personal
power, has brought the revolution to the edge of the abyss". Few
were able to read it, "but Stalin certainly did. His fury astonished
even those who knew his temper." The author confirms that Stalin
did demand Ryutin's execution, supported by Molotov and Kaganovich, but there was a Politbureau majority against, and "Stalin
had to be satisfied with a 15-year prison sentence". Ryutin served
his sentence first in Suzdal, then in a strict-regime prison in the Urals.
The evidence quoted suggests that he was brought to Moscow in
1937 as a possible participant in one of the show-trials, but, as he
did not appear, he must have refused to break, and was shot without
open trial. His family was almost totally destroyed too. One
daughter survived (and is shown in the newspaper holding a family
photograph). "She was the only one not reached by the Yezhov-
Beria headhunters. His wife Evdokia perished in 1947 in one of the
labour camps at Karaganda, his son Vasili, an engineer . . . , was
shot in Lefortovo prison; another son Vissarion, named in honour of
Belinsky, was sent to a Central Asian camp and shot there." (The
sufferings of innocent members of families of so-called enemies of
the people is a recurrent theme in these exposes.) The surviving
daughter tried for many years, in vain, to have her father's name
cleared; she wrote to Brezhnev and others, but it was not until 13
June 1988 that the plenum of the Supreme Court finally rehabilitated Ryutin.

A laudatory account of Ryutin, with long extracts from his
programme and declarations, was also written by A. Vaksberg, and
published in *Literaturnaya gazeta* (29 June 1988). His final trial in

1937 was conducted by Judge Ulrikh, an odious character who will be discussed further later in this chapter. Vyshinsky, equally odious, prosecuted.

In the chapter on Stalinism the (probable? likely?) role of Stalin and his then police chief Yagoda in arranging the murder of Kirov was already mentioned. It is possible to speculate openly about this, and also to denounce those who do so: thus, in the now-notorious "letter" by Nina Andreyeva in *Sovetskaya Rossiya*, Shatrov is accused of accusing Stalin of "murdering Trotsky and Kirov without a shadow of proof". It seems that some additional revelations may shortly be made, so I will leave this case aside, apart from making the familiar point that Kirov's murder (in December 1934) was used as a pretext for the mass terror that followed. It did not follow at once. We have seen that Gefter suggested that there was an opportunity in 1935 to adopt a policy of reconciliation on an antifascist platform, and that by 1936 Stalin had consciously rejected it. A number of writers have been discussing and puzzling over the purpose and sheer scale of the Terror. How many were involved? No one yet has tried to name a figure for total arrests. How many millions? Probably they simply do not know the totals. Perhaps soon evidence will come from official quarters. Until then, the writers confine themselves to those figures that have become known, e.g., on the military, which will be quoted later in this chapter. Medvedev wrote: "The terror of Stalin's time was explicable by the fact that Stalin needed to destroy the previous leadership. . . . The terror of the thirties was determined by Stalin's cruel character, as he knew no other way of dealing with his opponents. Most of these people had rendered major service . . . , their names meant a lot. So just to dismiss them seemed to Stalin to be dangerous, and so they had to be declared to be spies, wreckers, diversionists, one had to ascribe to them non-existent crimes, to attach nonsensical labels which nonetheless had an effect on the psychology of ordinary people" (*Sobesednik*, No. 18, 1988).

That explains the show-trials and also the fate of those very numerous old Bolsheviks who were shot without trial. But it was all very much bigger than this. I earlier expressed the view that the majority of Stalin's victims *in the thirties* were peasants. But Bestuzhev-Lada may be right: "Judging from the data available, the total who were repressed and perished in 1935–53 is hardly likely to be less than those dekulakized and starved in 1929–33" (*Nedelya*, No. 15, 1988). The methods used in interrogations have long been known, with many specific instances of brutality, sadistic torture, denial of sleep, and threats to wives and to children. Many memoirs describe the procedures; it is unnecessary to dwell on them here, other than to stress how openly all this has been described. But why the vast scale? Here it is useful again to quote Bestuzhev-Lada: "In principle the mechanism of terror is more or less clear. It was similar to that of dekulakization: a directive from above, threatening punishment for non-fulfillment, 'competition' between executants at all levels, from the centre to the provinces . . . with the main task of not falling behind others (recall Tvardovsky's 'blind, savage sentences for round-figure statistics'), and finally personal grudges or material calculations (to get the job, the property or the housing-space of the victim). . . . The net effect was a lava-like progression of the process, which apparently had at times to be restrained so that everyone would not be included." However, adds Bestuzhev-Lada, there are still unanswered questions: "Thus it is clear that the scale of the Terror exceeded many times the extent necessary to solidify Stalin's position after the policy failures [*provaly*] of 1929–33. In other words [this scale] was irrational in every respect, also from the angle of Stalin's personal interests." So—why did he pursue this process, why did he not stop it? To what degree was it controlled from above? Why were Yagoda and Yezhov, who headed the NKVD during the purges, themselves shot?

Why indeed did the NKVD obey, when so many of them perished? In a remarkable article, Evgeniya Albats (*Moskovskie novosti*, 8 May 1988) traces the career of a brutal interrogator, who abused and beat the great geneticist Vavilov, whose grisly fate has been fully described in articles devoted to the centenary of his birth. Alongside such crude and ignorant interrogators there were a few who "resisted illegality, who refused to 'beat out' confessions, refused to concoct 'cases', refused to participate [in the process]. They did exist!" She quotes, among several examples, the well-known name of T. Deribas, head of the NKVD in the Far East. In all the instances quoted, the individuals concerned had been shot, except for two who shot themselves. Medvedev and also Volkogonov quote a remarkably high figure of NKVD victims of the purges, 20,000, proportionately higher even than the Army's losses, which are put at 40,000.

Apart from the courts, which obediently passed sentence without bothering with evidence, there was the "special council" (*osoboye soveshchaniye*) of the NKVD at the centre and in the localities, which "could judge, as a rule, without the presence of the accused, without study of the crime, without calling witnesses, without a decision of the procurator, without any rights for the defence. There were also *troiki, dvoiki, spetskollegii*. In one day, 18 October 1937, a *dvoika* consisting of Yezhov and Vyshinsky 'examined' materials on 551 persons and sentenced all to be shot" (Albats).

While the author complains that most of those guilty of torture and concocting false evidence avoided punishment, she quotes the cases of no fewer than 38 police generals who lost their rank after investigation of their activities. An NKVD officer in North Ossetia, Boyarsky, "falsified accusations against 103 persons, of whom 51 were shot and the rest sent to camps where most of them perished. . . . Boyarsky personally used horrible tortures." He was expelled from the Party, but under the revised criminal code was not tried, because time had expired.

Many instances have been cited in the media of how ordinary and quite nonpolitical persons got into the meat grinder. Under a 1932 decree, peasants taking grain or any food from "their" *kolkhoz* without permission could be shot, or sent to labour camps for long periods if there were extenuating circumstances. The present secretary of the Union of Soviet Writers, Viktor Karpov, has related how, on the eve of the war, he made some remarks to a fellow cadet in an officers' school to the effect that there were more quotations from Stalin than from Lenin. This earned him a sentence in a labour camp, from which he was released in the middle of the war and sent to a penal battalion (he there distinguished himself and was promoted). (This was published in *Novyi mir*, No. 5, 1982, i.e., before Gorbachev, a rare piece of early *glasnost'*.) In Rybakov's novel the apparently real case is cited of a cook who prepared for some shock-workers a soup with the name *Lenivye shchi*, literally "lazy cabbage soup", and although he pointed to its name in a cookery book, he was arrested and sentenced all the same. Others have quoted such instances as the arrest of a number of young men who, because of a shortage of targets in a shooting gallery, used for the purpose paper which had a portrait of Voroshilov on the obverse side. The distinguished literary expert D. Likhachev was imprisoned because he expressed the view that the old orthography (the alphabet was modified in 1918) did have some advantages. He lived to tell the tale. Shalamov's extraordinary "Kolyma tales", of which more in a moment, cite two cases. In one, a man who had served in the Red Guards during the fighting in Moscow in December 1917 was asked, during a political study session, the name of his commander. He replied truthfully: Muralov. But because Muralov had been arrested, so was he. In another political study group, a railwayman was asked what he would do if Soviet power suddenly collapsed. He replied that since he had a large family to support he would probably go on working on the railway. For this he too was arrested and sentenced. As we shall see, to have been a prisoner of war was treated as a crime, and if one had tried successfully to escape that was seen as particularly suspicious. And so on and so forth.

We have already cited Tendryakov's story about the village half-wit's denunciations. Then there were the arrests of wives, some of whom were later shot, with children sent to orphanages or labour camps. In *Znamya* (No. 10, 1988), there appears the first installment of the memoirs of Larina, Bukharin's (then young) wife. It is a shattering document in which the fate of relatives of "enemies of the people" figure prominently. An example of tragedy: Tukhachevsky's mother was arrested and wept upon hearing of her son's fate, but, adds Larine, she fortunately did not know that all her other children were arrested too, that two other sons were shot, and that her daughters perished in labour camps. (No matter how many times such evidence is produced, the reader cannot but be taken aback by such purposeless savagery.) Larina's little boy, then eighteen months old, was taken away from her when she was arrested. She kept a photograph. A foul-mouthed jailer found it, tore it into shreds, and stamped on the pieces. This is not intended as a history of that dreadful time. I simply record that the facts are becoming known also about ordinary nonpolitical victims, of whom Khrushchev had hardly anything to say. Nor, despite requests to do so, did he ever refer to the cases of Bukharin, Rykov, and other victims of the show-trials who had been "oppositionists".

He did, however, specifically exculpate the military: Tukhachevsky, Yaki, Uborevich, and others were already declared innocent in 1956. In Brezhnev's time their fate became unmentionable. Nor was information published about the scale of the military purge.

This first came to public notice in an article in *Ogonyok* devoted to the case of Raskolnikov. A few words about this colourful character are needed. He played a major role in the revolutionary navy, and later became ambassador in Afghanistan and in Bulgaria. Recalled in 1938, he expected to share the fate of the bulk of the diplomats of the time (nearly all were shot) and refused to return. In France, in 1939, he wrote an open letter to Stalin detailing Stalin's crimes, listing his victims, denouncing the Terror. This was published in the French press. He died shortly afterward (apparently of natural causes). He was formally rehabilitated under Khrushchev, but under Brezhnev the reactionary cultural "commissar", Trapeznikov, denounced him as a deserter, so the article in *Ogonyok* was a second rehabilitation. In the course of this article, the author cited Major-General Todorsky's calculations, which have since been repeated by other Soviet publications. Presented in tabular form, they look like this:

| rank | total in rank | purged |
| --- | --- | --- |
| marshal | 5 | 3 |
| army commander, 1st class | 5 | 3 |
| army commander, 2nd class | 10 | 10 |
| corps commander | 57 | 50 |
| divisional commander | 186 | 154 |
| army commissar, 1st and 2nd class | 16 | 16 |
| corps commissar | 28 | 25 |
| divisional commissar | 64 | 61 |
| colonel | 456 | 402 |

It should be added that the same fate befell fleet commanders. That all this was done on the eve of war really does take one's breath away. Has any other army in history suffered thus from its own government?

In *Pravda*, on 29 April 1988, Boris Viktorov went for the first time into detail about the trial of the generals, using archive materials. Viktorov is a lieutenant-general of the military judicial service. On the pages of the records of interrogations there were some "grey-brown blotches" which proved to be blood. The actual trial was presided over by the same V. Ulrikh who presided at the open show-trials. This one was held in camera and took only a few hours. Tukhachevsky is quoted in the record of the trial as denying his guilt, asserting his loyalty, pointing out that his discussions with German staff officers and military attaches were all official and antedated Hitler's coming to power. Yakir had attended the German staff academy in 1929, and another of the accused, Kork, had been a military attache in Germany, so of course they had had German contacts. All rejected the accusations, denied any links with Trotsky. Feldman admitted to having had contacts with Pyatakov, who in turn is alleged to have sought collaboration with the military, but none of this was taken further during the trial. They were all accused of "wrecking" in order to weaken the Red Army. Thus Tukhachevsky, Yakir and Uborevich were "wrecking" by urging the strengthening of tank units at the expense of cavalry, an accusation made to the court by Marshal Budyonny. Some military members of the court also put hostile questions: Blyukher, Belov, and Alksnis. (All were shot in their turn. Apart from Budyonny, whose stupidity equalled the length of his moustache, only Shaposhnikov, of the military members of the court, survived until 1941.)

Whenever the accused tried to reply or explain, Ulrikh cut them short. Finally, a number of them did admit that they had discussed the desirability of removing Voroshilov from the post of commissar for war. They were not questioned as to their reasons, but this was treated as evidence of "preparing terrorist acts against comrade Voroshilov". In their concluding words to the court all said they were not guilty, all except one: Primakov, who made an accusatory statement which the author cites extensively: "I must tell the truth about our plot. Never in the history of our or any other revolution, has there been such a plot as ours. . . . Who was united beneath the fascist banner of Trotsky? What means were to be used by the plotters? All means: treason, betrayal, defeat of our country, wrecking, spying, terror. . . . Yakir had relatives in Bessarabia, Putna and Uborerich—in Lithuania, Feldman's links with South America were as close as with Odessa, Eideman is linked with the Baltic states." Those who read the record (after Stalin's death) were astonished, since Primakov had a fine reputation as a revolutionary cavalryman. As such he could have aroused Budyonny's jealousy, and he was arrested a year before Tukhachevsky, so "he could have had a prolonged going-over" (s nim rabotali).

So, asks the writer, what was the background to the so-called plot? In the records they found a note from Stalin to Ordzhonikidze, asking him to investigate a report (in 1931) that two ex-tsarist officers had been undertaking anti-Soviet activities inspired by Tukhachevsky, but presumably he was cleared, since he was given high military office. Other "background" items quoted: Brigade-Commander Medvedev under interrogation mentioned the existence of a "Trotskyist" organization in the upper ranks of the Army. Also in May 1937 on Yezhov's order a leading member of the NKVD, Arutuzov, was arrested, and "indicated" that he knew from German sources that there is a plot in the Red Army involving Tukhachevsky. (The word "indicated", pokazal, appears in inverted commas in the text.) He claimed to have informed Yezhov's predecessor Yagoda, who refused to take it seriously.

In the 1950s several interrogators were themselves interrogated. Space allows me to quote some extracts from the explanation given by one of them, Radzivilovsky: "Frinovsky [number two to Yezhov in the NKVD] gave me the task: 'We must develop a picture of a big and deep plot in the Red Army, so that its discovery would show the vast role and achievements of Yezhov. . . .' I accepted the task. I got from Medvedev, not at once, of course, the required statements concerning the existence in the Red Army of a plot and the names of its leaders. These statements were reported to Yezhov. He personally called Medvedev in for questioning. Medvedev declared to

Yezhov and Frinovsky that his statements were false. Then Yezhov ordered that Medvedev should be made, by whatever means, to return to his previous statements, and this was done, and his refusal to confirm them was not recorded. . . . The arrests of Tukhachevsky and the other plotters followed. . . . I cannot wholly deny my guilt, but I do wish that you realized in what sort of conditions we had to work." There followed the arrest of Feldman, who denied everything, until his interrogator (Ushakov) "insisted" at length. Ushakov in his statement "accused" a fellow-interrogator, Glebov, of allowing Yakir to deny his guilt. (Glebov figures on the list of NKVD men who were shot for trying to stop what was going on, cited by Albats, above.)

The author of the *Pravda* article also had access to statements made after their own arrest by Yezhov and Frinovsky, but these were not directly related to this case, though of great interest in providing evidence as to how these men thought and acted. Medvedev was shot four days after Tukhachevsky and the others. He too was "tried" in secret by the same "judge"—Ulrikh. His file included no evidence at all, other than his alleged confession that he held Trotskyist views. He declared at the "trial" that he was no counter-revolutionary and that he had been forced to give false evidence on the plot in the Red Army.

There followed a search for plotters throughout the army, "which became a campaign, hotted up by appeals for vigilance. Things got so that there could not be a military unit without at least one plotter."

According to Volkogonov (*Pravda*, 20 June 1988), Voroshilov announced to the Military Council on 29 November 1938 that "in the process of the cleansing [purge, *chistka*] we cleaned out 40,000 persons. . . . Out of the 108 former members of the Military council, only 10 remain." Volkogonov added that in 1939 the wave of arrests declined. "But still on 14 June 1939 V. Ulrikh, who just could not stop", reported to Stalin that there were still "a large number of cases not yet investigated concerning participants in right-wing-Trotskyist, bourgeois-nationalist and espionage organizations: 800 cases in the Moscow military district, 700 in the North Caucasus military district" and so on. He asked for instructions. "Stalin, instead of his usual 'agreed', issued an order that these cases be checked to ensure no errors." Volkogonov comments: "It was not Stalin that stopped the madness. The senseless bloody terror had reached the limit, threatening the functioning of the system itself."

Information has also reached the public about how major cultural figures were destroyed in these years. They had practically all been

rehabilitated in the fifties, but with few or no details of what had
been their fate. The list is a long one, and I will quote one exposé, by
the talented and courageous lawyer Arkadi Vaksberg (*Literaturnaya
gazeta*, 4 May 1988). The "trial" was again presided over by the
odious Ulrikh. The date is 1 February 1940, the location is "Beria's
office" at Lefortovo prison, an office which Beria used when he came
in to torture prisoners, but which was available for a "trial" when he
was not there. (In the memoirs of Gnedin, now published in the
USSR, Beria tortures him personally.) The accused was Mikhail
Koltsov, well-known author and journalist, accused of everything:
agent of French, German, and American intelligence, Trotskyism,
terrorism; he had confessed to everything, according to the act of
accusation. The record shows him denying it all. Ulrikh asked: "But
is this not your signature?" Kolstov replies: "I signed after torture,
terrible torture." Ulrikh in reply accused him of maligning the
(NKVD) organs, and duly sentenced him to die, on no evidence at
all. It all took less than 20 minutes. They next "tried" Vsevolod
Meyerhold, the great theatre director, who had been arrested on 20
June 1939. In the course of seven months' investigation, Meyerhold
"confessed" that he was a British and Japanese spy, a Trotskyist since
1923, that in 1933 he established links with Rykov, Bukharin, and
Radek, who told him to "wreck" the theatre, that Ilya Erenburg(!)
recruited him to a Trotskyist organization, while a well-known
Lithuanian diplomat-poet, Baltrushaitis, recruited him for the
British intelligence service. The record shows that in January 1939
Meyerhold refused to go along with his "confession" and wrote a
letter to Vyshinsky, which Vaksberg quotes: "I was laid on the floor
face down, I was beaten with a rubber whip on feet and back; they
sat me in a chair and beat my legs, causing internal bleeding, and
then they beat these red-blue-and-yellow weals with the same rubber
whip, causing such excruciating pain that it felt they were pouring
boiling water over me—I shouted and wept from the pain. They beat
me on the face with their hands. The interrogator always repeated:
'You will write [your confession], or we will beat you again, just
leaving your head and right hand. The rest we will turn into bloody
flesh.' So, on 15 November 1939, I signed [the confession]." He sent
a similar letter to Molotov. No reply. Vaksberg adds that Erenburg,
Pasternak, and Olesha were supposed to be part of the "plot",
indeed, Erenburg is supposed to have "recruited" Meyerhold, yet no
action was taken against them. Indeed, all three were alive in 1955
to join dozens of other leading intellectuals in praising Meyerhold
and urging that he be posthumously rehabilitated. Why, asks
Vaksberg, should Meyerhold have been accused of being a Japanese

spy "and not a spy for Ceylon or Honduras"? Because he did have a young Japanese trainee, Yoshido Yoshima, in his theatre. (It turns out that the unfortunate Japanese and his wife also went to their deaths "in Yezhov's cellars"; they have been "long ago rehabilitated".) Why also a British spy? Among his friends was a Russian with the English surname of Grey. (Tragicomedy? With a most tragic outcome for a world-renowned figure.) Meyerhold and Koltsov were shot on 2 February 1940, "and at that very time Ulrikh was condemning Robert Eikhe, only yesterday a candidate member of the Politbureau".

On 27 January 1940, Isaak Babel was shot, with others, having been condemned the previous day by Ulrikh. Again the investigators were given access to the files, and Vaksberg quotes extensively from them. The military procurator who reviewed the case (apparently in 1955 or 1956) stated in writing: "What the basis of the arrest was cannot be seen in the file, as the order to arrest him was signed on 23 June 1939, i.e., 35 days after his arrest." In this case the cause of the arrest seems to have been the friendship of Babel with Yezhov's wife. After Yezhov's arrest, his wife too was deemed to be involved in "an anti-Soviet terrorist plot" and to have "recruited" Babel. The record shows that after firmly denying all the accusations for three days, Babel suddenly "admitted" that he was a Trotskyist spy, recruited by Ilya Erenburg (!!) and Andre Malraux (!!), to whom he "sold secrets of Soviet aviation". Among the list of members of the "terrorist group" named in the Babel case, along with Erenburg, we find such prominent intellectuals as Leonov, Katayev, Olesha, Eisenstein, Mikhoels, the singer Utesov, "and many others". Since they were not arrested, presumably the "evidence" was kept on ice in case it was needed. The records of other cases show that people were beaten to give compromising evidence even against such loyal Stalinists as Andreyev, Zhdanov, and Kaganovich, for the same reason.

Babel on 10 October withdrew his "confession". He wrote: "I would like the investigator to note that . . . even here in prison, I committed a crime, by falsely accusing several persons." He wrote three times to Ulrikh, asked him to call witnesses, to allow him access to the procurator, a lawyer. "On 26 January in the course of a few minutes Ulrikh made everything clear, and next morning Babel's life ended."

Vaksberg states that relatives were told the victims had been sentenced to "ten years without right of correspondence", whereas the text of the sentence just read *rasstrel*, shooting. "Someone devised and introduced this dreadful euphemism." Many people for many years lived in hope, rumours spread that so-and-so was seen in

such-and-such a camp or prison. Boris Yefinov, the famous car-
toonist, heard that his brother Koltsov was alive, and Babel's wife
was actually "officially told" that he was alive in 1952! A Western
journalist imprisoned at Vorkuta described how she met Professor
Pletnev, sentenced in 1937 for "poisoning Gorky", in 1953. Yet he
was shot, with 154 people, in Orel prison cellars in 1941 (in the
group that included Spiridonova and Rakovsky, referred to in the
previous chapter).

Vaksberg praises those officers of the judicial organs who pains-
takingly reexamined the cases of those three men (and many others),
and praises Erenburg for his efforts to get them rehabilitated. He
goes on to name two principal villains—the interrogators Shvartsman and Rodos, ignorant sadists, whose work was praised by their
chief, Beria. These two were put on trial in 1956. Others he named
were not. He comments bitterly: if Babel, Meyerhold, and Koltsov
were "enemies of the people", then presumably these thugs were
"friends of the people". When Rodos, at his own trial, was asked
what he knew about Babel, whom he had tortured, he replied: "I
was told he was a writer." "Did you read even a line of his
writings?" Reply: "What for?"

I dwell at length on these cases because they demonstrate that it is
possible now to make public such details thirty years and more after
the victims' formal rehabilitation. There have been, and there will
be, others.

In *Literaturnaya Rossiya* of 20 November 1987, Lev Sidorovsky
writes about N. Vavilov, with quotations of his letters to Beria after
his arrest in 1940, and much is also said about his achievements, and
the way he was trampled on by Lysenko and his supporters.
(Vavilov died in prison in Saratov in a death cell.)

There were many economists and planners among the victims,
and some still await public rehabilitation. I will mention just one
case, that of the eminent statistician responsible for the ill-fated
census of 1937, O. Kaitkin. An old revolutionary and former
student at the Sorbonne, he played a big role in the statistical service
in the twenties, including the 1926 census. According to M. Tolts
(*Ogonyok*, No. 51, 1987), he was accused, together with colleagues,
of falsifying the results of the 1937 census, but the real "crime" was
that the population was shown to be well below the figure previously announced by Stalin himself. The author suggests that the
figure of 170 million, which was given by the census of 1939 by
another and doubtless frightened group of statisticians, could well
have been an overstatement. (The demography of the thirties is a
subject in itself, not to be pursued here.)

In this chapter I have deliberately not gone into the well-known show-trials of 1936–38, referred to in the previous chapter. Several publications (for example, *Izvestiya*, 7 Feb. 1988) have printed detailed reports and interviews about the process of rehabilitation, showing how the legal officials charged with the task scrupulously examined the "evidence" on the basis of which they were condemned before coming to the firm conclusion that the crimes were nonexistent. There is some discussion of the character of Bukharin: Was he, as some held, unbalanced and inclined to weep, as might be deduced from some statements made by his wife? No, asserted the legal investigator, he showed courage and consistency in his statements to the court. One must note a tendency in the Soviet media to concentrate on Bukharin. While one should welcome the way the discussion is conducted—the need for deeper study is recognised; he, like other politicians, can be right on some things and not on others—little is yet being said about other victims, except that they were not guilty as charged, of course. One must anticipate more articles on such men as Rykov and perhaps also Rakovsky. (An article by A. Senin on Rykov has appeared in *Voprosy istorii*, No. 9, 1988.) I say "perhaps" because Rakovsky was a distinguished supporter of Trotsky. Trotsky himself is now no longer an unperson, he can be and is quoted, but he cannot be judicially "rehabilitated" in a formal sense, in that he was never tried. Zinoviev and Kamenev have been cleared of guilt, and Kamenev has been cited in positive connections, as we have seen. One awaits news of others who were apparently disposed of without any trial at all, men like Preobrazhensky, who are still cited (if at all) in negative connections. This is linked with the needed reexamination of the policy prescriptions of the "left opposition" in the twenties. *Voprosy istorii* has announced the publication in 1989 of articles on Voznesensky and Sokolnikov, the memoirs of Vatsetis (first commander of the Red Army, shot in the purges) and of the cavalryman Mironov, and a denunciation of the Stalinist terror by A. Antonov-Ovseyenko (already published abroad). (The subjects of forthcoming articles include Ivan the Terrible and Rosa Luxemburg!) But to pursue this further would take us wide of the subject matter of this chapter.

Let us return to cultural figures. Anna Akhmatova's first husband, the fine poet N. Gumilev, was shot in 1921 in Petrograd. In the 1930s her then husband was arrested, and so was her son. She stood for hours outside a prison in Leningrad, with many others, and wrote a poem about it, the famous "Requiem". It passed from hand to hand, and was published in the West. I know most of this moving series of short verses by heart. When Gorbachev came to power, a skeptical colleague told Archie Brown, the distinguished political scientist, that he would believe that the changes were real if and when Akhmatova's "Requiem" were published. Published it was, in two literary magazines, *Novyi mir* and *Oktyabr*, in the spring of 1987. It was over twenty years after Akhmatova died, almost fifty years after the poems were written. But it demonstrates, in Bulgakov's words, that "manuscripts do not burn". It reminds one, too, of the power of poetry in Russia, a power lost in the West. Mandelshtam, who perished in a transit camp near Vladivostok in 1939, once quipped that only in Russia is poetry taken seriously, since only in Russia are poets killed for writing it. His own arrest had been largely due to some verses about Stalin: "He rejoices at every execution."

While on the subject of poets and the Terror, one must mention several other belated publications (there are others, too, but one cannot read everything). The talented poet Zabolotsky spent ten years in camps and survived. *Ogonyok* (No. 4 1988) reprinted a powerful poem about two old peasants freezing to death in the Kolyma complex ("On a Road Near Magadan"), dreaming in their last moments of their village:

Ikh nastigla sladkaya dremota,
V dal'ni krai, rydaya, povela

("Sweet drowsiness took them, sobbing, to their distant home".)

Then there is the belated appearance of Alexander Tvardovsky's long poem, "By Right of Memory", in *Novyi mir* (No. 3, 1987) twelve years after his death. Tvardovsky's father had been "dekulakized". The poem stressed the effects of terror, the universal fear, the falsehoods, the suffering. In passing, it must be added that Tvardovsky's own role, when he was editor of *Novyi mir*, has been singled out for praise by many: until he was removed in 1970, he had indeed done a great job. It was said that when he received Solzhenitsyn's *One Day in the Life of Ivan Denisovich* in manuscript, he started reading it in bed. On realizing its quality and importance, he got up: one cannot read so major a work without getting dressed!

Bulat Okudzhava, whose songs are universally known but were never directly political, had a set of short poems published in *Druzhba narodov* (No. 1, 1988). They are devoted to his father (shot), his brothers and uncles (shot or died in camps) and his mother (arrested and imprisoned).

Two other relevant works, well known in the West, spring to

mind: Solzhenitsyn's *Gulag Archipelago* and Evgeniya Ginzburg's camp memoirs. The Ginzburg memoirs are being serialized in *Daugava*, a Russian-language monthly published in Riga (Nos. 8 and 9, 1988) and are also in *Yunost*, beginning in September 1988. The same journal also printed an interview with her first husband, Aksyonov (father of the novelist), who also survived seventeen years of labour camp. As for Solzhenitsyn, it has been reported that two works that he wrote when still in Russia, *The First Circle* and *The Cancer Ward*, may soon appear. There are some evident difficulties with the tone and content of the *Gulag Archipelago*, especially its insistence that it all started with Lenin. But at the time of this writing it has been rumoured that Solzhenitsyn has been invited back to the Soviet Union. In *Knizhnoye obozreniye* of 5 August 1988 there appeared an appeal to "return Solzhenitsyn to Soviet literature".

Solzhenitsyn is still a problem area, however. It is widely known that *Novyi mir* intended to publish some of his work in 1989 and was told not to do so. It is not yet clear whether the ban concerns *The Gulag Archipelago* only or whether his whole opus remains for the time being under wraps.

Dombrovsky's *Fakultet nenuzhnykh veshchei* (*Novyi mir*, Nos. 9–11, 1988) paints a vivid picture of the terror in action; some of its most original scenes relate not only the processes of interrogation but also the discussions and mentalities of the interrogators and of the procuracy. The latter are shown to be forbidden to inquire into the details of the cases, even while called upon to "sanction" arrest and sentence. Cases where no evidence could be found, or where the prisoner could not be made to confess, were reported to the infamous *Osoboye soveshchaniye*, special council of the NKVD, which could and did sentence prisoners without any trial at all. However, in Dombrovsky's story, the interrogators received a circular which told them that reference to the special council could be seen as showing their failure to secure (or beat out) "evidence". The idea that, once arrested, a plainly innocent man or woman should be released is not even considered.

Conditions in the labour camps have now been described, with all their horror. Thus, *Argumenty i fakty* (No. 18, 1988) published an interview with Professor I. Kon, a famous medical specialist, who had fled from Romania to the USSR in 1938, served in the Soviet medical corps during the war, and was then arrested and sentenced. He survived because, as a doctor, he was used also to treat the camp commanders. He tells of prisoners being marched 12 kilometres to chop trees: "Those who collapsed in the forest were dragged by their feet along the narrow gauge railway, their heads bumping along the sleepers [ties]. Understandably, they were dead when they reached the camp." He referred to the criminals who held all the soft jobs in the camp and "pitilessly robbed the exhausted men, mostly 'politicals'".

But the most shattering of all was the publication, in *Novyi mir* (No. 6, 1988), of several of the "Kolyma tales" by Varlam Shalamov. His account of life and death in the worst of the camp complexes had been published in the West, and was greatly appreciated by Solzhenitsyn. Shalamov was also a good poet, and some of his poems had been printed earlier. In this issue there is a most moving one dedicated to Pasternak, about how, amid the horrors, with death ever present, he whispered his verses like a prayer.

Shalamov tells of many deaths: of a founder-member of the Komsomol, shot for not fulfilling his work-norm. Of a French communist "who was morally suffering: he could not believe that he, a Comintern member, could be here, in Soviet penal servitude. . . . Once the brigade leader punched him, just normally, but he fell and never got up. He was lucky to have been one of the first to die." A Dutch communist was there too, received a parcel from his wife containing a nightshirt and a photograph of the wife. Criminals stole both immediately, the photograph for masturbation sessions. The Dutchman went mad. An economist, Sheinin, "did not at first understand what they were doing to us, but eventually understood and calmly awaited death". A brigade-leader named Dyukov in 1938 formed a work brigade of peasants, since peasants worked better than intellectuals. But they were too hungry, and when they did not fulfill excessive norms, their food supply was cut. Dyukov tried to make representations, whereupon orders came down to "include the whole brigade and its brigade-leader on the list, and all were shot". A prisoner tried to be generous, "to share his last crust; this means that he did not live to see the time when no one had a last crust". The criminals, who unmercifully abused, beat, and stole from the politicals ("enemies of the people") were treated as "friends of the people", due for correction and not for punishment. "The gold mines turned healthy men into invalids in three weeks: hunger, loss of strength, long hours of heavy work, beatings. . . . The brigade was reinforced by new men, Moloch was sated."

The professors, party officials, engineers, military, peasants, workers, who filled the prisons to overflowing . . . were not enemies of the regime or state criminals, and when they died they never understood why they had to die. Their self-respect and their anger had nothing to rest on. Divided among themselves, they perished in the white desert of Kolyma, of hunger, cold, overwork, beatings, disease. They quickly learned not to support or defend each other. . . . The souls of the survivors underwent total corruption, their bodies lacked the qualities for physical labour.

To replace them after the war came the repatriated: from Italy, France, Germany, straight to the extreme north-east. These were very different men, formed by war, bold and willing to take risks. . . . Officers and soldiers, airmen and commanders.

One of Shalamov's stories tells of an unsuccessful attempt to escape, led by a major, one of the many Soviet ex-prisoners of war who ended in northern labour camps. Shalamov refers in this context to the efforts of Vlasov to recruit the prisoners of war for a Russian Liberation Army and how Vlasov's emissaries had been right to warn that on their return they would be treated as traitors.

Released at last, Shalamov ends with the words: "I returned from hell." His name recurs in Pasternak's correspondence; after his release they evidently met.

The publication of Shalamov brings nearer total revelation of how millions of detainees were treated, with brutality and killings on a vast scale. If this can be published, the truth can be, is being, told.

I will now quote from two very different accounts of postwar terror—for let us not forget that millions were still behind bars; indeed, if and when the figures are published, we may well see that the population of Gulag was as large in 1950 as it was in 1938. One of these concerns political leaders; the other, ordinary people. Let us never forget all the Ivan Denisoviches—Solzhenitsyn's "hero" was in camp *after* the war.

The "political" case first. This was the infamous "Leningrad affair", which led to the deaths of A. A. Kuznetsov, formerly secretary of the Leningrad Party and at the time of his arrest a senior Party secretary in Moscow; N. Voznesensky, chief planner and Politbureau member; and with them *all* the Party officials currently holding office in Leningrad, and, for good measure, those who *had* held office in Leningrad (among those shot were Party secretaries in Murmansk and the Crimea, because they were from Leningrad). Several hundred people were "repressed", including many Leningrad academics. After all the sufferings of the city in the siege, when close on a million died, it was a grisly fate that befell them. Khrushchev had referred to the affair and implied that Malenkov and Beria were to blame, but gave no details. Why did it happen?

A full account fills a whole page of *Komsomolskaya Pravda* (15 Jan. 1988). The background includes Kuznetsov's relative independence, his outstanding role in Leningrad's defence, his reluctance to shower paeans of praise on Stalin, his interest in the circumstances of Kirov's murder. Transferring him to Moscow, Stalin hinted, in conversations, that if he were too old to rule, Kuznetsov might become general secretary and Voznesensky prime minister (Zhdanov had just died); this was bound to upset Beria and Malenkov, who did indeed play a major role in what followed. Worse, Stalin actually gave Kuznetsov the job of supervising the NKVD/MGB (as the police apparatus was then called), and he did try to do so, greatly upsetting Beria and his gang. This was an example of Stalin setting his subordinates off against each other. The pretext for starting proceedings against the Leningrad Party organization was a report on a minor irregularity in a Party ballot. Then followed the concoction of a Leningrad-based conspiracy, supposedly intending to make of Leningrad a power centre, even a possible capital for the RSFSR (the Russian republic), which grew into accusations of treason and plotting. Rybakov in his novel stressed how Stalin already distrusted Leningrad when Kirov was secretary there. In that case too he called him to Moscow.

There was no public announcement of any trial or sentence. Indeed, Kuznetsov's widow, herself arrrested, discovered her husband was dead only after her release. Kuznetsov's daughter had married Mikoyan's son shortly before her father's arrest, but there was nothing Mikoyan could do, though he did look after Kuznetsov's young son after the mother's arrest. (This was, after all, the time when Molotov's own wife was in prison.) The article presents with remarkable clarity the atmosphere of the time. There is one unexpected touch: Kuznetsov's widow, after her release, told how her interrogator shouted at her in the usual manner, and then, turning up the radio, said to her: "Zinaida Dimitrievna, I do not believe what I am asking you." Then he turned the radio off and continued to shout at her. After her arrest she was chained, in solitary confinement.

At the time of their arrests the death penalty had been abolished. It was reintroduced in time for the execution of Kuznetsov, Voznesensky, Popkov (Leningrad Party secretary), Rodionov (RSFSR premier), and nearly 200 others.

Kuznetsov, according to this article, did not "fit" into the Stalin cult, often cited Kirov, visited Kirov's widow—"though Stalin's attitude to him [Kirov] was even then not a secret to many". So "Kuznetsov was not an innocent victim", in the sense that he was odd man out, "a white crow". When Stalin died, Mikoyan called on Kuznetsov's children and said: "Your father was no sort of enemy of the people."

It is interesting to note in passing that Mikoyan's son, in

*Ogonyok*, expressed the view that his father was guilty of having been one of Stalin's henchmen, that he did not do what he should have done.

At this same period (1948–52) there occurred the arrests and shooting of a number of prominent Jewish intellectuals. Of this I will write in the next chapter. I will end this chapter with short stories, told in the first person (but stories nonetheless), by Yulian Semyonov, better known as a writer of popular detective stories. In *Nedelya* (No. 11, 1988), he has two. One, called "Summer 1937", is about a child's reactions to the threatened arrests of his and his neighbour's parents. The other is called "Autumn 1952", and is set outside the Yaroslav transit camp, where a long queue of peasant women waits to receive news of, or to pass parcels on for, their loved ones. "It was a wave of arrests of *kolkhozniki*." The author paints a vivid scene, in which an old woman tries in vain to hand over some food for her sons, while a legless colonel on a wooden platform on wheels inquires about his student son, who has been arrested for "belonging to an anti-Soviet organization". Space limitations forbid further details, but the story is powerfully told. In the end the old woman with the parcel discovers that the young police lieutenant, who becomes gradually ashamed of the lies he tells and the role he plays, is a relative of hers and she cries out: "My God, my God, brother against brother, father against son, yet the heavens have not burst asunder. When? Oh Lord, when?"

The evidence cited in this chapter must surely convince any reader that efforts are being made to fill in the blank pages of the history of the Terror. Yes, there are still some to fill, but the progress made would have been regarded as astonishing and incredible just a few years ago.

*Novyi mir* (No. 7, 1988) reprinted long extracts from the memoirs of Evgeni Gnedin, which had been published abroad many years ago. Gnedin was the son of the famous (or infamous) Helfand-Parvus. He was brought to Russia by his mother as a child. He was press officer in the Commissariat of Foreign Affairs when Litvinov was dismissed, in 1939, and Molotov succeeded him. Gnedin was arrested, and he describes in detail the tortures and beatings to which he was subjected, sometimes by Beria, to try to force him to provide evidence against Litvinov. He had much to say about interrogation procedures and purposes. Among the "evidence" against him was a statement by M. Koltsov (the author and journalist) to the effect that they plotted in the apartment of the diplomat K. Umansky, yet Umansky was not arrested and was then ambassador to the United States! Gnedin's interrogators told him

that the NKVD was "now" (1940) working closely with the
Gestapo. They threatened to arrest his wife. He was transferred to a
super-secret prison, worse even than Lefortovo, Sukhanovo. He
mentioned something also noted by Solzhenitsyn, that the vehicles
which transported prisoners across Moscow were labeled MEAT or
BREAD. One of his fellow prisoners, a Kurd named Chinghiz
Ildirim, had been close to Ordzhonikidze and Kirov, and this was
the probable cause of his arrest. Gnedin had two years of prison,
then eight years of labour camp, then "eternal" exile, until 1955.
There are in his memoirs some thoughtful passages: "One's own
inner freedom in prison is above all the ability to remain oneself, to
preserve in reactions to one's surroundings an independence from
the influences of investigators, prison-guards and torturers. This
definition can be extended to the relationship of Man to a despotic
state and a despotic ideology."

In the same issue of *Novyi mir*, Vladimir Tsybin has a poem, a
"hutment ballad"—"half the country [was] in hutments, in Vorkuta
and Kolyma". In another poem, he pictures old men's wrinkled
faces, some earned in "Berlin" (the war), some in Magadan (Kolyma
. . . ). Altogether, there are clearly no taboos anymore in the way of
depicting the *Gulag* of the past.

The publication of Nadezhda Mandelshtam's memoirs (*Hope
Against Hope*) has been announced for 1989, and extracts have
appeared in the journal *Yunost'*. *Pravda* of 19 August 1988 printed
a long interview with M. Solomentsev, chairman of the commission
set up by the Politbureau to study the "repressions" of the Stalin
period. He gave details of its composition and its responsibilities. He
cited several cases of ordinary workers who were unjustly sentenced,
saying that the procedures are by no means limited to the famous.
They are still engaged in examining open and closed trials, some of
which surprised even the members of the commission. They are also
examining the circumstances of Kirov's murder. Answering questions as to how it was that courageous revolutionaries were made to
confess to nonexistent crimes, he pointed to the fact that even the
toughest could not withstand months of torture. He cited the case of
Krestinsky, who, "after having gone through the hell of the 'investigation', fearlessly told the [open] court of his innocence", whereupon Vyshinsky at once asked for proceedings to be resumed next
day, and "it is not hard to understand what kind of a 'going over' he
received, when at the next session of the court he admitted his guilt
and denied his own bold and truthful words uttered on the previous
day". He spoke also of the cruel fate of relatives, and of the
"monstrous" (*chudovishchnyi*) personal role of Stalin.

This chapter was already completed when *Znamya* (Nos. 7 and 8, 1988) published an autobiographical story by Anatoli Zhigulin. In 1947, together with a group of students in Voronezh, he formed an unofficial "Communist Youth Party", which aimed to change society and was critical of the worship of Stalin. They were arrested. Zhigulin spent years in Kolyma. As in the extracts from Shalamov, he draws a realistic picture of the horrors of the camps. "Mortality ... was very high. In the 'medical' special zone—more correctly it should be the dying zone—many died daily. The duty guard indifferently checked the number of the file against the number on the already-prepared tablet, pierced the dead man's chest thrice with a special steel spike, then stuck it into the dirty snow by the guard-hut and pushed the corpse out into freedom." He describes the "alliance between the criminals and fascist-collaborators and the camp authorities", and "the mass cruelties and sadism" which they inculcated. In commenting on and praising Zhigulin's work, V. Novikov, in *Literaturnaya gazeta* (17 Aug. 1988), refers to Solzhenitsyn's *The Gulag Archipelago*, the first such (positive) mention I had seen in the Soviet press.

A Belorussian literary periodical, *Literatura i mastatstva* has drawn attention to the wood near Minsk, where there are mass graves, 500 mass graves, of people who were shot there "daily" in the years 1937–41. After the publication (which shows that some provincial journals do show boldness!), the Belorussian government appointed a commission to investigate: "There is work to be done in the archives of the MVD and KGB." (All this was reported in *Moskovskie novosti*, 21 Aug. 1988. Alas, I do not know the Belorussian language.)

The same horror was the subject of an article in *Daugava* (No. 9, 1988) by V. Shershov. Some 510 mass graves have already been found, and many others are thought to exist. A rough official estimate puts the total number of victims in this area at 250,000–300,000! In 1939–40, some of those shot may have come from the Baltic republics, as some shoes that have been found were marked "Made in Riga". Who were the executioners? Who were the victims? Inquiries are continuing. In the same issue of *Daugava*, V. Yakobsons writes of Norilsk, in north Siberia, where there were 100,000 prisoners working, and Yulian Tarnovsky's "Norilsk ballads" were published, one of them in English. (It begins with the line: "This is barbed wire and we are jailbirds.")

More revelations will surely be appearing.

What of Lenin's time? It is significant that *Novyi mir* (No. 10, 1988) reprinted the letters that the famous novelist Vladimir

Korolenko sent to the Commissar for Education, Lunacharsky, during the Civil War, protesting about outrageous instances of Red terror. In a brief introduction, the editor, S. Zalygin, reminds the readers of the tragedy of civil war, but also of the fact that terror revived in peacetime ("in 1929–31, in 1937–38 and in the postwar years 1948–49").

In *Neva*, No. 11, 1988, A. Antonov-Ovseyenko tells the story of the fate of the old Georgian party leader Orakhelashvili, shot together with his wife in 1937. His daughter Ketevan spent eighteen years in labour camps, and her husband, a leading musician, was tortured to death in prison. Abuladze's now-famous film, *Repentance*, draws heavily upon the appalling experiences of this family.

*Novyi mir*, No. 12, 1988, printed some striking poems by Ivan Elagin, an emigre who recently died in America. He had penned verses to explain his unwillingness to return. "Maybe the man is still alive who shot my father in Kiev in 1938. He is probably on a pension. If he is dead, then there is the man who led him to execution . . . or the man who tortured him during interrogations. He is now probably on a very good pension. Yes, I could come back, since I hear that these men have forgiven me".

Finally, one must note the appearance of a remarkable film, *Vlast' solovetskaya*, a documentary about the first (and very vicious) concentration camp for "politicals", Solovki, which existed already in 1923. One of the witnesses of a massacre that took place there in 1929 was Academician D. Likhachev, who was then a prisoner.

# CHAPTER 5

# Religion, Nationalism, Morality

The areas mentioned in this chapter's title have been beset by taboos. The poet-balladeer Okudzhava has told how he had problems getting past the censor the harmless little phrase: "O my Arbat, my Arbat, you are my religion." The Arbat is a famous Moscow street. The word *religion* was what had to be fought for. Records of Russian religious music had to be presented as "history of Russian music", and a good choir conducted by Yurlov made a good job of them. Oddly, Bulgaria produced excellent records of orthodox liturgy. Nothing could be said about the persecution of the church. Nationalism as an internal Soviet issue could not be discussed seriously; it had all been settled within the brotherly multinational union. Questions of the relationship between religion and morality—indeed, serious questions relating to either—were seldom to be encountered, though of course some literary works were able to touch on them. One example, that of Chingiz Aitmatov, will be discussed in a moment.

I will begin with the Jews, another taboo subject for many years. Jewish history was (still is) a blank page. Jewish suffering during the last war, when millions were massacred by the Germans, was very infrequently mentioned. The "black book" on these atrocities, put together just after the war by Ilya Erenburg and Vasili Grossman, was never published in the USSR. In 1948–53, in Stalin's last years, a number of anti-Jewish measures were taken, and almost the entire wartime Jewish antifascist committee was arrested and shot, the Jewish theatre closed, its brilliant actor-director Mikhoels killed in a suspicious "accident"—and later denounced as an enemy. A campaign against "rootless cosmopolitans" sought to drive Jews out of cultural and literary activities, though without ever mentioning the word *Jews*. The announcement, in January 1953, of a plot by eminent doctors, most of them Jews, to poison Soviet leaders at the behest of international Zionism, was clearly intended to lead to further drastic measures. Among the victims of shootings (in August 1952) of the Jewish antifascist committee had been the leading writers in Yiddish: Fefer, Bergelson, Markish. They were tried in secret. Their wives learned of their executions only when they were posthumously rehabilitated in 1956. But these rehabilitations were given no publicity; the very fact that the Jewish antifascist committee had been dissolved, its members killed, remained a nonevent. It is not part of my task to discuss why all this happened. This is only a brief background note, to show what *glasnost'* has now allowed to see the light of day.

After Stalin's death the arrested doctors were released (some did not survive the interrogation). Under Khrushchev conditions improved, but there were numerous cases of discrimination, especially in access to higher education and to certain types of work (e.g., diplomacy, the military, foreign trade), and it was noticeable that persons sentenced to death for economic crimes included a grossly disproportionate number of Jews. Then, under Brezhnev, came a change of policy toward emigration: many left the USSR, to go to Israel or to Western countries, especially the United States. None of this was discussed in the Soviet media. There was at the same time a prolonged campaign against "Zionism", which, in some notorious instances, became anti-Semitic in tone. No reply to such attacks was ever allowed. The existence of anti-Semitism as a problem was repeatedly denied.

The Holocaust remained almost a nonsubject in the media, except for occasional allegations that "the Zionist leaders" collaborated with the Nazis. Nearly all the monuments erected at the site of massacres and mass graves failed to mention Jews (of course, there were also large numbers of non-Jewish victims). Yevtushenko's anti-anti-Semitic poem, *Babyi Yar*, attracted the ire of the authorities, and Shostakovich's thirteenth symphony, which quotes the poem in choral passages, was hardly ever played. The policy of saying as little as possible on Jewish questions should not be seen as anti-Semitic, since it was part of the general policy of avoiding open discussion of any awkward or embarrassing question, particularly under Brezhnev.

An exception to the silence on Jewish victims of the Nazis was the publication, in 1978, of Anatoli Rybakov's *Heavy Sand* (*Tyazhelyi pesok*), which dwelt on this theme. It has been published also in English. This is the same Rybakov who wrote *Deti Arbata*. Earlier, Vasili Grossman had written his great novel *Life and Fate*, which, as we shall see, has important Jewish themes, but he was prevented from publishing it—indeed, all known copies of the typescript were "arrested". It must be added that the main reason for this was not its "Jewish" pages, as shall be shown below.

With this by way of background, let us now see which taboos have been broken, and which have not. It is noteworthy that virtually everything to be mentioned occurred in 1987 and after.

Rybakov's *Deti Arbata* touched on Jews only tangentially, and this in two ways. Stalin, soliloquising, is shown to be uneasy about Jews: their religion and traditions do not predispose them to accept any supreme leader on earth. Then the least sympathetic of the novel's characters, who joins the NKVD, expresses anti-Semitic sentiments, as do his parents. Of course, the nonpublication of the novel before 1987 was due to other causes, but these passages too would have attracted the censor's scissors.

Next, chronologically, came the surprising publication in *Oktyabr'* of Grossman's *Life and Fate*. Further comment on this truly remarkable novel must wait its turn. Its principal theme has nothing Jewish about it, but one of the main characters is a Jewish scientist, Shtumm (possibly modeled on Landau, the great physicist), who suffers from petty anti-Semitic pin-pricks until the military importance of his researches is noted by Stalin, whereupon his colleagues show him all respect and solicitude. He is then shown putting his name to a politically demeaning letter, which a more principled colleague refused to sign. (It is my hunch that Grossman, an assimilated Jew who had to make many compromises, was getting a burden off his own chest through his fictional character.) Shtumm receives a letter from his mother, smuggled out of a ghetto shortly before its liquidation. This letter must move a great many of its readers to tears. The intensity of the writing is explicable in no small part by the fact that Grossman's own mother lived in Berdichev and was killed there along with all its Jewish inhabitants. Finally, in the novel a Jewish woman doctor, and an orphan she met on the way, make the journey to a death camp, and its procedures are described in painful detail. Grossman, as a military journalist, had been one of the first to reach the death camp in Maidanek.

The text published in *Oktyabr'* (No. 3, 1988) suffered a few cuts, and a two-page section devoted to an analysis and critique of anti-Semitism was omitted. The same journal in its September issue printed the missing pages, giving a somewhat specious excuse for having omitted them. Space permits but one brief quotation here: "Anti-Semitism can be met in the bazaar and in a meeting of the Presidium of the Academy of Sciences, in the soul of the old men and on children's playgrounds. Anti-Semitism has managed to migrate from the age of candles, sailing-ships and spinning wheels into the age of jet-engines, nuclear reactors and electronics. . . . Anti-Semitism is the mirror of the personal deficiencies of specific individuals, social organizations and state systems. Tell me of what you accuse the Jews, and I will tell you what you are guilty of." The passage in the novel immediately follows a discussion by two Germans on the design of gas chambers.

While Grossman's novel was being serialized, *Moskovskie novosti* (7 Feb. 1988) published an article by David Gai, titled "The End of the 'Doctors Affair'". It reminds the readers of the nature of the accusations, that "the beasts in human form had murdered Zhdanov and Shcherbakov, having been bought by the branch of American intelligence, the international Jewish bourgeois-nationalist organization 'Joint'". How and why did all this happen? The paper quotes a former minister of health, E. Smirnov. Stalin had expressed suspicion about the deaths of Zhdanov and Dimitrov, and Smirnov failed to reassure him about the doctor (Kagan) who had been treating both these patients. He goes on to quote one of those arrested, Rapaport, who will be cited here too, to the effect that Stalin was shaken by the recommendation made by Professor Vinogradov (*not* a Jew) that he cease all activity on urgent medical grounds, which made Stalin furious; he is said to have told Beria to "put him in irons". The first wave of arrests took place in November 1952. Gai in his article cites interviews with sons and daughters of those arrested, e.g., Lubov Vovsi, who tells that her father (who had been chief therapeutist of the Red Army in the war) was ordered to confess to having been an agent of Hitler and Germany, to which Vovsi said: "Not the Germans! My father and my brother's family were slaughtered by the fascists in Dvinsk"; to which the interrogator replied: "Do not speculate on the blood of your relatives." His wife Vera was also arrested.

It was Ryumin, a senior official of the MGB (as it was then known), described as "totally immoral, cynical, hungry for power and career", who "consciously falsified the interrogation materials". He had begun to prepare the case by arresting two doctors working in the so-called Kremlin hospital, Sofia Karpai and Yakov Etinger (Jewish names), and "Etinger could not withstand the prison treatment and died". Ryumin was shot, as was Beria, after Stalin's death.

There appeared simultaneously, in two different journals, an article by a 90-year-old survivor who figured in the second wave of "doctors' plot" arrests, Yakov Rapaport (*Druzhba narodov*, No. 4,

1988), and one by his daughter Natalia (*Yunost'*, No. 4, 1988), the latter preceded by an introduction by E. Yevtushenko, who told of how millions had believed the accusations, including himself, then a 20-year-old student in the Literary Institute in Moscow. He recalls how the only two Jewish students in the institute were shunned ("they were surrounded in the common-room by a vacuum"). Natalia, now an eminent chemist, recalls how the children were affected (she was a schoolgirl then), and also how various friends and colleagues reacted—some turned away, others courageously tried to help.

Yakov Rapaport's memoirs were introduced by the editor of *Druzhba narodov*, Sergei Baruzdin. He (at last!) linked the doctors' plot affair with "the most serious question of relations between nationalities. . . . It is now not a secret from anyone that the so-called campaign against cosmopolitanism, devised in the postwar years with the knowledge of Stalin and with the active participation of his closest associates, developed into a wild campaign, the victims of which included distinguished representatives of Soviet culture, literature, science, medicine. It is enough to recall the tragic fate of almost all the members of the Jewish antifascist committee—the outstanding actors S. Mikhoels and V. Zuskin, the old Bolshevik and colleague of Lenin's, S. Lozovsky, the writers and poets D. Bergelson, I. Fefer, L. Kvitko, P. Markish and others." (Lozovsky had been the party's man in the Jewish antifascist committee.)

This was the first open reference to the events which disfigured the years 1948–53, and which Baruzdin, in his excellent introduction, characterised not as a blank spot but as "black spot" in history. He then pointed his finger at the "extremist wing of the Pamyat' society", who have similar notions today.

Rapaport's memoirs begin by citing the accusations and listing those arrested. Some, he says, were "posthumously arrested", in that they had already died in prison before their arrests were announced. This included Etinger and also Shimelovich (through whom the plotters were supposed to have received their instructions from the Jewish organization "Joint"). Shimelovich had been shot along with the Jewish antifascist committee in August 1952. Rapaport also makes an important point: "One must say that Soviet society had been psychologically prepared for the emergence of the doctors' affair, or of something similar, during the campaign against cosmopolitanism, begun in 1948, when it turned out that the 'rootless cosmopolitans' were one and all of Jewish nationality. . . . There was even the removal of Mendelssohn's statue from the Great Hall of the Conservatoire. . . . Although directly there was no word of anti-Semitism, the general direction of the campaign was evident."

Equally evident was the anti-Semitic direction of the "doctors' affair", though there were some Russian names among those arrested. There were even rumours that they were not really Russian, "that Vinogradov was Weintraub, Zelenin was Grunbaum". Rapaport followed this by the first reference in a Soviet source to plans "that an open trial of the evil doctors would be followed by death sentences, some carried out in public, and this would inevitably lead to Jewish *pogroms*, as a result of which the Jews, to save them from 'the people's wrath', would be systematically deported to specially prepared reservations in Siberia". Prominent Jews were asked to sign a letter to the press along these lines. "I do not know the names of all the signatories, who must be seen as victims of the period, . . . but consider it my duty to name those who had the courage to refuse, while fully appreciating the possible consequences: People's artist Mark Reizen, Hero of the Soviet Union General Yakov Kreizer, and Ilya Erenburg. Luckily this document (letter) never saw the light of day, but the mere fact of its being written tells us much." (Let me add that a number of unofficial sources have described this episode, Erenburg among them. But never before had a hint of this appeared in a Soviet publication.)

As already mentioned, Rapaport believes that the entire case had as its origins Vinogradov's recommendation that Stalin cease all activity. Vinogradov, "admirable and experienced clinician", was right in his diagnosis, as was shown by Stalin's death in March 1953. Stalin's indignation gave to the police a reason to fabricate a plot. At first it had no Jewish aspect. This was suggested by Ryutin, apparently in an effort to discredit his chief, the minister of state security Anakumov, who supposedly concealed his knowledge of "a plot by bourgeois Jewish nationalists". (It is possible that Beria too was to be discredited, which would help to explain the release of the accused doctors immediately after Stalin's death, when Beria was still powerful.)

Rapaport recalls trials in the thirties which involved doctors; thus in 1938 several were arrested for supposedly poisoning Gorky, Menzhinsky, and Kuibyshev (but since only one had a Jewish name, I will not pursue this point here).

On being arrested in February 1953, Rapaport was promptly told, "You are arrested as a Jewish bourgeois nationalist and enemy of the Soviet people." On asking what he is supposed to have done, he got the reply: "That you must tell us yourself." He had a most unpleasant time, in painful handcuffs. Eventually the interrogator produced a set of motives: "the Jews are persecuted, kept out of jobs.... You yourself said that the directives come from the central committee, therefore you must fight those who issue them." But confessions were needed for something more serious than such grievances as (he quotes the interrogator) "Hyman was sacked, Abram was not appointed". Rapaport refused to confess. Vovsi and Vinogradov signed false confessions. Vovsi, years later, suffering from cancer, which required the amputation of a leg, said: "Can one compare my present state with what I felt *then*? Now I have lost a leg and remain human; *then* I ceased to be a human being." Rapaport was one of those who was saved by Stalin's death.

Evidence from a quite different and unexpected source appears in Konstantin Simonov's memoirs, published posthumously in *Znamya* (No. 4, 1988). Simonov attended a number of meetings between Stalin and editors and officials of the Writers' Union. At one such meeting, Stalin chose to criticise those who put a real (Jewish) family name after a literary pseudonym: "Why? who needs it? Why stimulate anti-Semitism?" So Simonov felt at the time that Stalin was not anti-Semitic. The question of Stalin's attitude toward the Jews had arisen frequently in conversation. His alleged dislike was attributed, in such discussions, to past struggles with the Jewish Bund, and with Jewish Party opponents like Trotsky, Zinoviev, and Kamenev. However, "Stalin also dealt pitilessly with the right-wing oppositionists, who were Russians one and all in names and origin", and he had close collaborators of Jewish origin, such as Kaganovich and Mekhlis, while Litvinov ran foreign affairs for a decade. The suspicious circumstances surrounding the death of the actor Mikhoels, the postwar arrests of Jewish writers, the appearance in brackets of Jewish names, especially of those selected for criticism as "antipatriotic critics", together with what he called "various favours shown to those dubious characters who were making or trying to make a career out of anti-Semitism", all this still did not convince him at the time that Stalin was responsible. "It did not fit my concept of the man, and seemed altogether senseless, inconsistent with the character of one who is the leader of the world communist movement." And yet "we did feel that something abnormal was going on. The problem of Jewish assimilation or nonassimilation, which in the years of our youth simply did not exist before the war, became a reality afterwards. Jews came to be divided between those who thought that their assimilation within socialist society to be a normal thing, and those who resisted this. During these postwar cataclysms, as well as shameless and open anti-Semitic outbursts there appeared in reply a concealed and obstinate

Jewish nationalism." Simonov states that, while he and his like never thought of criticising Stalin, "we several times speculated among ourselves as to who was the main initiator of the ever new manifestations of anti-Semitism. Who plays first fiddle here, who is trying to use for their own purposes some of Stalin's attitudes or sayings about the Jews, the existence of which we thought possible? Various people put forward various hypotheses, involving this or that member of the Politbureau of the time, or several at once." Simonov's own doubts were resolved after he was shown some documents, after Stalin's death, "which left no doubt at all that, in the last years of his life, Stalin's attitude to the Jewish question was quite opposite to that which he expressed in public". So he at least was clear as to Stalin's direct responsibility.

He goes on, in this same issue of *Znamya*, to speak of his shock over the doctors' plot and the anti-Jewish scenario of the previous year's Slansky trial in Czechoslovakia. He tells how, at this time (early in 1953), Alexei Surkov, acting head of the Writers' Union, "who was deeply contemptuous of, and hated, both anti-Semitism and anti-Semites", showed him a letter which had been passed to him by an official of the Party's Central Committee. To quote Simonov: "This letter is worth a brief citation even today, since it characterises a part of the atmosphere of the time, when a well-known man [we are not told who] could decide openly to undertake anti-Semitic researches of a kind which perhaps only fascists could think of." This man "drew attention of the central committee to the Jewish domination and pro-Jewish attitudes of *Literaturnaya gazeta*, under my editorship, which was explained by my own Jewish origins. He 'discovered' that I was not really Simonov but Simanovich, that I was born to the family of a Jewish tavern-keeper on the estate of countess Obolensky, who subsequently brought me up and adopted me." Simonov's reaction was to roar with laughter, and to say that he must tell his mother the story. His mother, as it happens, *was* of the Obolensky family (but they were princes, not counts—*knyazya*, not *grafy*), and had married a Colonel Simonov before the first war. But Surkov saw nothing funny in this at all. "Think of how low one has to fall to write such letters to the Central Committee, and what sort of atmosphere is it when a man can decide to write such letters." What indeed? (Surkov, whom I met several times, was a complex figure. On the one hand he was a typical literary bureaucrat, on the other he gave some material help to Mandelshtam, and made efforts to secure the publication of Akhmatova's poems.)

In the present context what is noteworthy is the publication of remarks on Jewish questions which were strictly off-limits for decades. They appeared at last in the same month (April 1988) as the Rapaport (father's and daughter's) memoirs.

An unusual article appeared in *Sovetskaya kultura*, 15 October 1988, by Tankred Golenpolsky. He cited his own difficulties in getting a regular job and mentioned the alleged existence of a numerus clausus ("quota") for Jews in higher education (allegations "never referred to, denied, or criticised"). Victims of discrimination desired to emigrate. Although ethnic Germans, Armenians, and Ukrainians have also emigrated, among the public the view is widespread that "the Jews are running away" (*begut evrei*), and the fact that American protests about emigration concern only Jews is seen by some as proof of a *zhido-masonski zagovor* (Yid-masonic conspiracy). He adds that if it were easier to go abroad and come back, fewer would wish to emigrate.

In *Druzhba narodov* (No. 11, 1988), among poems by Boris Slutsky is one entitled "Otchestvo i otechestvo" (Patronymic and fatherland). Some say you can tell (a Jew) by his patronymic even if he has a pseudonym-surname and an innocent-looking first name. Yes, there were princes named Slutsky, there was a tsar named Boris, but his (Slutsky's) father's name was Abram, he is Boris Abramovich, and will remain true to patronymic and to fatherland.

*Glasnost'*, however, gives freedom also to anti-Semites. We have already noted the clear implications of Andreyeva's letter published so prominently in *Sovetskaya Rossiya*, in which Trotsky's Jewish internationalism is combined with a barely concealed denunciation of Jewish emigration as a form of national treason. In doing so, Andreyeva undoubtedly expresses a significant strand of public opinion, irritated by demonstrations by "refuseniks" and by occasional reports of anti-Soviet activities by Jewish groups in the West. Her characterization of Jews (in the context, clearly Jews) as a "counterrevolutionary nation" produced a protest from G. Borovik in a speech to the 19th Party Conference. There were also the attempts (e.g., by Belov and Mozhayev, see above) to attribute various excesses, notably against the peasants, to Trotsky and other Jewish party leaders. Finally, there is the *Pamyat'* group, some of whose leaders are virulently anti-Semitic, though it is only fair to stress that their declarations do not appear in the legal press or media, which have several times criticised them. However, one consequence of *glasnost'* is the proliferation of unofficial, uncensored news-sheets and periodicals, of the most varied political hues. In these one can read about international judeo-masonic conspiracies. A series of meetings addressed by *Pamyat'* speakers have been reported from Leningrad, and have been the subject of protests: thus *Literaturnaya gazeta* of 27 August 1988 printed an angry letter from the (Jewish) General David Dragunsky, while in *Izvestiya* of 14 August there was a protest signed by 59 researchers of the Institute of Oriental Studies in Leningrad, accusing *Pamyat'* of "inciting hatred of non-Russians", of "ascribing to Jews, Latvians and other aliens the main guilt for the Terror, collectivization, the destruction of Russian cultural monuments". *Pamyat'* speakers oppose marriage between Russians and "aliens"; they "attempt to exert moral pressure on Jews active in culture, art and education"; they defend the Tsarist "Black hundreds"; they form "committees of national salvation", using Nazi-type slogans; they cite approvingly the forged "Protests of the Elders of Zion". Some teachers bring schoolchildren to their meetings, where leaflets are handed out. In his letter, Dragunsky referred to proposals to deport Jews and other aliens "to their places of origin". He reminded the readers of his own military service (he was twice Hero of the Soviet Union) and of the killing of his mother by Nazi death squads. How is it that such meetings are tolerated in Leningrad?

*Izvestiya* supported the letter of the 59, and said that the militia are taking steps to stop the meetings. (However, rumours persist that some Leningrad Party officials are quietly supporting *Pamyat'*, and the situation justifies serious disquiet.) There was also the exchange between the literary critic Eidelman and the novelist Astafyev, made semipublic (again through unofficial channels) by Eidelman. Astafyev accused "the Jews" of having killed the tsar (!), and, using offensive language, suggested that Russian literature should be off-limits to them (the correspondence was reprinted in *Detente*, No. 8). This should remind us that freedom to speak is also freedom to express opinions that are disagreeable. In a country where anti-Semitism has never been far below the surface, this has evident dangers. Official condemnations of "Zionism and anti-Semitism" show a desire to keep such trends in check. It cannot be said that *glasnost'* has led to total frankness on this issue. Thus, for example, neither emigration nor job discrimination has been the subject of serious discussion in the media, nor has the real role of Jews in Russian history or in the revolution. But it by no means follows that the opening of these issues to public debate would have favourable consequences for Russian Jewry, given the prejudices among significant segments of public opinion.

I will mention one other matter, which figures rather prominently in Solzhenitsyn's *Gulag Archipelago*: the role of Jews in the Terror and the NKVD. It receives mention in works published by emigrés:

thus, Sinyavsky recalls that many of his fellow prisoners expressed the view that they were victims of Jews in authority—this at a time, 1965, when there were no Jews in authority at all. The novelist Maksimov has one of his Jewish characters express the view that the Jews have played a sizable role in setting up the system, and so should not now emigrate and leave it to the Russians to pick up the pieces. Finally a (Jewish) *samizdat* poet, Garik, penned the following quatrain (my translation):

> The Jews are leaving, they are leaving Russia
> Away from Moscow they are going far.
> The world is strange for Ivan and for Vasya
> The Jews have left them neither God nor tsar.

Such thoughts have not spilled over into open publication. However, it is worth remarking that several brutal NKVD interrogators mentioned in the cases referred to in the last chapter do indeed bear Jewish surnames, e.g., Shvartsman. It is fair to add, though, that their victims were in many cases Jewish too: Isaak Babel, for instance, and also Koltsov, whose real name was Fridland (which did not prevent his brother from being named Boris Yefimov). Quite a few prominent Jews used pseudonyms. The "unmasking" of such pseudonyms was one tactic widely used in the anticosmopolitan campaign of 1948–52. The practice lends itself to evident abuse, as when genuinely gentile but villainous persons are alleged to be Jews in disguise. I once read (in an emigré publication) that *Djuga* is the Georgian for "Jew", that Stalin's real name was Djugashvili, and therefore ... Solzhenitsyn's *Lenin in Zurich*, unpublished in the USSR, makes a very Jewish Parvus-Helfand the main villain, while Lenin is presented as only "one-eighth Russian".

*Literaturnaya Rossiya* (20 Nov. 1987) printed four poems by Mark Chagall, translated from Yiddish. One of them is in memory of painters from his former home, who finished up in mass graves, or in Auschwitz or Maidanek.

> I see the flames, the gas, the smoke rising,
> the piles of shoes, of clothes, of teeth and hair,
> and ash and rubble, and I stand and pray,
> while David with his harp comes down from
> a painting with his psalms to help me weep.
> And Moses too appears ...

(Forgive my totally inadequate translation.)

It is also significant that Shevarnadze and Dobrynin met officials of the World Jewish Congress in Moscow, and that this was reported in the Soviet press.

There has been nothing new affecting Judaism as a religion, except that the general turn toward greater religious tolerance is having some positive consequences.

Religion has been linked in public debate and in some publications to the issue of morality, of a decline in standards of behaviour. The novelist Astafyev did this with particular effect in his "Sad Detective" ("*Pechalnyi detektiv*", Oktyabr', No. 1, 1986), without directly mentioning religion at all. Its principal character is a retired detective in a north Russian town, sadly observing crime, drunkenness, and delinquency and musing on the reasons for such things. His attempt to write about them meet with total incomprehension from the local literary commissar. He starts looking for ideas in Dostoevsky and even Nietsche. The author has little good to say about the liberal-minded intelligentsia. There is not a word about Marxism-Leninism, which plainly does not explain delinquency and crime, which cannot, 70 years after the revolution, be attributed to the remnants of capitalism. A grimly realistic picture is presented, with a gap where moral principle should be. Religion can be said to be present by implication, by not being.

Earlier, the Kirgiz writer Chingiz Aitmatov had succeeded in getting through the censorship with *I bol'she veka dlitsa den'*, where he raised at the same time the importance of folk memory and the significance of religion, in this case the Moslem religion. Being pre-*glasnost'*, this (in my view) admirable novel cannot be discussed further here. But in *Novyi mir* (Nos. 6, 8, and 9, 1986) Aitmatov published an even more challenging novel, *Plakha* (*The Executioner's Block*, or *The Scaffold*). In my opinion it is a less satisfactory literary work than its predecessor, but the moral and religious themes are even more pronounced. The "hero" is a former religious seminarist, expelled by the priests for having his own ideas about God, but deeply religious still. In Central Asia he encounters a gang of drug dealers collecting marijuana. Aitmatov's story moves to Palestine in Christ's time, along the lines of Bulgakov's magnificent *Master and Margarita*, but less convincingly so. The ex-seminarist, inspired by his religious beliefs, seeks to persuade the drug dealers to desist. The gang leader mocks his beliefs, and in the end the gang literally crucifies him. The novel includes highly critical remarks about the massacre of a local species of antelope in the steppes due to the local officials' anxiety to increase meat deliveries.

No religious question appears explicitly in Valentin Rasputin's *Pozhar* (*The Fire*), published in 1985. Set in a lumber camp in

Siberia, the centre-piece is a fire that breaks out in a storehouse, which, among other things, houses the food supplies of the settlement. Chaos and irresponsibility rule, the fire-fighting equipment is out of order, many steal what they can. The impression is conveyed of a sort of rootless, drunken, and alienated indifference. As in Astafyev's novel, religion is absent, and so is any moral basis for living. Rasputin's other works stress the loss, not replaced, of peasant traditions. His short story *"Proshchai Matyora"*, about a village condemned to be beneath the water in a hydroelectric project, has been made into a powerful film.

More remarkable yet is the appearance, several years after his death, of a novel by Tendryakov, *Pokusheniye na mirazhi* (serialized in *Novyi mir* in 1987). It begins with a discussion among Moscow computer programmers about the role of great men in history. Why not, they say, prove it by computer. Put all that there was in the programme, less the "great man", and see what would have happened. For example, put all that had occurred up to 1793 in the programme and have Napoleon killed at the siege of Toulon. They settle instead on Christ, whom they programme to be stoned to death several years before He was crucified, leaving Paul in a more dominant position (he was still converted on the road to Damascus).

Tendryakov proceeds with copious quotations from the New Testament, and from some apocryphal stories. Thus the computer programmers speculate as to why Jesus would not go out to meet his mother (Matthew 12:46–49). Tendryakov tries to show how Paul would have modified Jesus' teachings in His absence, and in particular takes up the question of Paul's view of the duties of slaves, which, in this interpretation, would not give them any reason to work. It needed Christ's emphasis that his "kingdom is not of this world". A ruler encountered by Paul finds his doctrines inoperable. So does the computer programme, which proceeds to resurrect Christ! In other words, Paul minus the doctrines preached by Christ in His last years on earth is not viable, because of the human relations aspect. Men can be made to work with whips, or because it serves their self-interest in this world or the next. Otherwise . . .

Developing this point further, Tendryakov figuratively leaves his programmers behind him (their computer games have been discovered and banned by their superiors), and moves into Campanella's Kingdom of the Sun, evidently aiming to show that this particular utopia would have disastrous consequences for the same kind of reason: its inhabitants would have no reason to work (because of what we nowadays call the "free rider" problem). So Campanella visits his Kingdom, finds that everything has disinte-

grated, there is abject poverty and oppression, and he himself is
thrown into prison. One is reminded of one of Tendryakov's own
stories about collectivization, quoted above: the peasant who gives
away his property and is free like a bird, but birds neither sow nor
reap. Utopias have a regrettable tendency to turn out to be very
different from what their authors had intended. Marx and Engels
are mentioned by name in another connection, but no reader could
miss the allusion.

So it was in a new atmosphere that 1988 saw the "thousand years
of Christianity in Russia". It provided additional stimulus for a
rethinking of the relationship between the state and the Orthodox
church, an opportunity for a look at the role of the church in Russian
history, a new opportunity too for the church to press claims for
amendment of the highly restrictive laws (especially that of 1929)
which effectively prevented it from doing anything other than
holding services (for example, charitable works were banned, as
presumably a form of "religious propaganda"). It should be recalled
that the Orthodox church, along with other religions, suffered the
most intense persecution in the 1930s, with thousands of priests
arrested and churches closed and destroyed. The full truth of this
aspect of the Terror has yet to be told, by church or by state. Stalin
eased the pressure during the war, when the church did its patriotic
duty. However, Khrushchev's ideological position caused him to
take a negative view of religion, and many churches were closed.
Under Brezhnev, too, restrictions were maintained. There was of
course no terror or *mass* arrests, but energetic priests who achieved
some influence found themselves behind bars, and smaller denomi-
nations (e.g., the so-called Initiative Baptists) and sects were frequently in trouble. The Ukrainian Uniate church was and is a special
case: it was set up in the sixteenth century under Polish authority,
providing Greek ritual under the authority of the pope. For centuries
it was regarded with deep suspicion by Russia's rulers *and* by the
Orthodox church. It still is, though its legalization is now on the
cards.

*Glasnost'* has affected Orthodoxy in several ways. First, cautious
but significant steps are being taken to bring the church into the
more open society. Three examples will illustrate this. In Moscow in
January 1988 a "round table on 1000 years of Christianity in
Russia" was held in a crowded cinema (I was present myself). It was
chaired by Yuri Afanasyev, who has been discussed in earlier
chapters. On the platform were seven priests and seven lay
academics, all of whom made brief statements about themselves.
(When one of the academics described himself as the Party secretary

of an institute, there was laughter in the audience!) Then there were questions from the floor. These included one on the role of religion in establishing moral principles for society and another on what the church will do to rehabilitate its victims of the thirties (a priest replied: there were victims also in the twenties; they need no rehabilitation from us; we hope that the state will do so). Someone asked how many monasteries there are; another asked if laymen can use the Danilov monastery library (answer: yes). There were also simple questions, such as what are the ranks within the Church. Afanasyev thought that there had been no such gathering for the past sixty years.

The radio programme broadcast from Red Square on the occasion of the First of May demonstration in 1988 included—to my astonishment—an interview of an archimandrite of the church on the subject of *miloserdiye*, a word midway between *compassion* and *charity*, a word which had gone out of use and has now returned, and not only in religious connections. Thus there are now Komsomol and other voluntary groups gathering money for charitable works. *Moskovskie novosti* on 26 June 1988 printed a note under the heading of "Doing Good": "Into one of Moscow's hospitals there came Baptists. They proposed to help look after the patients, to carry out any difficult work. They refused any reward." Then were quoted the remarks of the chairman of the "all-union council of Evangelical Christian-Baptists", Vasili Logvinenko. He spoke of the charitable work of Baptists abroad, and also explained that they participate in the Society for the Preservation of Monuments and "in the children's fund named after Lenin, of which, incidentally, I am a member of the governing board. But believers are not allowed, by the 1929 legislation, to participate directly in charitable works. However, times are changing: this year we petitioned the Central Committee and the State Committee on Religion to allow us a wider scope for charitable activities and our position was fully understood. More, we were at once met with a suggestion that we should work in the gerontological department of Psychiatric Hospital No. 1." The head of this department is quoted as welcoming the appearance of much-needed help: "The believers are very polite, kind, hardworking." Logvinenko reported that some fifty of his flock take turns going to this hospital, "to carry out their Christian and human duty of *miloserdiye*. . . . We are bound in duty by the Holy Scriptures, by the divine word, to help all who are miserable and in need." The author of the article remarks that some Baptists would prefer to work in a nonpsychiatric hospital located near their prayer-house, but this is not "yet" allowed. The clear implication is that a valuable precedent has been set, and not only for Baptists. (Indeed, it would be a safe bet, even in convertible currency, that a new law on religion, specifically allowing charitable works, and also some limited religious education, another very sore point, will be enacted before these lines are published.)

In *Znamya* (No. 8, 1988), D. Balashov, in the course of discussing the thousand-year anniversary, speaks of "the significance of ritual for Man, symbolic acts uniting the inhabitant of the land with his ancestors into a unified and unbreakable tree of national history. Without such a unification with ancestors there is no citizen, no personality, just a savage with a nuclear bomb instead of a stone in his hairy hand." Deploring the destruction of so many churches, he remarks that "humanity has to pay a high price for barbarism". Indeed, "nothing but unquestionable harm was done by the aggressive struggle against religion, in fact a struggle against Russian culture". And in *Novyi mir* (No. 11, 1988), in the last instalment of Yuri Dombrovsky's remarkable novel (*Fakultet nenuzhnykh veshchei*), a main character, a Jewish NKVD interrogator called Neiman, himself threatened by the purge (the action takes place in 1937) encounters a group of peasants by a nighttime bonfire by a river; they had found a drowned woman. A former seminarist intones a prayer, there is a discussion about forgiveness and sincere confession ("Christ forgave the sins of the thief who was crucified alongside Him"), and Neiman ponders his own situation: who could he appeal to, who could forgive his sins?

It is worth mentioning that the word "God" could not, for decades, be spelt with an initial capital letter. Only in the most recent years has this become possible, and it is now commonplace.

Recordings of church choirs have now become available, and a religious choir from the USSR has sung (beautifully) in the West. (I heard it myself in Cologne.)

*Yunost'* (No. 9, 1988) in an article by Y. Shcherbak, devoted to the Chernobyl disaster, cites the prophecy in Revelations, Ch. 8, 11 (the word Chernobyl means "wormwood", its usual Russian translation is *polyn'*), which appeared to forecast such a disaster. The author went to consult Metropolitan Filaret of Kiev, and his comment is printed in its entirety.

The Armenian earthquake was followed by *Pravda* printing a long article by the Katholikos of the Armenian church. And Soviet television showed, for the first time, the Pope's address on Christmas Day.

An unusual and strongly written article in *Moskovskie novosti* of 29 November 1977 discusses the Old Believers. It sets out their sufferings from the seventeenth century (when their leader Avvakum was burned at the stake) and "up to recent times". The author lists the many charitable acts of Old Believer merchants, one of whom founded the Botkin hospital and another the Moscow children's hospital, and another of whom financed the Moscow Arts Theatre and indeed also Lenin's "Iskra" (this was the famous Savva Morozov). The author, A. Nezhny, pointed out to a Moscow district soviet chairman that some old buildings, including a church which once belonged to the Old Believers, are used as storehouses or are in ruinous condition. Why not return them to the Old Believers parish, why not allow them to train a choir, before the ancient traditions disappear? Reply: "No, no choir." The author comments that "among the virtues of our Motherland, tolerance to dissidence is far from being in first place". At the beginning of the article is a quotation from academician D. Likhachev, eminent specialist on old Russian literature, on the Old Believers: "this living remnant of ancient Russian culture". The article is illustrated with a photograph of old bearded men, "parishioners of the Pokrovsky Old Believer church".

A final example is a televised discussion held in March 1988 on different worldviews, at a peak viewing time, which included a metropolitan of the Orthodox church, who spoke intelligently and was treated respectfully by the other three participants. He too mentioned the role of religion in establishing a code of morals in society. A few years ago the very idea of his appearance before a mass audience would have been considered both impossible and ridiculous.

*Literaturnaya gazeta* (15 June 1986) published an interview with the Polish primate, Cardinal Glemp, in Moscow in connection with the "thousand year" celebrations, the first visit *ever* by a Polish primate to Moscow! He spoke of the role of the church in Poland through the centuries, its close links with the people. And he specifically mentioned the need to clear up the question of Katyn.

Unofficial news-sheets, of which there are many in the Soviet Union today, criticise the church hierarchy for timidity, for failing to demand the repeal of restrictive laws. It certainly failed in the past to defend its more zealous priests from repressive acts. Rumour had it that some high church dignitaries were officers of the KGB. Be all this as it may, and rumours in a closed society can be baseless, the thousand-year festivities also brought Patriarch Pimen and the synod of the church to the Kremlin, and their interview with Gorbachev received considerable publicity. The report made (very cautious) references to past misunderstandings and injustices. Gorbachev promised to examine the church leaders' requests and to take the necessary action. The reports did not say what these requests were.

It would be wrong to assert, at the time of this writing (November 1988), that there is yet full honesty about the tragic history of the past or about legal rights in the present. This is plainly not so, or not yet so. But by the standards of recent decades there is progress, with hope of more to come.

A personal note: when I was in Moscow early in 1988 I expressed the view that religious tolerance would present no problem, that believers are, on the whole, good citizens, and that the Party's ideology could accommodate the existence of religion. The Soviet colleague with whom I was discussing the matter disagreed. In his view, the Party's rule requires it to combat religion, though not by the crude methods used in the past. I remained (and remain) unconvinced. Time will tell.

Nationalism is to be the subject of a special meeting of the Party's Central Committee, reflecting the officially recognised importance of an issue long beset with taboos. Some of the silences have been almost comic: thus, during Brezhnev's reign there were speeches and articles celebrating the fiftieth anniversary of the Kalmuck autonomous republic, and these passed with no mention of the "minor" fact that the republic had been abolished and all Kalmucks deported on Stalin's order in 1944! (Under Khrushchev the survivors were rehabilitated and returned to their homes, and this was not mentioned either!) The case of the Crimean Tartars, who were not allowed to return to the Crimea, drags on, with limited publicity.

The fate of the "punished people", i.e., those deported in 1944–45 on Stalin's orders, has been vividly described by A. Pristavkin (in the story *Nochevala tuchka zolotaya, Znamya*, Nos. 3 and 4, 1987), in which the victims were the Chechens, and also in *Ogonyok* (No. 35, 1988), where D. Kugultinov describes the deportation of the Kalmucks—men, women, children, officers, soldiers. The officers were "humanely" given some choice of where to go into exile; the soldiers were sent to a northern concentration camp and set to building a power station, and half of them died.

Many are the articles devoted to highlighting ecological disasters in various republics. In *Literaturnaya gazeta* (7 Sept. 1988), under the heading of "Save the Aral", the inland "sea" that is drying up, Adyl Yakubov wrote also of "the evil consequences of monoculture", and "of the social situation in Uzbekistan, of peasants working night and day on cotton plantations, of women who burned themselves to death, unable to get help in their despair, of children who for almost half of the school year have to toil in the cotton fields".

A. Minkin, in *Ogonyok* (No. 33, 1988), refers, not for the first time, to "the catastrophic situation in Uzbekistan in respect to maternal and infant mortality", that defoliants and pesticides threaten the health of women and children in the cotton fields, causing jaundice, birth defects, and miscarriages. An Uzbek researcher who wrote to *Ogonyok* to point all this out was dismissed from her institute.

The key events of 1987–88 are well known in the West, and need not be described here: the upsurge of nationalism in the Baltic states, and the conflict between Armenia and Azerbaidzhan over Nagorno-Karubakh. What is new and remarkable is press coverage of the events. Mass meetings of Latvians and Estonians were reported in *Pravda*, and the media also referred to conferences devoted to the anniversary of the incorporation of the three republics in the Soviet Union. Arguments are quoted concerning the element of coercion; thus, it was pointed out that there were hardly any communists in Estonia in 1939, and that the incorporation was a consequence of the Nazi-Soviet pact—totally unmentionable thoughts until quite recently. True, in these same articles the views expressed are said to be misconceived: there were indeed very few communists in Estonia, but it was said that this showed how efficient the repressive measures of the right-wing government were. More surprising yet were frank reports of demonstrations in the Baltic states on the anniversary (in April) of the mass deportations which had taken place in 1941, a few months before the war. The Party leaders were shown to be taking part, and one is left guessing whether this was to channel discontent into less dangerous channels or because the leaders themselves believed that these were indeed outrageous crimes and were only too glad to be able to say so. After all, relatives of a number of them could have been among the deportees.

*Moskovskie novosti* of 4 September 1988 printed a number of interviews concerning the Nazi-Soviet pact of 1939 and its impact on the Baltic states. It was there stated that 10,000 were deported from Estonia without trial in 1941, 20,000 in March 1949. In the case of Lithuania, the figures were 12,600 in 1941 and 100,000 "after the war". Reference was also made (for the first time, to my knowledge) to the "Kuusinen government" set up at the beginning of the war with Finland, and then forgotten.

Noteworthy, too, is the effort of the leadership of the Baltic republics to secure a greater degree of autonomy, including in the economic field. At the 19th Party Conference, as reported in *Pravda* on 2 June 1988, V. Vialas, the new Party first secretary of Estonia, spoke of the "recently born mass movement of a people's front [*narodnogo fronta*] to support *perestroika*", which called a meeting attended by 100,000 people. He spoke of "departmental super-centralized administration", which results in "over 90% of the entire economic potential of the republic being in the hands of ministries in Moscow". This "renders practically impossible recon-ciliation of their interests with the interests of the complex develop-ment of the republic". He urged greater economic powers and a solid financial base for the republic, "a return [*sic*] to Lenin's principles of federation as the basis for national and inter-republican relations". Meetings of intellectuals ("creative unions") have brought up "a whole number of sharp issues in the area of economics, culture, social development, national relations, ecology, the creation of a legal order [*pravovogo gosudarstva*]". The first secretary of the Latvian Party, Pugo, spoke of "the notable sharpen-ing of national feelings" in his republic, and joined many other speakers in condemning the neglect by the central ministries of environmental questions; he also requested constitutional amend-ments to give greater powers to the republics, giving as an instance the fact that the design of tarts in Riga bakeries, until very recently, had to be cleared with a Moscow office! There, too, a national front has been formed.

*Moskovskie novosti* (No. 31, 1988) recently carried a report on the "Estonian people's front", in which citizens with various views can "participate in *perestroika* apart from and outside the Party". The movement to create such an organization began in connection with ecology—protests against a plan to build a large fertilizer plant. The article refers to Estonia's alleged reputation as "a nation of dissidents", where people believe that "Estonia was illegally annexed". The author of the article claims that all this is exagger-ated, though "there are nationalist people in the republic". Alas, I am unable to read Estonian, Latvian, or Lithuanian. Their press must be well worth following by those who can.

The first secretary of the Lithuanian Party, R. B. Songaila, re-quested the stopping of the construction of a nuclear power station, and went on to the need to grant "greater independence" (*samos-toyatel'nost*) to the union republics. The Constitution should be amended accordingly. By June–July 1988 the old flags of these countries were flying in public places, without hindrance.

While the Soviet readers and viewers have been left with no doubt as to the seriousness of Armenian-Azerbaidzhan clashes, or the upsurge of nationalism in the Baltic republics, complaints have been heard that reporting was far from complete. Thus, I heard from a participant in one of the large gatherings held in Lithuania that the central press substantially softened the tone of the discussion and resolutions. However, the proceedings had been fully broadcast by Lithuanian radio and TV.

The Ukraine has been remarkably quiescent, at least as far as the centrally published media are concerned. However, the 19th Party Conference saw some vigorous words from a Ukrainian writer, words for which not too long ago he would surely have begun an involuntary journey eastwards (they would, of course, not have been printed). As reported in *Pravda* on 2 June 1988, B. Oleinik, after stressing that his motherland (*rodina*) was the Soviet Ukraine, part of the USSR, went on as follows: "Since in our republic persecutions started long before 1937, publicity should be given to the causes of the famine of 1933, which took the lives of millions of Ukrainians, and to name all those guilty of causing this tragedy." He went on to deplore in his turn the "distortions of Lenin's nationality policy", and its negative effect on the use of the Ukrainian language, which is disappearing from administrative papers (*deloproizvodstva*), from use in government and Party. "In many towns there are now no schools in the national language. In almost all higher educational institutions the students are deprived of the possibility of studying in the language of their mothers." He demanded "most-favoured nation treatment for the language, action against those who prevent the development of the national culture". He protested against nuclear power stations being built in the Ukraine, recalling that when the Chernobyl complex was being built the ministry mocked "the Ukrainian syndrome", asserting that there was nothing to worry about, "that the reactor could be safely mounted under the bed of a honeymoon couple". He complained of the "haughty and contemptuous attitude of some Union departments to Ukrainian interests, that this is "an insult to national dignity". Water shortage is serious, and now there is a proposal to build a Danube-Dnieper canal, which would "put into the Dnieper the drainage [sewage] of all Europe".

There may be much more in the Ukrainian press.

Turning to Central Asia, the media have given wide publicity to the truly appalling instances of corruption in some of these republics. The name Rashidov, Party secretary in Uzbekistan, has become a byword for abuse of power for personal gain; Rashidov had his own men throughout the local hierarchies. *Pravda* and *Literaturnaya gazeta* in 1987 published some truly extraordinary exposures of abuses: state farms run by gangsters who terrorised the peasants, using their own private police (some of them criminals they "bought" from prison), with even their own prisons and, when necessary, executions. All those whose task it was to prevent such outrageous illegalities were simply "bought". Cotton output statistics were shamelessly padded. A high proportion of the Party and state officials in the Central Asian republics ended up in prison. Niyazov, the new secretary in the neighbouring republic of Turkmenistan, reported that 31 members of the republic's Central Committee were dismissed, 80 officials were deprived of their seats in the republican soviet, so that they could be dealt with. The publicity given to such abuses is new: previously "the honour of the uniform" required cover-ups. Words such as "feudalism" and "mafia" abound in the media. It is evident from these reports that the republics themselves were incapable of cleaning up their own affairs. The dismissals were initiated by Moscow, and most of the investigators of the abuses had Russian names: the principal detective-investigator (Gdlyan) was referred to by one speaker at the Party conference as more colourful than Maigret. Several attempts to kill him—or to buy him off—were made, and reported.

There had been tales told of unpleasantness between Uzbeks and Tadzhiks, and this too was openly referred to in an interview printed in *Pravda* (25 June 1988), which spoke of "frequent reports that Tadzhiks who live in Uzbekistan have serious complaints about the restriction of their legal rights by the local authorities". The (new) first secretary of the Uzbek Party, Nishanov, admitted that this was indeed so, quoting several instances involving language and culture, including the omission of the fact that the great mediaeval scholar-scientist Avicenna (Ibu Sina) was a Tadzhik! He promised measures to prevent such undesirable practices, to ensure closer collaboration with Tadzhikistan.

The novelist Chingiz Aitmatov found it necessary to write a long article (in *Pravda*, 12 Feb. 1988) to defend his fellow Central Asians from the taint of being corrupt. He pointed, with justice, to the fact that the victims of these outrages were Central Asians, especially the peasantry. "I feel deeply for this exhausted Uzbek mother of many children, who getting up for work at dawn, was able at last to see the crooked director [of her farm] led down the road in handcuffs, as she ran weeping and cursing him for her sufferings on the sunlit cotton plantations, for her heavy labour whose fruits were doubly and trebly misappropriated by the Ferghana mafiosi . . . cursing him for her miserable life and poor shack, where there is not even space for a hen because cotton is planted right up to the walls, cursing him for her half-educated children, who had to work half the year on the plantation, . . . for her timid tractor-driver husband who found himself in mediaeval slavery." And a whole long paragraph along similar lines.

The troubles in Alma Ata in December 1986 were linked in the Western press with the replacement as first secretary of the Party of a Kazakh by a Russian, Kolbin. This was the first such disagreeable event that was speedily reported in the national press. It is easy to see in this an unjustified interference with a national republic. However, not only is the majority of the population of Kazakhstan not Kazakh, but there too there developed a deep-lying corruption, based on traditional clans, which the Kazakhs themselves were unable to correct. It needed an outsider, someone not linked with the local clan-based mafias.

It seems clear that the mafias used nationalism in their response to Kolbin's appointment. The same seems to be happening in Uzbekistan: rackets need to be protected from outside interference, even if one has to appeal to Islamic tradition and to Uzbek national feeling. (One thinks of the case of Noriega in Panama; resentment about U.S. pressure can be used by him to stay in power with some popular support.) And of course corruption was by no means confined to the national republics: Brezhnev himself set an example, and we will have occasion to refer to the well-publicized case of Shchelokov. The word "mafia" was also used by Yeltsin in referring to rackets in Moscow itself, and several sources have hinted that the then Party secretary in Moscow, Grishin, was lucky not to be prosecuted.

However, the most widely publicised issue, in and out of the Soviet Union, concerns the Armenia-Azerbaidzhan dispute over Nagorno-Karabakh, the predominantly Armenian enclave within Azerbaidzhan. The Armenian demands to have it transferred to them, clearly supported by the Armenian Party, touched off an appalling massacre of Armenians in the industrial town of Sumgait, and also got out of control in Armenia itself. The rights and wrongs of the case are not our concern here. The essential point is the reporting of what occurred in the national press—not complete, to be sure, but extensive. Riots, killings, strikes, demonstrations are reported. Grievances in Nagorno-Karabakh are reported too, as well as steps taken to try to meet some of the demands. However, the Constitution does say that the boundaries of Union republics shall not be altered without their consent, and it is clear from the speech by the first secretary of the Azerbaidzhani Party, A. Bezirov, that they do not consent ("The further development of *perestroika* and democratization is contradicted by demands for a change in the national-territorial settlement"; *Pravda*, 20 June 1988). Meanwhile, he sadly reports that some Azeris have fled from Armenia, some

Armenians from Azerbaidzhan. He makes no attempt to hide the gravity of the situation. He refers to the "long-standing traditions of collaboration" of the two peoples (which is not quite what history teaches, since Armenians were massacred in Baku in 1918). Yes, he accepts that both nationalities had much to complain of, but "unfortunately in meetings and processions . . . there are also those behind whom there stand influential anti-*perestroika* forces. These are corrupted clans, shady operators in the shadow economy linked with criminal elements. . . . They seek to provoke people into nationalist activities." (Note the reference here, as in respect to Kazakhstan, to corrupted *clans*.)

Andrei Nuikin (*Novyi mir*, No. 2, 1988) also takes up this issue, in connection with the disorders in Alma Ata. In Kazakhstan until the late sixties or early seventies "it did not matter to what clan one belonged". Old men remembered the clans. But "suddenly . . . they began to be the basis of business and ideological links, the main factor in cadres policy". Even in higher education, "rectors and deans surrounded themselves with devoted fellow clansmen, often professionally incompetent or even semi-literate". Nuikin goes on: "We used to sigh and attribute this to 'national characteristics', 'remnants of feudalism', 'for them clan links matter above all else'. But what sort of national characteristic is it that was absent until the late sixties? What 'remnant of feudalism' which was not seen for decades?" His explanation: these "traditional" links were revived so that certain individuals could "occupy high posts, acquire a lot of money, power, respect, privileges, fearlessly to accept bribes, enter into criminal conspiracies". It helps create "an environment within which one can calmly steal, to surround oneself with unprincipled, dependent and unclean 'colleagues'. In Kazakhstan "it took the form of clan-favoritism. Sometimes it is disguised by religious links, sometimes by departmental 'patriotism'. We now have also scientific mafias". In capitalist countries the pursuit of self-interest was seen as normal, but "our ideologies . . . neatly managed to persuade us that this was inapplicable to Soviet reality, . . . that our embezzlers, bribe-takers and magnates believe in another ideology. Which ideology? It would be interesting to know."

Of course this is not the whole story by any means. However, in Central Asia, at least, the resistance of local corrupt officialdom to intervention from Moscow, a resistance which can appeal to tradition and even to Islam, can at times serve as cover for local rackets.

As mentioned earlier, a special plenum of the Central Committee is to be devoted to nationality problems. They are complex indeed, but they are at least partially out in the open in this time of *glasnost'*.

# CHAPTER 6

# Literature and the Media

In previous chapters, I have noted some examples of political-historical and religious literature that has been published at last, so I need not repeat those examples here. The same applies to literary works about the Terror. This chapter will be devoted to the appearance of books and stories, old and new, Soviet, emigré, and translated, which could not be published before and which have not already figured in previous chapters.

We begin with foreign works. Many British and American writers have been translated, but selectively so. Just to cite one example, Graham Greene is known for *Our Man in Havana* and *The Honorary Consul*, but an intelligent review of his works draws attention to, and welcomes, the expected appearance of *The Power and the Glory*, complete with the "whisky priest" in Mexico, and other novels too. His recent novel, *The Human Factor*, was serialized in *Ogonyok* in January-February 1988. One of that journal's literary prizes for 1987 went to John le Carré. Raymond Chandler's *Farewell, My Lovely* appears in *Podyom* (No. 8, 1988). In these respects, too, the times are a-changing.

There are, of course, books and authors that have seemed quite out of bounds: Orwell, for instance. Now *Animal Farm* has appeared, and *1984* is on the *Novyi mir* list for 1989. A fascinating article in *Moskovskie novosti* (26 June 1988) begins by saying that "the famous work of this outstanding satirist, written in 1945, is at last accessible to Soviet readers". This relates to *Animal Farm*, which "reminds us of some particularly odious dictatorships of the first half of the 20th century". The author then draws the reader's attention to a coincidence: a Russian historian named N. Kostomarov, who died in 1885, wrote a short piece entitled "Animal Uprising", which contains some remarkable parallels with Orwell's novel. The author, Vitali Tretyakov, prints extracts from the speeches made to the animals by, in Orwell's case, Major (the boar), and in Kostomarov's case, the senior ox. Both lead rebellions of domestic animals against Man. Both end unhappily, but for different reasons. As Tretyakov remarks, "both for Kostomarov and for Orwell the rebellion of the animals is a metaphor for a people's revolution". In Kostomarov's work, the rebellion fails because of "organizational and intellectual lacks": the animals simply cannot manage their own lives. Whereas "Orwell, under the influence of actual events in the first half of the 20th century, examined another variant: the degeneration of the revolutionary regime. But this possibility too was indicated in the story of Kostomarov. It was directly linked with the behaviour of those whom both the Russian historian and the English writer designated as 'pigs'."

Kostomarov is very little known; he was the illegitimate son of a Russian landowner and a Ukrainian peasant serf-woman, and Tretyakov suggests that his neglect, even as a historian, in the Soviet period was due to his having been labeled a Ukrainian nationalist. Orwell could not possibly have heard of or read Kostomarov, so the author rightly concludes that this must be seen as a fascinating coincidence.

*1984* brings to mind two other books, both Russian. One is Chayanov's peasant-utopian novel, set coincidentally *in* 1984, mentioned in Chapter 3. This has been referred to in articles devoted to Chayanov's rehabilitation, but not (so far as I am aware) published, though another of his science fiction works has been. The other is Zamyatin's *My* (*We*). We know from Orwell's correspondence that, before writing *1984*, he did read Zamyatin's novel, in a French translation. Zamyatin wrote *My* in Russia, but it was published abroad. He was allowed to emigrate in 1931. The book's appearance, serialized in *Znamya* (Nos. 4 and 5, 1988) was an event which, like so much else that has happened in the cultural field, would have seemed totally incredible in the real 1984.

*My* was intelligently introduced to the Soviet readers by the distinguished critic Lakshin, who had made major contributions to *Novyi mir* in the years it was edited by Tvardovsky. "The novel was written at the height of war-communism, which provided a basis for the author's fears of barracks-socialism in a semiliterate country containing strong 'Asianist' elements." Yes, he got some things wrong, "but more important are his frequent direct hits . . . including gas chambers, which reminded us of Hitler's monstrous inventions. Or, alas, things all too well known to us: demonstrations in honour of the *Blagodetel'* (The Benefactor), elections with prearranged results held on the Day of Unanimity, total subordination to the will of one man, supervision by invisible 'guardians', and so on. Even so grim a detail as the Unitary State's triumph over hunger, achieved by starving part of the population, could appear as a sad forecast of what happened in the famine in the Ukraine in 1932–3."

*My* was a remarkable achievement indeed. I have always preferred its way of disposing of the critical sense to that in *1984*. The hero is *not* persuaded to "love Big Brother", as in *1984*, but a surgical operation on the brain removes the "critical" part of it. But to return to Lakshin: "Of course, anti-socialist propaganda could use Zamyatin for its own purposes, as it did in even greater measure with the novels of Orwell. But can anything valuable exist which could not be used abusively? Of course any fable, and Zamyatin's story is a fable, and not a very pleasant one, contains 'a moral for youth'. But to be angry about a fable that has 'no roses round the door'—does this not mean giving oneself away, that the cap fitted? Contrariwise, a straightforward and healthy reaction, free of complexes of guilt and fear, shows self-confidence; let us listen to the gloomy predictions, and let us avoid the disasters foretold."

The serialized publication in *Novyi mir* in 1988 of Pasternak's *Dr. Zhivago* was not unexpected, and anyone who first read it in 1988 would surely have had in mind the question: What on earth had the fuss been all about? The novel's literary merits and shortcomings can now be sensibly discussed. By the standards of *glasnost'* there is barely a subversive page. Like so much that was banned in those years, it is rather the spirit of the work that upset the literary bureaucrats. The eminent literary specialist D. Likhachev, in his introduction to the first installment, cites Pasternak: "Revolutions are made by activists, limited fanatics, short-sighted geniuses. In a few hours or days they overthrow the existing authority, the old regime. And then for decades people bow before the short-sighted spirit that had made the revolution." Clearly, such sentiments would upset a man like Khrushchev, or Brezhnev. Several authors have used the opportunity to criticise the literary bureaucracy, their fellow authors, and themselves, for condemning Pasternak's novel unanimously with one abstentient at a "disgraceful" meeting of the Writers' Union, a novel hardly any of them had read. A typical expression is one by a humorous writer, Alexander Ivanov, who, in a serious mood, spoke of "being already a mature person when began the disgusting and disgraceful baiting [*travlya*] of Boris Pasternak". What did he do in this and subsequent cases? Nothing, and this calls for repentance. It is not true that no one spoke up. Of the literary men, Kaverin repeatedly put his name to letters of protest. Then there was Andrei Sakharov, whose courage and sacrifice entitles him "to eternal gratitude". Ivanov went on: "and when in Leningrad they demeaned and persecuted Yosif Brodsky, accused him of parasitism, compelled him in the end to leave the country, where was I? As it happens, I was in Leningrad. I will take this opportunity to congratulate this major poet for his Nobel prize" (*Moskovskie novosti*, 26 June 1988).

Discussions around *Dr. Zhivago* have enabled participants to express varying views about the novel's literary qualities. A *Pravda* critic had some reservations, but was strongly criticised in his turn by participants in a "round table on *Zhivago*" reported in *Literaturnaya gazeta* (22 June 1988). One of the participants, Gulyga, made the point that, for *Zhivago* and its author, Stalin and "1937" were consequences of something deeper, and that something was the civil war: "it was then that began the great tragedy of our people, its self-destruction [*samoistrebleniye*]". *Novyi mir* (No. 6, 1988) recently carried a very long and thorough account of the background to Pasternak's work on *Zhivago*, by V. Borisov and E. Pasternak. It is a gold mine for anyone interested in Pasternak. The sources used include literary archives, private letters to, from, and about Pasternak, and quotations from works published abroad, e.g., the book by Ivinskaya. There are details such as that when, in 1937, Pasternak was asked to sign a letter condemning Tukhachevsky and the generals, he refused. Whereupon Stavsky, the literary functionary, abused him ("Think you are Tolstoy, hey?"), and his name was included in the published letter all the same. Stress was laid on the (Christian) religious aspects of his thought, as is indeed clear from the *Zhivago* poems, all now published. The story surrounding the Nobel prize and his troubles arising out of the publication of *Zhivago* abroad are fully documented. There is much about his difficulties in earlier years. A volume of his poems, set up in type in 1947–48, was destroyed by order. Ivinskaya was arrested in 1949. We learn that even his translation of Goethe's "Faust" was condemned for overemphasis on the irrational!

*Novyi mir* (No. 11, 1988) printed the correspondence between Pasternak and Ariadna Efron, the daughter of the poet Marina Tsvetayeva. She had returned to the USSR with her mother from Paris in 1937. After her mother hanged herself, she had been arrested and exiled to a remote north Siberian village. Pasternak gave her material and moral support in what clearly had been a miserable life.

*Yunost'* (No. 10, 1988) printed an interview with the writer Vladimir Voinovich, who recounted how he was persecuted, libelled, and virtually compelled to emigrate (he now lives in West

Germany). His famous story about the soldier Chonkin is about to be published in the USSR and made into a film.

The same issue printed more of V. Shalamov's *Kolyma tales*, as well as correspondence between Shalamov and Pasternak.

Which brings me to the appearance or reappearance in Soviet literature of emigrés of different vintages. It used to be said that it would be all right if you were long dead. So Chaliapin, Rachmaninov, and Ivan Bunin became acceptable. Stravinsky, too. These rules no longer apply. The appearance of V. Nabokov's long essay on Gogol in *Novyi mir* was followed by several other of his works; we have yet to see his novels, but (presumably with the exception of *Lolita*, and maybe with no exception) this could come any time now. *Literaturnaya gazeta* (17 Aug. 1988) published a full-page discussion of Nabokov with American participants! At least Nabokov was an emigré of the first postrevolutionary wave. More surprising was the reprinting of poems by Brodsky, in *Novyi mir* (No. 12, 1987) and *Znamya* (No. 8, 1988). This was followed by the even more surprising reappearance in the Soviet journals of Alexander Galich, who, though dead (he was accidentally electrocuted in Paris in 1977), was well known through *samizdat* for politically satirical songs. The same Alexander Ivanov followed his self-criticism about Brodsky with an apology for not defending Galich, who was also in effect forced to emigrate. A few of Galich's verses were reprinted in *Novyi mir* (No. 5, 1988), and others in *Znamya*. One of these, well known to me from *samizdat* and publication abroad, is a clever satire on marriage and off-duty sex among small-time Party bureaucrats. His more directly political verses have yet to appear, but that he was published at all represents a remarkable change. Some sketches by V. Nekrasov, who also died in Paris, have also appeared in *Znamya* (No. 8, 1988), with more publications planned. It is not all smooth sailing. A speaker at the 19th Party Conference condemned *Ogonyok* for publishing a critique on Lysenkoism by a man who turned out to have "deserted his country", an emigré named Soifer. However, this was a personal view, not an official ruling, and it may be that the name Soifer had something to do with it, though both Galich and Brodsky were/are also Jews. So is Naum Korzhavin, another emigré poet, whose study of Akhmatova is on *Novyi mir*'s publication list for 1989, and whose poems appeared in *Oktyabr'* (No. 8, 1988). (He has recently visited Moscow.)

A special case is that of Nikolai Gumilev, Akhmatova's first husband and a major poet in his own right; he was shot as an alleged counterrevolutionary plotter (with sixty others) in Petrograd in 1921. A few of his poems found their way into a literary anthology published in 1962, but there was no more of him until 1987–88, when several of his poems were published, with comments about his quality, and also some short prose pieces (in *Literaturnaya Rossiya*, No. 18, 1988). Like many of his poems, the stories are mainly about the exotic East. Gumilev was not a "political" poet, and his neglect was attributable to his having been shot by the Bolsheviks. *Novyi mir* (No. 8, 1988) published a moving poem about Gumilev's fate.

Also making a comeback is Maksimilian Voloshin. Some of his poems, often on grandiose historical themes, were published in the twenties. He died in 1932, virtually unknown to the Soviet reader. *Novyi mir* (No. 2, 1988) recently published one of his "epics", placing the Bolshevik violence in the context of older Russian history, including Ivan and Peter. (In another poem there figures the quotable line, *Veliki Pyotr byl pervyi bol'shevik*, "Peter the Great was the first Bolshevik".) Also republished are some works by the romantic poet Bal'mont, who was popular before the revolution and died in emigration.

Returning to prose, one must welcome the appearance of a number of works by Mikhail Bulgakov which did not figure among those published after 1956. Bulgakov is rightly regarded as the pride and joy of Russian twentieth-century literature, and *The Master and Margarita* as a masterpiece. This had been published in 1967, but a large number of his stories and plays remained out of public sight, in some cases since the twenties; others never saw publication at all. Now we have, among others, "The Heart of a Dog", a delightful science fiction satire on Soviet life, and plays: *Zoikina kvartira* and *Bagrovyi ostrov*. "Heart of a Dog" has been turned into a play. The collected works of Bulgakov, long known to be under discussion, may soon appear. Studies of his work and career can now refer both to his association with the Whites in the civil war and to his painful conflicts with censorship and the literary bureaucrats. Also published is his letter to Stalin: when all his works were banned, he asked to be allowed to emigrate, or to work in the theatre in any capacity. Stalin suggested that the Arts Theatre employ him, which they did.

By 1970 the Soviet public did have at its disposal a large part of Bulgakov's works (I saw four of his plays in Moscow in 1969). This could not be said of the man many regard as another master of Russian prose, Andrei Platonov. His major works were unpublishable for generations. Now we have *Chevengur* and *Kotlovan*. It is easy to see why, for them to appear, there had to be major changes in the outlook of the leadership and in censorship. Platonov himself earned a humble living, fought in the war, and died, apparently forgotten, in 1951.

*Chevengur* was serialized in 1988 in *Druzhba narodov* (Nos. 3 and 4). In introducing its belated publication to today's readers, Natalya Ivanova tells how she read the original typescript, with the author's corrections in blue ink and the editor's remarks in red. "Particularly thickly underlined were any paragraphs containing the words 'socialism' or 'communism'." Platonov put naive thoughts into the mouths of semiliterate peasants, so he "was accused of heresy in relation to the holy and untouchable concepts, as seen by watchful editors of the twenties. Yet at this very time it was not the writer Platonov but quite other [political] activists who were distorting and destroying the idea [of socialism]. These blood-red penciled corrections on the long pages of paper grown yellow through years of hopeless waiting represent an impressive documentation of coercion. I hope that in Moscow, where *Chevengur* was written at the end of the twenties, in the future Platonov museum (though in our fine capital there is still not even a memorial plate on the house where he lived and died) these pages marked in red will be exhibited under glass, as a lesson to future generations."

So what was *Chevengur?* A fantastical tale, in which one character, resembling Don Quixote, sets out on a horse named *Proletarskaya sila* ("proletarian strength") to rescue the body of Rosa Luxemburg from its infidel keepers. An idealistic schoolteacher, Dvanov, and several other simple persons, march on to communism in an imaginary country town. Their fantasies are interrupted by the coming of NEP, which they misinterpret in their own way. The local Party secretary interprets NEP as "the revolution allowed to go forward spontaneously as the proletariat wishes. Whereas until then the revolution was hauled forward by apparatuses and institutions, as if the state apparatus were really a machine for building socialism." A middle-aged man is much more skeptical: "When they took power, they promised that the very next day the whole world would achieve happiness, and now you say that objective circumstances prevent this. The 'popes' [priests] also said that the road to paradise is blocked by Satan."

But meanwhile the Chevengur comrades build "communism", where "property is not collected, it is destroyed". Work itself was declared to be productive of exploitation. In the villages horses belonging to the better-off peasants are handed over to the poor. The property of the petty bourgeoisie is confiscated, redistributed, wrecked. Nothing works, since nobody does. "For each and for all only the sun worked, declared to be the world proletariat. Work is declared once and for all to be a remnant of greed and animal-like enjoyment of exploitation, because labour facilitates the creation of property." Asked about supplying the proletariat with food, comrade Chepurny, one of the enthusiastic comrades, "was indignant: 'Look over at the steppe, things are growing there, go and tear up some edible grasses and wheat and eat it. The sun is shining, the earth is breathing, the rain is falling—what more do you want? You want to drive the proletariat again into needless effort? We have got beyond socialism, we are one better." On another occasion he says: "Since we now have communism, we should not distract the proletariat from it by having meetings." Another of the naive believers, Kopenkin, worries about the bureaucratic consequences of organization: "Should we not at once liquidate the 'Friendship of poor-peasants' commune, since when life becomes complicated it will be impossible to tell who oppresses whom." Another such remark: "An official position [*dolzhnost'*] is as bad as [private] property."

Platonov's imagination extends to having members' votes designated in advance—one is appointed to vote against, one to abstain. There is also a serious-comic exchange of views among the comrades, doubtful about the revolutionary nature of women, since, instead of marching onward to communism, they want things like coloured scarves. They "knew that in the past there was always love for women and reproduction too, but this was a sort of alien natural activity, and not folkwise and communist. . . . The beauty of woman existed also under capitalism, as did mountains and stars and other non-human events." They also thought of animal liberation: "We will let the cattle go free. They are almost human, but backward because of age-long oppression." They take over the church as their headquarters, and discuss what slogan to write on the entrance, to replace the church's own: "Come to me all that labour", which turns out to "speak entirely against capitalism"—so they leave it.

This is, of course, a satirical fantasy, with grotesque features mixed in with anti-utopia and poetic imagination. However, it also hits very real nails on the head. There is a description of how the comrades in Chevengur expel all those they consider to be bourgeois, a scene which seems to me to anticipate the doings of Pol Pot, or the deportation, in the early thirties, of thousands of former gentry families from Leningrad. Then they order all the prosperous peasants of a nearby village to hand over their horses and other belongings to the village poor. Thereby Platonov anticipates dekulakization as described by Tendryakov in the first of his three stories cited in Chapter 4. Platonov also shares with Tendryakov the view the latter expressed in his "computer" novel cited in Chapter 5. In fact, in both, Tendryakov tries to show that some utopian models fail to provide any motive for working: one recalls his *kulak*'s remark that, once free of property, he is free like a bird, but birds neither sow nor reap. One wonders whether Tendryakov was not inspired by Platonov, some of whose works were published abroad and probably circulated, as did much else that was banned, among Moscow literati.

Platonov's *Kotlovan*, written in the early thirties, is directly concerned with the violent events associated with forcible collectivization. Earlier, I mentioned a scene in which *kulaks* are driven out of the village by the poor. (No doubt there were instances in which the efforts to foment "class war" in the villages did have such an outcome.) But the main moral, as summarized by a Soviet commentator, is "that to build socialism by forced labour [or "serf labour", *krepostnym trudom*] is not only impossible but monstrous [*chudovishchno*]" (Ivanova, *Druzhba narodov*, No. 4, 1988). Platonov presents the cruel inhumanity of the period through the eyes of a little girl, with great effect. *Kotlovan* appeared in *Novyi mir* (No. 6) in 1987. Platonov's evidently negative and sometimes ironic attitude toward the process of collectivization ensured the novel's prolonged nonpublication.

Another "resurrection" was that of Daniil Kharms. Unlike Platonov, he was arrested repeatedly and died of hunger in a Leningrad prison in 1942. But like Platonov he was a most original stylist, with a line of humour all his own. He wrote imaginative "futurist" poetry, some fantastical stories and children's tales, as well as plays. An article about him in *Novyi mir* (No. 4, 1988) sees him as a predecessor of Ionesco and Beckett, influenced by Gogol and by the poet Khlebnikov. He himself also mentioned Edward Lear and Lewis Carroll among those whom he particularly admired. After his final arrest, his wife, dying of hunger in the siege, managed to get his papers and manuscripts to safety. One of his stories appeared in *Druzhba narodov* (No. 10, 1987). We are promised the publication of more of his works.

Also welcome was some new material on and by the original and committed revolutionary writer Artem Vesyoly, who was arrested in 1937. *Novyi mir*, in May 1988, published an account of how he wrote his epic novel, *Rossiya, krovyu umytaya* (*Russia Washed with Blood*), parts of which appeared in 1932, together with some unpublished fragments which have survived. (The KGB supplied to the Writers' Union the titles of four literary manuscripts confiscated when he was arrested; they could not be found.) In 1937, shortly before Vesyoly's arrest, *Komsomolskaya Pravada* published a denunciatory review-article. *Novyi mir* published alongside the fragments some memories of Vesyoly (his real name was Kochkurov) by his son. The latter doubts the official date of death (February 1939), because a fellow prisoner, Emelyanov, recalls sharing a cell with Vesyoly at Lefortovo prison: "Artem was taken to interrogation every night, and in the morning he was *carried* back"; this in March 1938. He was rehabilitated in 1956, and some selected works were published in 1958.

In this issue of *Novyi mir* there is some hitherto unpublished material which was to have formed part of the novel in its full form. One character in the novel was a certain Fil'ka, and one can readily see now Vesyoly's style and subject would have upset literary commissars in the thirties: "Fil'ka joined the party, he found a niche in the Cheka. In the villages the Chekisty raged . . . and their evil fame spread. From Firsanovka the priest was deported. There was no one who could christen or bury. . . . In a Tartar village they rode around drunk, shooting many dogs and wounding a woman. Tax-avoiders were bathed in icy water and made to stand barefoot for hours in the snow. . . . They ate six geese without paying. Requisitions and confiscations right and left, with beatings in the place of a receipt. . . . They beat the chairman of the district soviet half to death for 'carrying on in the old ways'." Following numerous complaints, Fil'ka and his two fellow chekisty were removed. Fil'ka became "grave commander": he ensured that a large pit was dug, accompanied the condemned on their last journey, shot them in the back of the head, and, after cleaning the blood from his boots with snow, went home to eat pork cutlets and to sleep with a lavish woman "who was juicier than the cutlets". An editorial note points to the fact that such as Fil'ka really did exist in real life. Vesyoly, under his real name of Kochkurov, had been chairman of a local soviet in Samara province and editor of a local newspaper in 1920, in which he denounced "disgraceful and illegal" acts by the local Cheka, and this led to an inquiry and to the dismissal of the "adventurers who had penetrated into the Cheka". Of course, Vesyoly's writings in no way accorded with the way such things were expected to be presented. There is a parallel here with Isaak Babel's justly famous *Konarmiya*, which painted the brutalities of the time in their true colours and was also denounced. A short story, also reprinted in *Novyi mir*, titled "*Bosaya Pravda*"("*Barefoot Truth*") concerned both the neglect from which former Red partisans suffered and abuse of power. This was published in 1928, and earned a "severe reprimand" for the editor of the journal *Molodaya gvardiya* for having published it.

Two more "resurrections" deserve a mention. One was the talented poet Nikolai Klyuev, of peasant origin, whose poetry reflected his roots and quickly got him into trouble. He was arrested several times and disappeared finally in 1937. Some of his poems were published in *Novyi mir* (No. 7, 1988) and *Druzhba narodov* (No. 12, 1987). *Novyi mir* (No. 8, 1988) printed letters sent by Klyuev from his exile in Siberia, between 1934 and his death in prison in 1937. These are exceptionally moving documents of the sufferings of a sick man, whose warm clothes were stolen by criminals in transit, and who was left penniless, living in a corner of a room, dependent on money sent to him by loyal friends, one of whom was another poet, Klychkov. Both were accused of being "kulak writers" because Russian peasant folk traditions played an important part in their writings. Both perished. The addressee of many of the letters was Klychkov's wife, whose surname was Gorbacheva. One of the editors of the letters, which are accompanied by full explanatory notes, was the son of Klychkov, godson of Klyuev, who, as is clear from the letters, was a deeply religious man.

There is also the case of that remarkable novelist Boris Pilnyak, another victim of the Terror. His fate was probably in no small part due to his novel, *Tale of the Unextinguished Moon*, published in 1926, which was based (in thin disguise) on the supposition that the commissar for war, Frunze, had been deliberately killed when ordered to undergo an unnecessary operation. The novel was republished in *Znamya* (No. 12, 1987).

Before leaving the theme of literary victims, it is desirable to return to the denunciation of Akhmatova and Zoshchenko in 1946, which took the form of a resolution condemning two journals, *Zvezda* and *Leningrad*, for publishing them, together with the notorious speech by Zhdanov. (It is not surprising that we hear of a successful petition from Leningrad University staff and students that it no longer bear the name of Zhdanov.) How and why did it happen? A long article in *Izvestiya* (21 May 1988) is devoted to this topic. Since it cast so long a shadow, and since it was only in 1987–88 that the episode was denounced as the outrage that it was, it is worth devoting some space to this disgraceful piece of political-literary history. The article begins by citing extracts from the text of the decision of the Central Committee: Zoshchenko was an "evil-intentioned hooligan", Akhmatova was "harmful to the upbringing of our youth", her poems "could not be tolerated in Soviet litera-ture". Similar or even harsher words were used by Zhdanov in his speech (Akhmatova became "half nun, half whore"). Records now published show that Zhdanov told the Leningrad committee that the matter was put on the agenda by Stalin personally. However, the author of the *Izvestiya* article (A. Ezhelev) notes that Zoshchenko had been harshly criticised in 1944 in the journal *Bolshevik* on the initiative of the Leningrad Party, according to Zhdanov himself, who was then its head. So maybe he suggested the matter to Stalin in 1946. Be that as it may, Zhdanov made the opening statement. One of the Leningrad authors who was present knew shorthand and took down a full text of what transpired, and it is only proper that *Zvezda*, one of the "guilty" journals, has announced that it will publish it in full.

The author's name was Levonevsky, and his account is of interest also in terms of the atmosphere it conveys. Thus six litterateurs were requested to go to Moscow. Once there, they were instructed by the then head of agitation and propaganda, Alexandrov, "not to leave their hotel, to speak to no one by telephone, not to meet Moscow writers, not to contact anybody". They were then taken to the 'Orgburo' hall of the central committee, and on the way Surkov saw them and cheerfully gave them each a copy of a Zoshchenko story with the author's photograph on the cover! So Surkov, though an official of the Writers' Union, could not have known what was coming. Zhdanov criticised both journals for publishing weak and bad works, before turning to Zoshchenko and Akhmatova, who "fell under the influence of petty-bourgeois ideology, of literature hostile to us". Stalin spoke repeatedly. Thus after the author V. Vishnevsky denounced Zoshchenko for "always dragging out in to the open old dirty linen, writing about invalids, beerbouses, militiamen, etc." (*sic*), Stalin said: "Writers think that they are not in politics. . . . They write something nice, and that's it. And yet there are bad, harmful passages and thoughts which poison the consciousness of youth. Why do I dislike such men as Zoshchenko? Because what they write resembles an emetic. Can we tolerate in responsible positions those who allow such stuff to be published? . . . Our journals are not private enterprises. . . . They do not have the right to adapt themselves to the tastes of people who do not wish to recognise our regime." (Stalin knew perfectly well that Zoshchenko was hugely popular!) "Whosoever does not wish to restructure himself [*perestraivatsa*, the verb from *perestroika*!], like Zoshchenko, let him go to the devil. It is not for us to alter our tastes, it is not for us to adapt our tastes to those of Zoshchenko and Akhmatova. Can Anna Akhmatova be an educator [*vospityvat'*]? Can that fool, that circus-clown Zoshchenko, educate?"

Why all this? Levonevsky comments: Stalin "wished to put an end to those intellectual 'liberties' which Stalin was compelled to tolerate during the difficult war years. . . . Akhmatova, who had not been published for nearly twenty years, having been declared to be expressing the mood of a past world, suddenly produced fine patriotic verse in the war days, and soon her earlier lyric poetry was reprinted. On top of this, in 1946 in Moscow there were Akhmatova poetry readings, which, according to Konstantin Simonov, were 'tremendous triumphs, even demonstratively so'. This was a triumph of a totally nonconformist writer! No more was Zoshchenko a conformist, he was after all a satirist, and was highly popular. . . . No satirist could be forgiven for this. . . . In addition, Zoshchenko and Akhmatova were part of Leningrad", a city with a great intellectual, architectural, and revolutionary past, which inevitably "competed with the capital as a spiritual centre, which could not please Stalin, who wanted strictly centralized state". The author then makes the very reasonable connection between the literary *pogrom* of 1946 and the "Leningrad affair" of 1948 (described in Chapter 4), which destroyed "thousands of leading cadres, major specialists, scientists, cultural figures. . . . All key posts in the Party and Soviet apparatus were then filled by officials sent from other places. Thus the 'dangerous' spirit of Leningrad was extirpated and burnt out. . . . What was done to Leningrad on Stalin's initiative in these years, after the war and the siege that cost the city a million lives, imposed very heavy loss to its spiritual traditions, felt still today."

At this point I would like to put in a personal note. I met an economist in 1988 who said: "In Leningrad all the senior economists were shot in 1948, and in their place were appointed young stupid dogmatists. They are now old stupid dogmatists, who oppose *perestroika*!" So 1946–48 has a contemporary significance, which is why I have put this episode into this chapter, though it could just as well have been treated in the chapter on the Terror. The author Ezhelev, in his *Izvestiya* article, also points out today's moral: "Today we publish books which could have cost the interested reader his liberty if he were to read them. However, the metastases of authoritarian thinking are not easily overcome. There is still administrative interference with creative activities, silly prohibitions, fear of life's truth and of its critical interpretation in the press and in art. In one place they cut back [the showing of] *Repentance*, in another they 'persuaded' the theatre director not to put on a Shatrov play, elsewhere they put on the shelf an allegedly 'blackening' documentary film. In each of these facts one sees the same deadening spirit of authoritarianism, which so openly showed itself in the events of 1946."

In the same issue of *Izvestiya* the 85-year-old writer Veniamin Kaverin writes movingly and eloquently of Zoshchenko and Akhmatova, how the attack on them was a way of slapping down the postwar hopes for relaxation of restrictions and for humanity. "The very choice of these authors, who were deliberately left at liberty so as to prolong for years the effect of the blow, show that this was so." He writes indignantly about the foul epithets used in attacking Akhmatova, "whose works have taken their place in the heights of world poetry and were labeled with the single expressive word 'rubbish' [*khlam*]." Zoshchenko effectively used laughter, "laughter that served humanity at all times." They won in the end. Anna Akhmatova is crowned with glory worldwide, recognised and deeply loved in her own country. Zoshchenko transcended death to win "one of the first places in our literature. But what sacrifices, what sufferings, he had to undergo! . . . We have no right to be silent about them." Kaverin has completed a book-length account of the literary events and personages he has known in the course of a long life. It should be well worth reading. However, he told *Literaturnaya gazeta* (15 June 1988) that this manuscript (called *Epilogue*) is still being held up—he did not say by whom or why.

In this interview, he stated that a judicial investigator currently engaged in the formal rehabilitation proceedings of Osip Mandelshtam had visited him, and asked him (inter alia) how he could explain that the sentence on him for his anti-Stalin poem (in 1934) had been so mild. As is known, Mandelshtam was rearrested in 1938, and Kaverin cited evidence to the effect that he died of hunger in a Far East camp, rummaging for food in rubbish bins.

There have been a number of other "resurrections" of long-dead authors, or the belated publication of previously banned works of such authors. Let us now look at the publication of books written more recently, but unpublishable until *glasnost'* came. Some have already been analyzed in previous chapters. This includes Shatrov's plays, Rybakov's *Children of the Arbat*, and Tendryakov's novel and stories. *Life and Fate*, by Vasili Grossman, has been mentioned in connection with its Jewish aspect. However, it is not this which gave the greatest offence to the censors. The book appeared several years ago in many languages, including English. So it would be sufficient briefly to enumerate the previously unpublishable elements in it, omitting what was already discussed in Chapter 5. The appearance of this novel in the USSR surprised many people, despite what we have heard and seen about *glasnost'*, and that included me. It was, of course, a welcome surprise.

First, the novel includes scenes in both Nazi and Soviet concentra-

tion camps. The horrors are reserved for the former, but there are
painful scenes in which old communists in a Soviet camp hospital
sadly discuss the past, including the crimes they themselves committed against so-called *kulaks*, one of whom is lying dead beside them.

Second, there is more than a hint that the Soviet system in Stalin's
time resembled the Nazi regime. The words to that effect are put into
the mouth of an SS officer, but the thought is there. Readers will
ponder over the idea that, paradoxically, the victory at Stalingrad
completed the transformation of the regime into national-
bolshevism.

Third, the hardships and conditions of civilian life in wartime are
pitilessly presented.

Finally, the heroic deeds of the soldiers at Stalingrad and of
devoted professional military commanders are contrasted with the
less-than-honest behaviour of the political-commissar types. Thus
when an officer delays his attack until an artillery bombardment can
create favourable conditions for its success, although the attack is
successful, they write an adverse report on him, and he is recalled to
Moscow; the reader is left to guess whether he is being recalled for
promotion or court-martial.

Prior to publication, *Life and Fate* was introduced to Soviet
readers in an article by S. Lipkin in *Moskovskie novosti* (18 Oct.
1987). He confirmed the story, told in the West, that in 1961
Grossman had been received by M. Suslov, then the chief Party
ideologist, who told him that this work could not be published in
less than 200–300 years. "The same figure was cited to Grossman by
three officials of the Union of Writers." Grossman submitted his
manuscript to *Znamya*, and its editor, Kozhevnikov, referred it
elsewhere, whence came the order to confiscate every copy. Lipkin
quotes from the letter sent by Grossman to Khrushchev: "How can
we understand that at the present time a writer's rooms are
searched, his book removed, a book no doubt imperfect but written
with my heart's blood in the name of truth and love of humanity. I
beg you to free my book, so that my manuscript is discussed by
editors and not by members of the Committee of State Security."
Lipkin's article ends with the words: "As with the works of his
friend Andrei Platonov, Grossman's best novel is now to be given to
us."

It is, as its readers know, a book of vast sweep and great literary
power. It was praised by a number of reviewers before publication,
which took place more than twenty years after the author's death.

Another novel which attracted attention was Vladimir Dudintsev's *Belye odezhdy* (*White Coats*). Dudintsev came into promi-

nence, as we have seen, in Khrushchev's time with *Not by Bread Alone*, which upset officialdom. This time he published a well-structured, intelligent adventure story, set in and around a genetics institute under fire from Lysenko and his crew. The main character is sent to the institute by a Lysenkoist academician (surely a caricature, under another name, of Lysenko himself) to extirpate genetic heresy—and for Lysenko genetics itself was a heresy. However, this character is two-faced: he is in fact anxious to limit the damage, and falls in love with a research worker in the institute who is a key member of a secret "cell" of real geneticists, fruit-flies and all. There are effectively pictured scenes at institute meetings at which some courageous geneticists defend themselves, and are dismissed. Since disagreement with Lysenkoism was seen at that time as tantamount to antistate activities, the secret police become involved too. Interestingly, the two secret policemen in the novel are at daggers drawn: one of them is anxious to arrest geneticists, and indeed the hero's loved one is arrested and sent to a labour camp. But the other policeman is sympathetically presented; he goes out of his way to warn those threatened with impending arrest, and ultimately commits suicide. Dudintsev's tale can be enjoyed at the level of a detective story, but it also carries a powerful sting in the tail, reminding the reader of the triumph of politically reinforced obscurantism over real science. It may be said: so what, this is old hat, Lysenko has been discredited many years ago. But no, it is not as simple as all that. In Brezhnev's time a dissident had on his list of "crimes" the fact that he opposed Lysenko in 1948. When he replied that the Party had condemned Lysenko's theories, his accusers were far from satisfied with such an explanation: his claim to have been right at that time implied that the Party had been wrong at that time. This impugns Party infallibility. Now, as is clear, infallibility is no longer claimed.

Another novel which created a stir appeared many years after its publication in the West (in Russian). This was Alexander Bek's *Novoye naznacheniye* (*New Appointment*). It is built around an imaginary commissar of heavy industry *Onisimov*, who rose to his high position in the thirties, but fell from grace after Stalin's death, being shunted aside into an ambassadorship in a place resembling Norway. To be fair, one has heard that an important reason for not publishing the novel earlier was the protest of the widow of a real heavy-industrial commissar, Tevosyan, whose career seemed to be the basis of the novel; i.e., Onisimov was a thinly disguised Tevosyan. As already noted earlier, this novel was used by Gavriil Popov for a long and penetrating review of the nature of the

"Administrative system" and of the devoted, self-sacrificing, and totally uncorrupted men (like Onisimov-Tevosyan) who made the Stalinist system function. In the novel (and in real life) Onisimov (Tevosyan) hated Beria, but Beria (or someone like him) was an integral part of the system—"the subsystem of fear", again to quote Popov.

Bek's novel highlights the defects as well as the virtues of that sort of commissar. He expects instant obedience, he obeys his master even at the cost of implementing what he knows to be wrong and wasteful. He has no time for initiatives from below. And when finally he has to find a successor, he recommends an obedient and tame subordinate, an example which commentators like Popov will generalize: the system cannot produce high-class captains of industry from within itself (Onisimov-Tevosyan was brought forward by the revolution), elites can degenerate, a theme to which we will return. Interestingly, Onisimov-Tevosyan falls afoul of Khrushchev over the latter's plans for the reorganization of planning; he speaks his mind, something he would never have done to Stalin, and is "rewarded" with a second-class ambassadorship. (This was how Stalin himself dealt with some oppositionists in the twenties, before he started killing them, and this was also what happened under Brezhnev: thus Yakovlev, at present a Central Committee secretary, was sent for several years to Ottawa.) Popov draws the moral, pointed to by Bek: the "new appointment"—i.e., a more or less honourable sack—showed that the "Administrative system" still existed after Stalin died and after the first wave of Khrushchevian de-Stalinisation. Even if it was no longer necessary to tremble, it was still necessary to obey—though disobedience no longer threatened life or liberty.

Daniil Granin's *Zubr* was also used by Popov as a peg on which to hang an article, specifically on the role of the independent mind under Stalinism. But this is not in fact what Granin's novel (or semibiography) is about. The chief character has his own name, Timofeyev-Resovsky, an eminent geneticist, a colleague of Vavilov. He is sent by the Soviet academic establishment to work in a laboratory near Berlin. The laboratory and its work are undisturbed when the Nazis come to power, except for the sacking of Jewish scientists, which is shown to be of concern to Timofeyev, since, in Granin's words, "like all true Russian intellectuals he hated anti-Semitism". Much is said in the novel about his contacts with eminent Western scientists, and about the Russian emigré community in Germany and France. When, in 1937, his return to Russia is requested, he refuses to go. Vavilov was already in trouble, many of his friends were arrested. During the war he works in his laboratory; his son undertakes anti-Nazi activities and is killed. The Soviet victory brings him into contact with a senior industrial commissar (minister), Zavenyagin, who realises how important his research could be in a military context (it is not made clear just how). However, the NKVD gets him first, and by the time the minister is able to find him, he is half dead in a Siberian labour camp. He is revived, and works in a secret establishment as a free man. His nickname, *Zubr* (*auroch*; figuratively, "diehard") gives the novel its title. Apart from much incidental detail, the chief "unmentionable" is simply praise for an independent-minded intellectual who was what used to be known as a *nevozvrashchenyets*, a "nonreturner", who stayed abroad, in Nazi Germany too.

Returned to literature is one who did not leave the USSR, Yuli Daniel, who had been sentenced along with Sinyavsky in 1965 (see above). Some of his poems were published in *Novyi mir* (No. 7, 1988). (Daniels died in January 1989, and Sinyavsky visited Moscow that month.)

Mention should also be made of the belated publication of Lidia Chukovskaya's *Sofya Petrovna* in *Neva* (No. 2, 1988). Chukovskaya is the daughter of that fine literary critic Kornei Chukovsky. This novel has been published in the West, and so have her highly informative notes about her friend, the great poet Anna Akhmatova. Another of Chukovskaya's works, also (thus far) published in the West, relates in detail the procedures for her expulsion from the Writers' Union. Presumably, she will be or has been readmitted with apologies. *Sofya Petrovna* tells of a mother's anguish when her son was arrested during the Terror; it is a moving and effective short novel.

As well as novels, there has been an upsurge in the publishing of essays and reviews, in the "thick journals" but also in a variety of other formerly dull and orthodox publications. Indeed, the number of dull and orthodox publications has sharply diminished, and there is in fact competition for readers, which takes the form of offering the unusual and controversial. Unpleasant events, such as riots and strikes in Armenia, show up on television, complete with frank interviews with strikers. Past efforts of newspapers to provide news had usually been blocked by the established habit of looking at news from the standpoint of political-social usefulness. An illustration is provided in the memoirs of Adzhubei, which have been quoted earlier. A train crash occurred near Moscow. Rumours spread, "200–300 killed, many injured". *Izvestiya* sent its reporter to the scene and found that there were just two killed. So *Izvestiya* wanted to publish a report. This needed the say-so of the so-called Ministry of Transport (so called because in reality it runs only the railways). The ministry said no. The reason? "What for? Whoever knows, knows. Whoever doesn't, won't find out. You would write that two had died, but then everyone would suppose the figure was much higher." So nothing appeared. Now, after some initial hiccups with regard to Chernobyl, disasters large and small make the press with reasonble speed: such was the case, for instance, with a recent collision between two ships in the Black Sea, where many were drowned.

In contrast to the silence which had followed the earthquakes in Tashkent and Ashkhabad in pre-*glasnost'* days, the Armenian earthquake was fully reported, with harrowing photographs and detailed descriptions of the tragedy. This represented a big advance on the reporting of Chernobyl.

Journalists live in a different world today. They are encouraged to investigate, to denounce abuses, to criticise fearlessly. However, this remains difficult in the provinces, where the Party secretary is still master of all he surveys, and that includes the press. One of the speakers at the 19th Party Conference (Masaliev, first secretary in Kirgizia) actually expressed outrage at the fact that some mere journalists dared to criticise "elected officials" (*Pravda*, 30 June 1988). He was criticised in his turn. (And, I might add, how had he the nerve to refer to *elected* officials when the "elections" had hitherto been quite phoney!?) This question must be seen as a subitem within the much larger question which is being fully discussed, having been raised by Gorbachev too: How is one to set limits to Party dominance in a one-Party state? It is no use providing legal remedies if the law and the judges are also under Party discipline. We will be returning to this theme in the next chapter.

Felix Dymov expresses the new atmosphere well, in an article titled "What Is Not Forbidden Is Allowed!" (*Literaturnaya Rossiya*, 17 June 1988):

We learned to read between the lines ..., trying to deduce future demotions and transfers by studying who is next to whom in the [official] photograph and how far from number one. ... Only in the last months have our periodicals printed the letter from Raskolnikov to Stalin and of Ernst Henry to Erenburg. But the texts of these letters were circulating in our country, typed and retyped. As do other documents, not yet published.

Is it not time to finish with the old thought-categories? One cannot hide from the people. ... Alas, the old categories are indestructible. At one time radio receivers and typewriters were registered: Still today for some reason we have to put official typewriters under seal and hand them over to be guarded on the eve of holidays. Yet today the number of privately owned typewriters equals official ones . . . and yet we still take precautions. Against what? Against leaflets or anonymous letters? Abroad one can anywhere have access to a Xerox machine and can copy anything for a few pence. With us, duplicating technology is under incredible supervision. . . . In all countries we can buy detailed plans of our cities, but for ourselves we publish unbelievably distorted and primitive diagrams. Only the influence of old stereotypes can explain the ban on cooperative publishing houses. [Such were publicly proposed—A.N.] There is fear of losing monopoly on information. Yet the state has announced an overall programme of computerisation, which cannot but lead to a loss of this monopoly. The phenomenon of Vladimir Vysotski, which did not fit into the usual literary and popular-musical genres, would have been impossible without tape recorders. Their appearance means the loss of government control over what people hear. With videos it practically loses control over what people see. With computers . . . control will be lost over what people read.

At the Party Conference, conflicts among the writers came into the open. Yuri Bondarev launched a strong attack on an alleged clique of writers who dare attack such authors as Rasputin, Belov, and Astafyev. This clique criticises faith and hope in the motherland as if this were "chauvinism", mentions the traitor-general Vlasov, disapproves of the editor of *Nash sovremennik*. The illustrated weekly *Ogonyok* was one of his targets. When G. Baklanov, editor of *Znamya*, spoke, he counterattacked. He cited a telegram: "Will no one answer Nina Andreyeva and Yuri Bondarev?" Amid interruptions, which required an intervention from Gorbachev to silence, he went on: "A classic of our literature, Andrei Platonov, worked as a janitor. . . . Only now, as a result of *glasnost'*, his works are published. Alexander Trifonovich Tvardovsky did not live to see his poem in print. Bek . . . also died before his novel's publication. Suslov promised Grossman that his novel will not be published for 200 years. . . . All three authors died of cancer, a quick-acting cancer. Perhaps doctors could explain this." He contrasted the present concern about prisoners of war and the missing in Afghanistan with the attitude toward prisoners of war in the Stalinist past. He added: "it needed political wisdom and courage to withdraw our troops from Afghanistan. Neither of these qualities were needed to send them there." This is open debate indeed, and amply reported in the media.

Another totally "untouchable" theme was real life in the armed forces. *Moskovskaya Pravda* on 3 June 1987 already raised the question of the treatment of conscripts when they report for duty.

This, under the heading of "Forbidden Territory", produced a flood of readers' letters, and a further and bolder article on 5 August 1987, with extracts from the letters. These raised more painful questions. Recruits are abused, their belongings stolen. Medical examinations are perfunctory. Recruits are bullied unmercifully by second-year soldiers. This so-called *dedovshchina* (the word is used in the article) is described as "a sickness which, fortunately, is far from having infected all military units. But unfortunately, we cannot say that [such] disorders in the army are isolated occurrences." The journalists who tried to investigate further had the doors slammed in their faces by the military: "As soon as the correspondent tried to check the allegations made in readers' letters, it was transparently hinted that a way would be found to deal with excessively bold newspapermen. They could, for instance, be recalled to army duty (as reservists), and then . . . ."

*Moskovskaya Pravda*'s report included a critical letter from a conscript who had completed his service in Afghanistan (and who signed his name): "What is disgusting is not what is described in your article, but the fact that you write about it though you well know that those responsible will suffer no more than a minor admonishment, and then only in those military offices which you named. You are just engaged in showing-off criticism [*kriticheskoi pokazukhoi*]." But gradually even these doors were forced open, despite military counterattacks (e.g., in their own *Krasnaya zvezda*).

Korotich's own *Ogonyok* in June 1988 printed a letter from a mother whose son was killed by a senior rating in the navy, and a major scandal broke in July 1988 when a bullied and ill-treated young soldier went berserk and shot several of his tormentors, the case being given press publicity. (Of course, bullying of young soldiers has occurred in the British army too, though hardly on such a scale.)

On a different theme, B. Mozhayev and Ludmilla Saraskina, writing in *Moskovskie novosti* (No. 31, 1988), referred to the problems encountered by the former in getting his works published and on the stage. Lyubimov, of the Taganka theatre, wanted to put on a play based on his story "The Life of Fedor Kuzkin", but the then minister of culture, Furtseva, said no. In 1970, Lyubimov's novel *Muzhiki i baby* (published in *Don* in 1987) was also blocked, despite support not only from Tvardovsky but also from *Glavlit* (the censors!). The "blockage" came from literary colleagues.

*Znamya* (No. 5, 1988) published a poem written by Vladimir Lifshits directly after Tvardovsky's death in 1971, but unpublished then. To avoid public demonstrations, the authorities kept people away from the funeral, while official speakers "praised the poet whom they had defamed" and dismissed (the previous year) from the editorship of *Novyi mir*. Lifshits's poem deliberately imitates the style of Tvardovsky's wartime verses, hugely popular, on the soldier "Vasili Tyorkin", whom the reader can imagine hitchhiking to Moscow to attend the funeral: "Why cannot the people bid farewell to the people's poet," he asks. A police officer replies: "We are ordered not to let people through, people are buried in accordance with their rank [*kto kakoi imeyet chin*], so go away." The would-be mourner goes to a bar to drink, there "freely to remember Russia's poet". So, as Vanshenkin says in his introduction to the poem, Tvardovsky's own simple hero was forbidden to say a decent goodbye to his creator.

A word must be said about the press treatment of Andrei Sakharov, after his return from his Gorky exile. Interviews with him have been printed, also an article by G. Zhavoronkov in *Moskovskie novosti* (15 May 1988), praising him, referring to his 1968 and his 1975 memoranda, condemned then, but now "there are clear parallels between what he then said and the ideas which we put forward today". The article mentions the false reports previously published, e.g., about his and his wife's "riches" and family history. He gave his money to the Red Cross and to help build a cancer clinic (his first wife had died of cancer). The father of Elena Bonner, his present wife, was shot in 1937, her mother returned from Gulag in 1954. The Sakharovs live simply—a photo shows him doing the washing-up. The author of the false report once visited him in Gorky to ask for an interview. Sakharov showed him a copy of the book which contained the libels and asked for a written apology. When this was refused, Sakharov said: "Pity that duels are now no longer allowed," and gave him a slap in the face.

Of one thing there is no doubt at all: Soviet papers have become much more interesting, and it is quite a struggle to buy many of them because not enough copies can be printed to satisfy rising demand. In fact, in August 1988 there was a public scandal over limitations imposed on new subscriptions of the most popular of the "cultural" journals. *Literaturnaya gazeta*, one of those "limited", complained in its issue of 21 August that no limits were placed on subscriptions to *Nash sovremennik* and *Molodya gvardiya*, both known for their conservative position. The reasons adduced for the limitation were shortage of paper and the overburdening of the posts.

The same issue of *Literaturnaya gazeta* had challenging articles on criminals and their links with "corrupted officials", noting, among other things, that Uzbek village girls coming to town to study are "placed in an underground brothel". The issue contained descriptions of several criminal gangs and their doings, and coins an interesting word, *bandokratiya*, to define the amalgamation of *nomenklatura* and organized crime which can replace *burokratiya* (author: Vladimir Sokolov). Also in the same issue was a fascinating interview with Vladimir Dudintsev, in which he tells of his many troubles following the publication of *Not by Bread Alone*, and the odd position of Simonov, who published it but denounced it (and, when no one was looking, gave Dudintsev a knowing wink!). In 1957, Dudintsev was called in to the KGB, a general questioned him, and, at a time when Khrushchev said that there were no political prisoners, this general showed him photographs of such prisoners. For many years he could not be published, and survived thanks in part to generous gifts, often sent to him anonymously. Dudintsev stressed the importance of behaving honourably, recalling the times when doctors and professors did not take bribes, referring to "certain regions where degrees are bought and higher-degree dissertations purchased for large sums". Now there are still "anti-*perestroika* attitudes among the top Party posts". Asked for his view of Nabokov, he expressed strong approval for everything he had read except *Lolita*, which disgusted him. One could fill many pages just by citing and summarizing the contents of this one journal.

The cinema saw the first grass-roots revolt of the *glasnost'* era. In 1986, at the elections of the official Cinema Association, the slate of the officially nominated executive committee was rejected, and nominees from the floor of the conference were elected instead; Elem Klimov, a talented director, became the association's head. Great had been the irritation with the bureaucrats' negative attitude to original film-making. All the evidence points to the fact that this was not prearranged; it was a genuine election. Indeed, the story around Moscow was that the cultural authorities were taken by surprise and accepted the outcome, but then took care that the solution adopted by the Writers' Union represented a compromise—a new joint secretary, V. Karpov, and a mixture of old and new on the executive.

Anyhow, the new Cinema Association speedily set to work, deciding to review all the films made and not shown in the previous decade. We have all benefited from the consequences. The biggest sensation was the showing of *Repentance*, the Georgian film that has also been shown in the West, an allegory on Stalinism, though Stalin's name is not mentioned and the small-town dictator who, so to speak, stands in for him in no way resembles him physically. One cannot attempt here to review the large number of films now taken off the shelf to which they were confined by the former cultural bureaucrats. I will confine myself to one, as an illustration of the atmosphere: *The Cold Summer of 1953*. The setting is a northern village, its miserably low living conditions faithfully portrayed. In this village live two exiles, both having served sentences in labour camps. One is an ex-army officer who was captured by the Germans and escaped. (This was very often "rewarded" with a long sentence, a recurrent theme in recent literature.) The other is an engineer who had been sent to study in England and was therefore arrested and given a long sentence as a "British spy". Into the village comes a gang of criminals, released under the "Beria" amnesty (after Stalin died and before his own arrest, Beria ordered the release of criminals from labour camps; the amnesty did not affect "politicals", whom Khrushchev was to release in 1955–56). The criminals kill the village's one policeman, terrorize the inhabitants, seek to rape a young girl. The two "politicals" fight back; the ex-officer's military skills enable him to dispose of the bandits, but the engineer is killed by them. The film ends three years later: the ex-officer, now amnestied, returns to the city, which is draped with slogans for May Day. He seeks out the engineer's family. Like so many others, they had tried to save themselves by renouncing him—indeed, before his arrest he urged them to do this. The ex-officer tells the wife of her husband's fate—she had had no news for fourteen years—and gives her her husband's sole possession, a much-repaired pair of spectacles. She sits silently holding them, while her son launches into a justification: "He told us to renounce him, we could do nothing."

I will mention just one other film which I personally found human, moving, and realistic: *Twenty Days Without War*. A military correspondent travels on leave to the distant rear, visiting his wife, who is also assisting in making a war film, the unreality of which dismays him. There is a love interest, a sort of Russian *Brief Encounter*, portrayed with restraint and good effect. But above all what lingers is the unvarnished reality of life behind the front: mud, overcrowding, the sad goodbyes to newly enrolled youngsters off to war on overloaded trains. Talent there is. Clearly, we will see more of value from Soviet cinema.

Theatre too has had its share of *glasnost'*. The historical plays of Shatrov have been mentioned already. A new and vigorous Theatrical Society was formed in 1986, and articles by its leaders, notably Oleg Efremov, argued eloquently for greater freedom. Indeed, this has been achieved to a substantial extent: theatre directors, at least in the capital, may put on plays on their own responsibility, without the endless and frustrating delays which arise in getting them cleared by *Glavrepertkom*, the chief repertory committee of the Minstry of

Culture. Once again, there are more problems in the provinces. Thus Efremov and several colleagues wrote to protest the attempts being made in some places to block the production of Shatrov's controversial plays, and also complained that the committee of the Theatrical Society is ignored when decisions are taken to appoint or dismiss theatre directors: the bureaucrats at the ministry and the local authorities do their own thing.

It used to be said, only half in jest, that directors of theatrical companies were often those local officials who had failed in everything else. This thought was repeated, in the present tense, in a discussion on theatre reported in *Nedelya* (No. 11, 1988): "Seryozha, tell me, where do directors come from? As a rule [*sic*] they appoint someone who has been unable to cope with other work." A "director" (*direktor*) is the theatre's principal administrator, who may or may not actually direct (produce) a particular play; that person is called a *rezhiser* (*régisseur*). It has been widely reported that many provincial theatres have very small audiences, and that the pay of actors is deplorably low. (Efremov told a gathering at which I was present that the "salary" was as little as 120 roubles a month; an average industrial worker earns over 200. In Moscow, actors can pick up extras from TV and radio, but in the provinces life is tough for them.)

In the same discussion, there was also an interesting point made about the powers of the theatre director, with Efremov among others arguing that he ought to be in charge, and not subject to control from below by the actors.

When all the difficulties are allowed for, there certainly has been progress. One welcomes development in recent years in a profusion of studio-theatres, experimental groups, with their own repertoires and real autonomy. One such, the *Teatr-studiya yugo-zapada*, appeared in 1987 at the Edinburgh festival fringe, presenting *Hamlet* in Pasternak's translation with success. (They played in Glasgow too, and I had the pleasure of seeing them on their home ground in Moscow in 1988.) The Tbilisi "Rustaveli" theatre has appeared in the "official" Edinburgh festival. The Leningrad "Maly" theatre has toured Britain and North America with a new play with such a previously taboo subject as prostitutes—and some stage nudity, too, which contrasts with past puritanism.

Several new plays deal with important social-economic themes. Thus, a young playwright has adopted for the stage Ovechkin's *Rayonnye budni*, the first part of which, as we have seen, appeared in print as long ago as 1952. It deals with abuses of power in the village, and the dictatorial attitude of the Party official Borzov,

whose name has become widely identified with the type who bangs
the table with his fist and demands grain deliveries of the state
regardless of peasants' requirements. His slogan: *gosudarstvu
nuzhen khleb* ("the state needs bread grains"). In Ovechkin's stories
he is succeeded by a more caring official, Martynov, but he too runs
into difficulties in his dealings, both with his own superiors and with
the peasants and the farm managements. Commenting on Ovechkin's sketches in *Novyi mir* (No. 12, 1986), A. Strelyany points out
that the same problems exist still thirty years later: "It is so
*zlobodnevno*, that it might have been written by Saltykov-
Shchedrin." This sentence may need explaining. The untranslatable
word *zlobodnevno* means "relevant today", with the implication
that the matter is acute and troublesome (the word is made up of
*zloba*, anger, and *den'*, day). Saltykov-Shchedrin is a nineteenth-
century satirist, so there is the further implication that the abuses in
question have existed for over a hundred years, let alone thirty!

A play entitled *Kolyma*, by I. Dvoretsky, was published by *Neva*
(No. 12, 1987). I do not know if it has reached the stage. It is a play
within a play, the former being set in the Kolyma camps.

This is not the place to discuss in detail the state of the theatre in
Russia in the late eighties, nor am I qualified to write such a piece.
All that is attempted here is to show the sort of play that can now
appear, which formerly would have been rejected out of hand by the
guardians of public morals and political respectability.

It should be added that controversial plays are also shown on
television, and are thus seen by millions all over the country. This
includes some of Shatrov's plays. Television also presents free,
unscripted discussion on many controversial issues, including (as we
have seen) the participation of orthodox priests, plus questions to
ministers and other officials, particularly on matters economic;
there are virtually no economic grievances or malfunctions that do
not also receive critical attention on television. Since nearly all Soviet
citizens have television sets, this fills a gap left in those places where
the press is still timid and uncritical.

Music, too, is much freer, despite the survival of the old gang in
the Composers' Union. Modern pieces can be played, modern
composers' works are performed, and composers are allowed to
travel. One thinks of such talented men as Shnitke. Jazz and rock
bands proliferate. High-level pop, represented, for instance, by Alla
Pugacheva, no longer has to be hidden away from the censor-
bureaucrats, and large editions of her records are produced. The
unofficial cult of Vladimir Vysotski, who died tragically young, is
now official, with large editions of his poems and records available.

The issue of youth alienation, legitimation of rock music and its iconoclastic lyrics, the appearance of such films as *Ne legko byt' molodyn* ("It is Not Easy to be Young"), which touches also on the drug problem, the emergence into the light of day of such issues as prostitution—all these are further examples of much greater openness. It has its limits. Thus, while the grievances of "Afghan" veterans are given considerable publicity, it is in private conversation that one hears that ex-soldiers who served in Afghanistan are potential recruits for right wing or neo-Fascist extremism. The politics of all this should not be oversimplified. "Stalinists" do exist—those who bitterly resent criticism of the despot, seeing in this a denigration of their own work and sacrifice. This view found expression in Nina Andreyeva's article (see Chapter 3) and occasionally appears in letters printed by such anti-Stalinist journals as *Ogonyok* and *Znamya*. However, some nationalist supporters of *Pamyat'* cannot forgive Stalin the destruction of peasant culture and historical and religious monuments. Also, some who are genuinely and deeply concerned with the preservation of Russian culture are by no means the supporters of the chauvinist and anti-Semitic wing of the *Pamyat'* organization. The latter very seldom appears in the media, except as an object of attack. Nor are directly anti-Semitic views printed, despite the (alas) rather widespread feelings on the subject. There are also a minority of economists and publicists who equate "socialism" with the *existing* economic system and derive from this the conclusion not that it should be reformed but that socialism as such as failed and should be replaced. Such a view may be illustrated by the following "joke":

Q. What is socialism?
A. It is the longest road from capitalism to capitalism.
   (A variant: A. The longest road from feudalism to capitalism).

Such views are not likely to be tolerated, they are beyond the limits of *glasnost'*.

Abstract art, too, is tolerated. No more do we hear of unofficial exhibitions being attacked with bulldozer and fire hose, as happened in Brezhnev's time. Painters unorthodox in method and subject can now function, and even exhibit and sell works abroad. However, the Academy of Art remains in the hands of the old guard. This matters because of their control over the supply of canvases and paints, and of exhibition halls. Deprived of top-level support, they are in retreat. So the future is much less bleak than the past, when paintings by such great artists as Chagall and Malevich were hidden in cellars, and even French impressionists were seen as shockingly modern by the mediocrities who, in Stalin's time, earned good pay by producing statues of the Father and Teacher, and endless copies in oil of older pictures. (I lost count of the number of times I saw Vasnetsov's painting of "Three Knight-Errants" [*Tri bogatyrya*] in hotel lounges in the fifties.) When Chagall revisited Russia, his pictures were extracted from the cellars. Anyhow, art too is now much freer, and more controversial.

A challenge to the old gang is mounting. Writing in *Moskovskie novosti* (29th Nov. 1987), Vladimir Dashkevich reminds the reader of the decisions taken in 1948 on the report of Tikhon Khrennikov. The executive of the Composers' Union contained none of the talented musicians: missing were Shostakovich, Prokofiev, Khachaturyan, Mravinsky, Oistrakh, and Richter. The "musical officials of various ranks", the "musical *nomenklatura*" still decided what should be played. In 1968 the then deputy-minister of culture "categorically rejected the new wave of new symphonists, such as Shnitke, Denisov. . . . He described Vysotski's songs as "turbid rubbish". . . . What today is the Union of Composers? In my view, it is an overorganized bureaucratic machine. . . . Its administrative structure has greatly expanded. . . . Almost 500 persons who are part of it claim to represent *all* of Soviet music and greatly limit the opportunities of other members to have their works performed." And so on. But the would-be reformers have not yet won.

It is sometimes said that culture, literature in particular, can actually benefit from restrictions and obstacles, providing for the authors a motive for circumventing and overcoming them, and also grievances to respond to. A tragic and dramatic history "helps" too. However, if the history gets suppressed, if "sincerity" is regarded as irrelevant (and a mere mention of it as heretical), if even tragedy must be optimistic (and there was indeed a play called *An Optimistic Tragedy*), if so-called socialist realism requires a false picture of reality and causes Shostakovich to be accused of writing a formalist fugue, and a Russian trying to paint like Dufy or Picasso to be deprived of the possibility of showing his pictures, then the scene becomes grey and bleak. Life *should* be an obstacle race, but some obstacles at least should be surmountable.

In the theatrical discussion in *Nedelya* mentioned above, a participant (Igor Kvasha) remarked that "until recently our theatre existed so to speak compulsorily, we were compelled to put on such-and-such plays". To which Sergei Yurski replied that the right to experiment "is not pure joy: previously everything was forbidden, now everything is allowed. . . . Paradoxically it is a time of [self-] restriction of desires."

I must end this chapter by stressing the actively negative role played by the various cultural unions and associations until the most recent times. There is ample evidence not only that they did nothing to protect their members, but that they actually initiated restrictive measures and condemnations. An art historian who emigrated in Brezhnev's time asked the question: Where is the chief obstacle to good painting to be found? Not in the censorship, not in the Central Committee of the Party, but in the Academy of Arts, whose leaders hate talent and originality, and run to the Party ideologists to beg them to stop such heresies. The disgraceful performance of the Writers' Union in respect to Pasternak has been mentioned already. Its Leningrad branch initiated the persecution of Brodsky. This union also obstructed for years the publication of Mandelshtam's poems, and contributed to the dismissal of Tvardovsky from *Novyi mir*. Some of the union's officers at that time—Gribachev, Sofronov, Mikhalkov—were fully and drearily as orthodox as the worst official of the Party's cultural department. Nor can we confidently assert that this was due to the undemocratic nature of elections to the executive. It is likely that the majority of the members shared the views of their executive committee, or else believed or pretended that the Party's ideological-cultural views should at all times prevail. Those in this second category were ready to switch their opinions as soon as the Party did so. It is about such persons that Gorbachev and other reformers speak scornfully, varying the word *perestroilis'* (the verb derived from *perestroika*, in the third person) to *pristroilis'* (implying trimming, time-serving). Many bureaucrats are doing the same outside the cultural area, too. In the scientific sphere, one recalls Khrushchev's outrage when he asked the director of an agricultural research station why he recommended a particular crop, and he got the reply that "it was the line of the Party". Khrushchev exploded: the expert should give the Party advice, using his expertise. But that did not prevent Khrushchev from ordering the dismissal of another director of another agricultural research centre (in Siberia; the issue was fallowing) when the advice displeased him. Khrushchev's impulsive and contradictory personality is no longer with us. The problem of the relationship between the ruling party and the creative intelligentsia, the scientific and managerial strata, remains open.

The publication plans for 1989 now (in August 1988) being announced include a survey of the ideas of Russian (non-Bolshevik) philosphers such as N. Berdyaev, S. Bulgakov, Vladimir Soloviev, and P. Struve; more works by Nabokov, Platonov, Tendryakov, and Shalamov; Nadezhda Mandelshtam's memoirs, *1984*, and more. So it seems that *glasnost'* marches on.

# CHAPTER 7

# Politics, Sociology and Law

One could say that at the height of Stalin's power the Soviet Union became totally depoliticised. True, political slogans were omni-present, Party propagandists duly propagated the Party line, and there was a high level of formal participation: 99.9 percent voted in elections for the only candidates, and millions acted as deputies in local soviets, or as agitators. However, the Party line itself was infallible, and all votes were always unanimous; one did as one's superiors ordered, or at least pretended to. This situation persisted long after Stalin's death, though of course without the pathological excesses of mass terror. No autonomous body could be contem-plated, all had to be controlled by designated Party functionaries. Nor was there any sign of *public* discussion among the leadership itself, debates being behind closed doors unless or until the victors could describe those ousted as an "anti-Party group" (in 1957) or as guilty of "hare-brained schemes" (in 1964). In published material on Party meetings or Supreme Soviet sessions there was virtually no sign of anything that could be called "debate": no one actually took up a point made by another speaker and agreed or disagreed with it. No one ever abstained from voting yes.

This is not to say that speakers at Central Committee plenums or Supreme Soviet sessions made no criticisms. They frequently did so, drawing attention to some local lack or reproaching a ministry for some action or inaction. There was seldom any reply, there was no feedback, no "public opinion". It would be wrong, however, to imagine that the system conformed to the pure totalitarian model, that the hierarchical principle was at all times observed. Especially after the despot's death, functionaries acquired considerable possi-bilities for manoeuvre within their spheres of responsibility. One could analyze the polity in terms of many rival interest groups, competing for resources and influence with each other. This was (and is) particularly the case in matters economic. I characterised this as "centralized pluralism" (in my *Soviet Economic System*); a Soviet critic preferred the word "polycentrism". The topmost authority, the Politbureau, had to be obeyed, but in a vast country with a large bureaucracy and many institutions, the sheer complexity and vast amount of decision making made total supervision impossible, necessitated delegation of authority, permitted a complex array of informal links. A Hungarian economist once told me: remember, in a so-called command economy many commands are written by their recipients.

Party control was and is exercised both through the Party's own institutions, dominating or duplicating those of the state, and through its power of appointment to all posts of influence. This requires a few words of explanation, the more so because the most recent reform discussions have put these procedures in question. *Nomenklatura* has a double meaning: it is a list of functions, jobs, alongside each of which is the name of the Party committee responsible for filling it, or at the very least ensuring that it approves the appointment. It also designates individuals deemed capable (politically cleared) for such appointments. Collectively, the *nomenklatura* is a sort of all-inclusive Soviet "establishment", covering every sort of post of significance, from industrial manager to editor, from trade-union secretary to the minister of nonferrous metallurgy. Some of these offices are nominally elective, but hitherto the holders have been designated or approved by the appropriate Party committee or its personnel department.

In several of my own works I have suggested that the *nomenklatura* of the Central Committee, those deemed important enough to concern this body, might be seen as the ruling class or stratum of the Soviet Union. The question of the applicability of the word *class* (and of who is in it) has been the subject of debates among Western Marxists. There could be no such debate in the Soviet Union until very recently. Let me illustrate the sensitivity of the issue with a (true) story involving myself. Ten years ago I was in Moscow for a political science conference. A Soviet scholar approached me and said: "You are Alec Nove? You have written an article called 'Is the Soviet Union a Class Society?' May I discuss it with you?" I naturally replied in the affirmative, and asked: "Have you read it?" My colleague answered as follows: "In my institute I study Western interpretations of the USSR, and in this capacity I am allowed to read anything that is behind two locks. Unfortunately this article of yours was behind *three* locks!" The reason for this was not that I was personally seen as particularly dangerous; I even found three of my books in the open catalogue of Moscow University library when I was there in 1969. No, the reason was the sensitivity of the subject. The nature of Soviet society was itself a taboo subject. Officially, there were two friendly classes, the workers and the kolkhoz peasants, with a stratum (not a class) of Intelligentsia, and that was that. Furthermore, "contradictions" essentially afflicted class societies, notably Western capitalism.

No wonder sociology and political science had problems establishing themselves as academic disciplines. The Soviets did participate in world congresses in sociology and in political science, but the subjects remained barely recognized in the USSR itself. An Institute of Applied Sociology was created, but it was severely mangled in 1972. It is noteworthy that the chief "mangler", Rutkevich, who was appointed to run it in that year, was roundly denounced by a group of social scientists, including Zaslavskaya, when he was nominated for membership of the Academy in 1988. He was not elected.

Nature abhors a vacuum. Able academics sought to fill it for several years before *glasnost'*. The efforts of such men as Burlatsky, Shakhnazarov, and Kurashvili were recorded at the time by Archie Brown (see his contribution to *The State in Socialist Society* (N. Harding, ed., State University of New York Press: 1984). Interestingly, Shakhnazorov held, indeed still holds, an official position as a Party functionary. Temporarily silenced as sociologists, some were able to write in the "disguise" of economists or ethnographers. Tatiana Zaslavskaya, whose interests straddle economics and sociology, was elected academician. The Siberian branch of the Academy of Sciences sheltered several of this species of what I would call "constructive dissidents", i.e., those who prematurely advocated *perestroika*. It is there that Zaslavskaya penned the memorandum or paper which, in 1983, was leaked to the West and printed here, and which earned her a reprimand. Its interest lies, *inter alia*, in the evidence it provides as to the state of *unpublished* discussion in the last Brezhnev years. We should never forget that, once the Stalin Terror was over, freedom of speech substantially exceeded freedom of the press. There is a Russian saying: *chto napisano perom, ne vyrubish toporom*, "What is written with the pen cannot be chopped away with an axe".

Zaslavskaya raised in sharp form two basic points, which now are the staple of published discussion, but required courage at the time she raised them. One, to be further developed in the next chapter, was that the economic system had become obsolete, a hindrance to the forces of production. (Similar ideas had been expressed also by Aganbegyan, in another memorandum, which had also been partially leaked to Western correspondents, and which, so it is said, led to his being barred from foreign travel at that time.) The second, which raises fundamental issues as to the nature of Soviet society, referred to contradictions in that society, the fact that its "monolithic" nature was a myth, that there were divergent interests, not least in the ruling stratum itself, and that no reform project could be realistically advanced which did not take into account these divergent interests and the different ways in which any reform would affect them.

Thus, intelligent critics were in place to take advantage of *glasnost'*, when gradually the new "Gorbachev spirit" penetrated the social sciences, overcoming conservative obstruction. At first a discussion on contradictions had to tread carefully: yes, they did exist, it had been wrong to deny this, but under socialism contradictions were not of an explosive nature, they were not irreconcilable—they were, so to speak, benign rather than malignant. However, Polish events in 1980 did suggest that they could become explosive unless correctly handled. Now the brakes are off: since Gorbachev himself spoke of a "precrisis situation" in the Soviet economy and society, of the need for *revolutionary* change, it was pointless to deny that the contradictions that existed were as real as they were anywhere, even though there was no class of exploiters and of exploited.

Or was there? Was there a ruling class in the allegedly classless society? This utterly heretical view does now appear in print, though it is also disputed, as it is also in some of the Western discussions of this very subject. All serious arguments about obstacles to change refer to the privileges and power of high officialdom, of the disease and might of "bureaucratism", and some dig deeper: who are these "bureaucrats", why do they have so much power, what connection does this have with property relations, with the nature of the political system, with the absence of the market? For example, an article in *Moskovskie novosti* of 26 June 1988 is headed: "Remove Our Property from the Bureaucracy", and one sentence reads: "The people's property has become the property of the bureaucrat", with "dictatorial forms of control, and hidden forms of exploitation". Then what of legality? The extreme forms of arbitrary terror of Stalin's time are facts of history, but still today illegality and (nonsanguinary) arbitrariness are all too frequently met with. Gorbachev was a student in the faculty of law, and the pleas of reform-minded lawyers have become loud and clear, as we shall see.

*Pravda* and *Izvestiya* used readers' letters to raise for the first time in living memory (in print) two vital issues, which had been strictly taboo. On 13 February 1986, *Pravda* printed an analysis of letters which included one which asserted that "in discussing social justice, we cannot close our eyes to the fact that party, soviet, trade union, industrial and even Komsomol leaders often objectively deepen social inequality by utilizing all kinds of special buffets, special shops, special hospitals, and so on. Yes, we have no egalitarianism [*uravnilovka*], the leadership should have higher money incomes. But other privileges should not exist. Let the boss go like other citizens to an ordinary shop and stand in line with everyone else". I recall that when I told a colleague who had studied the USSR for many years that this had been printed in the Soviet Union, and in *Pravda* too, he simply refused to believe me. It seemed to him that the mention in public of such things was inherently contrary to the very essence of the system.

Then *Izvestiya* published a short letter, pointing out the phoniness of elections, in a language which Western specialists used to describe them, but which none of us expected to see on page one of *Izvestiya*! There is only one candidate to vote "for", one puts the unmarked ballot paper in the box; to take out a pencil or go into a booth is a sure sign to whoever is watching that one is crossing out the name of the candidate (the only way to vote against). The author of the letter expresses the wish to have several candidates to choose from. (Indeed, the Russian word for "elections", *vybory*, is the plural of the ordinary word for "choice", so having no choice is something of a linguistic mockery.)

Another established principle has been questioned, and now finally laid to rest (at least I *hope* it is finally!): this is the habit of presenting all decisions as unanimous. Adzhubei, in his memoirs, reports having asked Khrushchev, after the latter's forced retirement, why this practice continued; after all, people do disagree with one another, so why not put matters to a real vote? He said that Khrushchev replied: "The Party is old, it has long-established habits." Since 1933, to judge from the record, it seems that the Central Committee of the Party too was unanimous on every occasion—except that in 1957, on a vote expelling Molotov, Molotov abstained! There must have been disagreements, splits, maybe real votes—for instance, when Khrushchev won in 1957 and lost in 1964—but in public the myth of unanimity was maintained. Until 1988, *every* vote in the Supreme Soviet has been reported as unanimous on every issue, every occasion. It seemed important for the regime to have these 99.9 percent votes at elections, a monolithic "parliament" and Party. Since the Party dominated the soviets at all levels, they too were supposed to be of one mind. In the Party itself, elections had long been reduced to a formality: the leadership coopted its own members—local Party secretaries were nominated by the upper-level secretariats and/or the Central Committee apparatus, with the nomination always unanimously voted by the comrades below them.

Party congresses were in principle the determinants of Party policy, and they elected the Central Committee. In practice, under Stalin and since, they became mass meetings at which the delegates approved unanimously the proposed slate of Central Committee members, any changes in the Party programme, and whatever policy declarations the current leader made. Under Stalin there had been only one congress, the 18th, between 1934 and 1952. He did not even bother to pretend to observe the formal statutes. Since 1956 (the 20th Congress) they have been held every five years, with the approval of the draft five-year plan on the agenda. It is with this background in mind that one must view the extraordinary events at the 19th Party *Conference* in May–June 1988 ("conferences" used to be held between congresses, but not since the war). Gorbachev spoke in an unusual way, leaving questions open for debate and decision, thereby—as they admitted in a Moscow radio discussion—surprising and confusing some delegates, who had never seen or heard anything like it. There were even votes at the end on various resolutions, some actually proposed from the floor, and these were *not* unanimous! The conference itself was featured prominently in the media, including television, with no attempt to soften the contours, to hide disagreements, or to censor the more radical or critical speeches. So the Soviet public, through the media, got a quite unusual view of real politics. To a reader of reports of conferences or congresses held in the past fifty years and more, the contrast is truly astonishing.

For many decades the dismissal of senior Party officials was seldom explained, and never had the "victims" the opportunity to explain or defend themselves. There is a long list of members of the Politbureau, or ministers, dismissed under Khrushchev and under Brezhnev: Kirichenko, Aristov, Belyaev, Pogdorny, Polyansky, and so on. No reason was given. (At least in the case of Molotov, Malenkov, and Kaganovich, Khrushchev characterised them as an "anti-Party group", giving them no chance to reply, of course.) Was Gorbachev going to be different? At first it seemed he was not. Out went Grishin and Romanov, with no reason given. Then in November 1987 came the Yeltsin case. Yeltsin, alternate member of the

Politbureau and secretary of the Moscow Party, an outspoken opponent of privilege and corruption, made an apparently tactless speech at a Central Committee plenum and was sacked. Rumours spread about what had occurred, and there were even some pro-Yeltsin unofficial demonstrations in Moscow, but no explanation, no text of his or anyone else's speech was published. This attracted criticism and public protests, this was not *glasnost'*. It was evidently decided that this was a mistake. So Yeltsin was given the floor at the 19th Party conference, where he made a long defence of his position, and of having given an interview to the BBC and other foreign journalists. He ended by an appeal to the conference for his political rehabilitation. Several speakers commented, mostly unfavourably. Ligachev criticised him severely, and at the end Gorbachev spoke at length to explain what had transpired at the meeting which led to Yeltsin's dismissal. This was all carried by the Soviet news media.

Nor was Gorbachev immune to criticism. His own proposals for limiting the length of time high office could he held, for combining the offices of local Party secretary and chairman of the local soviet in one person, and for redefining the role of the Party itself were the subject of openly expressed doubts, queries, and concern. So were the totally new proposals, put to the conference by Gorbachev, about a new kind of legislature: a congress of people's representatives plus a smaller and apparently full-time Supreme Soviet, and a president, which would be a post of real power (unlike the one held by Gromyko) and no doubt intended for whoever is at that moment the leader of the Party. This is not the place or time (it is premature) to speculate on how a reformed system would or could function. The point is that it was put forward as a proposal, by the general secretary himself, and that this did not prevent several delegates from saying that this was new to them, they needed time to consider the implications, that they had doubts.

Reading the press account of the discussions, one felt that this was quite a different world to the one we had known, when speeches followed a set pattern, as did the editorials of *Pravda*: a list of achievements, some criticism of shortcomings (preceded usually by the word *odnako*, 'however'), and a coda promising an onward march to victory, interspersed with praise for the general secretary. Nothing like this at the 19th Congress.

The number of examples which could be quoted could fill a book. It is worth first citing here the speech by the chairman of the Theatre Association and a leading actor, M. Ulyanov (*Pravda*, 30 June 1988). First about bureaucrats: "What is this invisible and untouchable creature? Everyone knows him but no one actually sees him.

Like the mythical snowman. . . . As if it is the Evil spirit, as they used to say in the old days. Well, yes, in those days men were ignorant, though they worked hard, fed themselves too, though they believed in evil spirits! [laughter, applause]." He went on: "Why is the bureaucrat all-powerful? Because he wins not through logic, not through a good decision, but by the power he has acquired. Having seized power he surrounds himself with men like him, and will not part with his power to anyone. This is what the *nomenklatura* has been invented for, this is a caste which cannot be touched. . . . Hence the astonishing adaptability and unsinkable nature of the *nomenklatura*, hence also the stifling of talent, since comparisons are odious." There could still be a resurgence of a cruel "cult". "Why not? Do we have today legal, juridical, political, constitutional guarantees . . . , laws that would protect us from possible uncontrolled arbitrary rule [*administrirovaniya*]. . . . No." He advocated a search for effective legal guarantees. Furthermore, he went on, there is a lesson to be learned from "the bitter and frightening affair of the article by Nina Andreyeva" [in *Sovetskaya Rossiya*]. "This article left us in a state of shock [*vrasplokh*]. Many, not all, but many, already stood to attention and awaited the next order." At this point Gorbachev interrupted: "Mikhail Alexandrovich [Ulyanov], she has written a letter. We just got it now. The members of the Presidium [of the conference] will read it. She holds to her view." Ulyanov continued: "Well, you see! The point is not her, the point is how her letter scared us. It is this that is frightening [applause]. If instructions had been issued, many would instantly rush to carry them out, without thought or hesitation. Since [the article] had appeared in a newspaper, then it was seen as an instruction. So even if they were upset, the vast majority stood still and waited for directions. . . . Were it not for the article in *Pravda* [which attacked Andreyeva], which shook up the hesitant, the silent, the expectant, how do you think today's conference would have gone? That is the depth to which the habits of obedience has eaten into us!"

Ulyanov went on to speak very strongly about the "heavy hand of the provincial and republican leadership" and the overdependence on them of the press. "We have a one-party system, but in nature everything is based on the struggle between opposites. So here we need the press. . . . Yet a speaker at this conference rostrum said 'some journalist dared to criticise an elected official'. One can lose faith in *perestroika* after such declarations!" Gorbachev in his interjection supported "a pluralism of opinion"—in itself a remarkable phrase, first heard in speeches and articles in 1987 (before then, "pluralism" was treated as an unacceptable bourgeois notion).

Ulyanov ended with a reference to the hopes raised by the Khrush-́chevian "thaw", dashed under Brezhnev, when there occurred "the monstrous flowering of corruption, bribery, ignorance and simply primitive behaviour, which expressed itself in a shameful game of awarding each other medals". No wonder people took to drink. There must not be yet another disappointment.

Although Ulyanov's was a particularly colourful peroration (one must bear in mind his eminence as an actor), there were plenty of other "meaty" speeches. Thus, Yeltsin not only defended his record—he stated that the proposal to combine the role of Party secretary with the leadership of the local soviet "was so unexpected that a worker who spoke here said that 'he cannot yet understand it'. I as a minister can say: 'Me neither.' . . . This is too complex a question. I would like to suggest an all-people's referendum on the issue [applause] [*sic*]." Then he said (*and* it was fully reported): "We have become accustomed to blame the dead. Especially as there will be no comeback. Now stagnation is blamed just on Brezhnev. And where were those who for 10, 15, 20 years, were in the Politbureau and are still there? . . . They voted for a fifth star for one man [yet another Order of Lenin for Brezhnev] and allowed a crisis in society as a whole. Why was the sick Chernenko nominated [as leader]?" He then accused Solomentsev, then a member of the Politbureau, of failing to take action against senior officials who had become "bribe-taking millionaires". He spoke of a "deep-lying rot" and of "a mafia which, I know from my Moscow experiences, definitely exists". "We can be proud of socialism . . . , but in 70 years we have not settled the main questions: to feed and clothe the people, provide services, resolve social issues." There are still (he said) some "secret" questions, such as the Party's own budget. One sees "luxury houses, villas, sanatoria on such a scale that one feels ashamed when representatives of other parties [from abroad] go there". He went on: "In my opinion if something is lacking in a socialist society, then this must be felt by all without exception [applause]. Differences in labour input should be regulated by differences in pay. We must, finally, liquidate the food parcels for, so to speak, the 'starving *nomenklatura*'." (Not many years ago, the very existence of *nomen-klatura*, the very word, was hardly ever allowed to appear in print.)

When Ligachev spoke, before turning to sharp criticism of Yeltsin, he criticised what he considered to be excesses in historical writing: "Can we agree with the presentation of Soviet people—in our own printed publications!—as if they were slaves, fed only by lies and demagogy and subject to pitiless exploitation?" He also said that in his own family some were shot and expelled, and he echoed

Yeltsin in his description of the Brezhnev period: "Our country was moving into crisis, widespread was abuse of power, corruption, bribery, discipline slackened, drunkenness ate into our society, our international standing declined. And at the very top there was moral degeneration. . . . The party faced grave danger." In March 1985, when Gorbachev was elected, "there could have been quite different decisions. There was such a real danger. . . . Thanks to the firm position taken up by Politbureau members Chebrikov, Solomentsev, Gromyko and of a large group of first secretaries of *obkomy* [provincial committees], the March plenum took the only correct course." (In other words, Gorbachev's election was a close-run thing.) S. Kondrashev, writing in *Moskovskie novosti* (26 June 1988), stated that it was widely believed that the alternative candidate was V. Grishin, "who had an unsavoury reputation among muscovites". In the end "we, supporters of *perestroika* were lucky". Ligachev vigorously criticised Yeltsin's record. He did not avoid the issue of privileges of officials. Official data on this should be published, he said, so people know the truth, rather than "the ersatz from *Moskovskie novosti*". (!) As for pay, the average pay of Party officials he gave as 216 roubles a month (little more than the average wage for the country as a whole), and anyone elected to work in Party organs loses money if transferred from specialist duties in the economy. "For this reason, it must be said, the quality of Party officials declines." Another delegate, Saransky, had made the same point. And, indeed, by implication so had Yeltsin; the problem is hidden perks, not pay; the perks make up for the modest pay.

A truly original and challenging notion was put to the 19th Party Conference by a science administrator, G. Zagainov. Not only did he advocate a maximum of two five-year spells in high office, but he urged "competitive elections, with direct secret ballot. For the general secretary and members of the Politbureau, with the obligation for [candidates for election] to publish their programme. And it would be excellent if their views as to the solution of this or that problem in some respects differed. Outstanding characters with different life-experiences would naturally have their own specific points of view. Unfortunately members of the Politbureau, the secretaries, tend to speak on specific issues, which does not permit us to judge their general [policy] position." He considered that *Pravda* should be the organ of the Party as a whole, and not of the Central Committee, and that its editorial board should be elected by the Party Congress, so that the paper would feel able to criticise members of the Central Committee. There should be an end to cooptation to high positions. Democracy, he said, also requires the emergence, along with the formal leadership, of "informal leaders", and he cited as an example Churchill's influence in the years in which he held no office.

I would like to add a small but significant additional point. A worker, V. Nizhelsky, was speaking. Gorbachev twice interjected remarks, whereupon the speaker said: "Do not interrupt me [*ne sbivaite*], this is my first speech from such a rostrum". Unimaginable a few years ago!

The Supreme Soviet meeting in Novembver 1988, its last under the old constitution, saw all the resolutions pass, but not all the votes were unanimous. The reported speeches were far more critical and business-like than on any previous occasion.

Let me now pick up Ulyanov's plea for real legal guarantees, and turn to the question of legality, justice, observance of the law, and equality before the law. On this vitally important subject much has been written and spoken. One of the most forthright of the critics has been Arkadi Vaksberg, writing mainly in *Literaturnaya gazeta*. The satirical *Krokodil* also joined in. A cartoon showed a judge and his two assessors in the room to which they retire to consider their verdict. In front of them is a telephone. One of them says: "The telephone does not ring. We will have to decide the verdict ourselves." Vaksberg, in one of his articles, specifically mentions the existence of a direct telephone line to the judge's room from the Party secretary's. The Constitution states: the judges are independent and subordinate only to law (*podchinyayutsa tolko zakonu*). A Soviet satirist rewrote these three words: *podchinyayutsa tolko raikomu*, are subordinate only to the district Party committee. This situation is now openly talked and written about, reflected in the ironic phrase "telephone law". To his credit, the chairman of the High Court, Terebilov, has joined in the debate, as we shall see.

First, Vaksberg. On 30 December 1986 in *Literaturnaya gazeta*, he took up with most unusual frankness the weak spots in Soviet criminal justice: the domination of the prosecution (procuracy), the almost total absence of not-guilty verdicts, the dependence of the judge on local Party officials, the low level of knowledge of the law, failure to heed the principle that the prisoner must be proved guilty (in Soviet law as in many others the "presumption of innocence" exists, in that it is for the prosecution to prove its case, but in practice this has not been so). Defence lawyers have little status, influence, or pay. He cited an instance when the accused said in court that his confession had been made under extreme duress: he was beaten. The man was found guilty as charged. Asked why she

did not heed his claim that his confession had been beaten out of
him, one of the two assessors, who sit with the judge, replied with
charming naiveté: "But unless they are beaten, would the accused
confess?" The procuracy was shown to be less than scrupulous in
pressing charges, and proof of injustices did not lead to any
consequences for those guilty of them. The whole tone of the article,
the many examples quoted, pointed to a harsh verdict on Soviet
justice.

He returned to the charge in *Literaturnaya gazeta* of 27 January
1988, in an article devoted primarily to a denunciation of the sinister
Andrei Vyshinsky, the prosecutor in the Moscow trials of the thirties
and active collaborator in the Terror. The details of Vyshinsky's
odious career need not concern us. It is, however, worth quoting the
story behind the article's publication. It was preceded with an
editorial note as follows: "Recently the French newspaper *Le
Monde* published the following: 'during a discussion evening . . . in
Moscow, the Soviet playwright Shatrov stated that an article on the
procurator-general Andrei Vyshinsky . . . which was to have been
published in the next number of *Literaturnaya gazeta*, has been
banned by the official censorship. "I am much concerned about the
fate of *perestroika*," said Mikhail Shatrov in the presence of several
hundred people, mostly intelligentsia, waving [the manuscript of]
the article by Arkadi Vaksberg. This incident . . . did take place. But
for what purpose did the secretary of the executive of the Union of
Writers M. Shatrov 'wave' the article which was not yet ready for
the press!? He should have telephoned, and would have learned that
it was subject to normal editorial work. . . . Now it has been
completed and the article is herewith presented to the readers'
attention. We hope that '*Le Monde*' will report this."

I heard from a most reliable source in Moscow that Shatrov's
speech before an audience which included not only a French
correspondent but also a U.S. senator, helped to secure publication. I
naturally asked why. Surely to attack Vyshinsky cannot be ill
regarded, since the phoniness of the Moscow trials is openly
recognised? I was told that, so to speak, the sting was in the tail.
Having finished with Vyshinsky, Vaksberg quoted some of those
who joined him in kicking and abusing his victims. Thus, the literary
critic Lev Nikulin on Bukharin: "animal-like monster",
"comedian", "pseudo-simpleton cheat", "shaking little tenor",
"pulls faces", "strikes poses like a provincial tenor", (what a master
of words!!). Others on the same page of the newspaper denounced
the accused as "typhus lice" and "bloody monkeys". He went on:
"Why do I recall all this today? To settle belated accounts [with such

men]? To tickle the nerves? No, of course not, I do so to observe the origins of those deformations from which we strive to cleanse ourselves today."

Vaksberg then went on to cite more examples of injustices, of improper acts by the procuracy *now*, and he repeatedly pointed out that this has its origins "in those days". Thus:

> When today we are compelled to return to the most elementary juridical principles, to their most basic norms, without which there can be neither law nor justice, when we combat the accusatory deviation with the priority of statements obtained in the preliminary investigation, without observation of the necessary rights for the accused, when we repeatedly try to discredit the so-called queen of proof [*tsaritsy dokazatel'stv*], the admission of his own guilt by the accused, when we do all this, what are we combating? "Some mistakes" and "certain deficiencies"? The inability of some jurists to understand current instructions? No, it is the whole outlook, which creeps up on us from those days. A couple of years ago one prominent juridical functionary, speaking in a very respectable auditorium, replying to a journalist's question, described the presumption of innocence as "bourgeois rubbish". I think he spoke sincerely and genuinely, using terms which entered firmly into his psyche. After all, he studied in the forties, and probably studied conscientiously, and this is what was taught then.

Vyshinsky's book, *The Theory of Judicial Proof in Soviet Law*, "contains much that today sounds unthinkable, incredible, but they were the juridical bible of thousands of lawyers who practice still today". There one learns that statements and confessions of the accused "have the character and significance of basic, most important and decisive proof", that "the principle of two opposing sides, and that of equality in the process of accusation and defence, are bourgeois survivals". In recent years, Vaksberg goes on, there have been cases where the investigators committed "grievous illegalities", and "the accused spoke . . . of beatings, threats, blackmail", whereupon the court's reaction was invariably "that this is a slander on our glorious investigatory organs. Whence this indestructible and criminal procedure. From those days. . . . "

Clearly, it is these passages in the article which could well have caused the editors to hesitate about publishing it. Shatrov's manoeuvre evidently helped to overcome these hesitations!

Vaksberg published another article in *Literaturnaya gazeta* (4 May 1988) under the general rubric "morality and law", following readers' letters stimulated by his attack on Vyshinsky. Some were hostile to Vaksberg, and praised "the great Vyshinsky." Several

asked for more details as to how he and his like dealt with major
cultural figures, and it is in response to this that Vaksberg wrote
about the grim fate of Meyerhold, Babel, and Koltsov (see Chapter
4). He again reminds us that unjust "justice" did not cease with
Stalin's death. He cites the case of Khudenko, "who perished in
prison, victim of lies and insults": he was the man who ran a
successful state farm in Kazakhstan and was sentenced for breach of
regulations, because he used effective incentives to motivate the
labour force in ways which, as will be seen in Chapter 8, are now
regarded as right and necessary. No, he insists, this and other
deplorable cases of recent decades are not a rerun of "1937", but
"the habit of obediently implementing someone's hasty opinion,
without taking into account the real interests of society, become for
some jurists a sort of second nature, . . . a stereotype of professional
behaviour. The country has to pay too high a price for this." He ends
with some fine words:

> Fidelity to the law requires courage and conviction, to reject any
> pressures, any illegal order. Otherwise an honest man should resign, to
> find a job which does not require heroism and excessive risk. The
> constitutional principle that "Judges are independent and subject only to
> the Law" ends with a full stop. It does not continue with the words "and
> also to those who place themselves above the law". If there are those who
> are above [the law], then there is no legality, no fairness. There is no
> justice.

Another article by the same author, in *Literaturnaya gazeta* of 18
May 1988, takes as its subject the career and the fall of Nikolai
Shchelokov, formerly minister of the interior and in that capacity in
charge of the regular (not the secret) police, among many other
things. All that the public knew of him was that, having been a
Brezhnev protégé (Brezhnev nominated his son-in-law, Churbanov,
as his first deputy), he was dismissed and stripped of the rank of
general. The rest was (almost) silence. Press reports did speak of
abuses and misappropriation, but few knew any more.

Vaksberg then refers to over a hundred volumes of court materials
and evidence about Shchelokov and other corrupt senior officials of
the Ministry. The Ministry received nine imported cars for official
use. One Mercedes went to the minister, one to his son, a third one
to his daughter, a BMW to his wife. The police discovered a criminal
who had illegally acquired works of art of great value, museum
pieces. Out of 73 objects, 53 were acquired by the minister (value:
250,000 roubles). He ordered the import of crystal chandeliers, at
the Ministry's cost, for himself, his family, his friends. He acquired a

number of apartments, including one for his son's sexual adventures, and also for his personal dentist, his personal tailor, and so on. His personal masseur was on the books as a research worker in a ministerial institute, and his daughter's servant was also on the Ministry's payroll. He "acquired" old books from a library. In two years, 36,000 roubles were spent on flowers for the family. A solid gold watch, nominally a gift to a visiting foreign potentate, was presented to him on his birthday. The ministry spent 42,000 roubles on fur coats for his family in just three years. And so on and so forth.

Vaksberg asks: How could such a man have acquired vast power, "decided the fate of thousands (or more)"? Can it be explained by the temptation of power, by "degeneration"? But this man "succumbed to temptation" for years, repeatedly. He goes back to history, to the victims of the Terror of the thirties. "Not only the direct victims, the millions of innocents who perished in those years, but the indirect [consequences], the locusts who flew in to eat up the people's wealth, corrupted ignoramuses, who grabbed power, rushing in to take the place of those slandered and killed. These were ignorant swindlers, who tried to impose their 'culture', their 'morality', their way of life". For them ideological phrases are a sort of cover, "rules of the game", no more, a means to rise where they can enjoy the dolce vita. There was no "degeneration"—such people remain themselves. Shchelokov's son was already made the head of the international department of the Central Committee of the Komsomol (communist youth), without the slightest qualification for the job, "not even the pretence of one". The orgies he held in his apartment were videotaped, presumably by him, and may be seen. The son also had allocated to him (the Moscow soviet certified him as in "most urgent need") a building site near Moscow, and the ministry paid for the construction of a luxury villa, which, however, was not completed when Brezhnev died. Investigations into fraud and misappropriation at lower levels—previously blocked—led to Shchelokov himself. First his wife and then he committed suicide, so it ended tragically. Vaksberg asks questions about how such people, and their children, get appointed and promoted—indeed, how appointments and promotions were decided (in secret), and by whom.

It appears that Brezhnev's son-in-law, Churbanov, is alive but not well: he has been tried and sentenced.

This was one prominent case, the subject of the kind of investigative journalism which is in itself a product of *glasnost'*. Vaksberg states that, before his suicide, Shchelokov complained bitterly of unfairness: no doubt he felt singled out—others in his milieu were doing the same, by all reports no one more so than Brezhnev himself; Shchelokov followed their example. This brings me to the question of degeneration of elites, but first let us complete our survey of questions of law and legality.

Terebilov, the chairman of the Supreme Court, had much to say on the subject in *Literaturnaya gazeta* (27 Apr. 1988). Judges' status must be raised, they must be protected from being punished by local organs of power, who should in no circumstances issue them any instructions. Indeed, this should be an offence in law, according to Terebilov.

The desirability of restoring trial by jury, introduced in Russia in 1864, and the superiority of a jury system to the existing judge and two assessors were argued by Z. Chernilovsky in *Sovetskoe gosudarstvo i pravo* (No. 9, 1987) and by I. Gryazin in *Novyi mir* (No. 8, 1988). The latter points out that lack of legal guarantees were to some extent compensated for by bureaucratic inefficiency ("not all private cattle were destroyed, not all 'enemies of the people' were sent to Siberia or shot, maize was not everywhere sown and not all flower-sellers were arrested"). The author stresses that the Constitution in its present form has no juridical force or status. Radical change is necessary to establish a true legal order. The right to demonstrate should be clearly set out, and should not depend on who happens to be on duty at the militia headquarters.

In *Ogonyok* (No. 43, 1988), A. Yakovlev discusses the many inadequacies of the present legal system. Thus, he points out that the so-called rights of enterprises, cooperatives, and family leaseholders cannot be real if they are dependent on administered allocation. Freedom depends on the right to *sell* (rather than on the obligation to *deliver*) and to *buy* (rather than merely receiving what is allocated). He also urges the replacement of the two assessors who sit with the judge by a more numerous "jury" (*prisyazhnye*).

In *Pravda* (23 June 1988), B. Lazarev took up the question of how to establish a legal order, a law-based state. Up until now, many important social relations have been governed not by laws but by government decisions and departmental normative acts. For example, there are no laws on the procedures of planning, or price fixing. There is "lack of legal culture among government officials and economic directors, which is inconsistent with the idea of a legal order."

The Party's journal, *Kommunist* (No. 2, 1988), continued a discussion on law and *perestroika* begun in three of its last issues in 1987. The main contributor was the same B. Lazarev. He "accepts the notion of a general legal reform with considerable fears.

Of course we must cleanse the Augean stables and bring law into line with the new social requirements. But every time the basic question is one of implementing laws. How would this be done and by whom? . . . Alas, the general level of political and legal culture today" worries him. It is said that "everything should be allowed that is not forbidden", but clearly this principle cannot apply to the actions of officials, who should follow a different principle: only that is allowed which is permitted. In any case "our laws have many gaps". Lazarev advocates a constitutional court, since the procuracy is "evidently helpless faced with departmental illegality [*vedomst-vennym bezzakoniyakh*]". He too stands firmly for "real and not pseudoautonomy of the juridical organs".

A. Agsamkhodzhayev (Uzbekistan) spoke of "exaggeration of achievements, a tendency to present what should be as what is, which, to our general regret, found its expression in the Consti-tution. Can we really fully agree that in the USSR there is a mature socialist society?" He was unhappy with amendments to the law, not yet operational, concerning the rights of citizens to appeal against illegal official acts. Lawyers have too little influence in the drafting of legislation. Local soviets interpret in various ways the formal rights of citizens to hold meetings and demonstrations. The law should give citizens the right to information.

The Western press reported the roughing up of demonstrators in Moscow on the tenth anniversary of the invasion of Czechoslovakia. Unusually, this episode was critically reported in *Moskovskie novosti* of 4 September 1988, with reference to some tough men in grey who seized some of the demonstrators. The author of this report (L. Miloslavsky) put questions to a local militia colonel and recounted the experiences of a demonstrator who had been arrested.

V. Chernyshev, for the Collegium of (defence) Advocates, protests about forced confessions, literally "beaten out of" the accused, and no one was and is held responsible either for the beating or for sentencing innocent people. "Who will answer for the fact that for years these people were incarcerated? . . . Such facts are too frequent to be ignored." He mentions "the chase after a high percentage of solved crimes" as a motive for illegal behaviour of the prosecution. He asks—as do others—for defence counsel to be given access to the accused as soon as he or she is interrogated. He also says that defence lawyers should be better paid, should have more facilities.

While the horrors of prisons and labour camps under Stalin have been freely described recently, the same was not true of prisons and labour camps (now known as "colonies") until today. Now, this taboo is also disappearing. For example, *Izvestiya* (4 and 7 Aug.

1988) recently made far-reaching criticisms of harsh conditions, arbitrary punishments, and illegalities, as when a good worker's release is prevented by the camp administration of trivial breaches of regulations. It was pointed out that putting the so-called colonies on *khozraschyot* made matters worse, since there is an economic incentive to overwork the prisoners. Detainees, too, must have legal rights. This must be seen as part of the theme of "the rule of law", which turns up in the press repeatedly. Needless to say, none of this guarantees that the abuses described will be ended, but publicity is, as the French say, a *condition préalable*.

In *Moskovskie novosti* (14 Aug. 1988), Yuri Feofanov discusses "The Mafia—inevitable or paradoxical". Why, he asks, has our own mafia suddenly come to light, complete with gangs, protection rackets, murders, even "lavish funerals" of victims? But "the most dreadful are the links between criminal gangs and the bribe-takers, the close contact [*srashchivaniye*, literally, "growing together"] of the criminal elements with the corrupted governing apparatus". Examples cited by Feofanov include the Uzbek party apparatus and Brezhnev's family, his daughter Galina in particular. He cites *Nedelya* as to the "price" actually paid to obtain the gold star of Hero of Socialist Labour: up to one million roubles. He notes that under Stalin, Hitler, and Mussolini (named together in one paragraph!) in "totalitarian regimes", organized crime was effectively combated. There is a temptation now to deal with the corrupt and criminal elements by ignoring legal guarantees, the presumption of innocence. This should, in Feofanov's view, be resisted. A legal order is essential, and the Soviet mafia should be dealt with without the transgression of the law by authorities. In *Ogonyok*, T. Gdlyan, who has played a leading role in investigating official corruption, pointed out that some of the delegates to the 19th Party Conference took bribes, and spoke of the "vast network of corruption" which is gradually being revealed.

This is not the place to discuss the proposals, which surprised many delegates, which Gorbachev made at the conference concerning constitutional reform. What is remarkable in the present context is the anticipation of his proposals in an article by F. Burlatsky published two weeks earlier, in *Literaturnaya gazeta* of 15 June 1988, entitled "On Soviet Parliamentarism". There he argued for an elected president, who should also be the leader of the Party, with a cabinet whose names he would submit to a properly functioning Supreme Soviet parliament (full-time), with a constitutional court. He stated that Khrushchev had already considered these ideas. He asserted that leaders should have skills in theory and oratory. He also wrote: "Russia had some elements of a democratic tradition (peasant communes, *zemstvos*, the duma) but never had a liberal one, i.e., individual freedom from state intervention, there was no concept of the inalienable rights of Man. It was and is considered that we are all servants of the state." (I recall how the late Leonard Schapiro used to deplore the lack of legal sense and traditions in Russia, pre- and post-1917.)

Gorbachev's own speech to the 19th Party Conference is available in translations, but some references to it are necessary in the context of the discussion of legality. He noted that "the existing political system was for decades adapted not to the organization of social life within the bounds of laws, but mainly to the implementation of willful [arbitrary, *volevykh*] instructions and orders. . . . It is this ossified power system, and its command-and-pressure methods, that today stand before the basic problems of *perestroika*." High on his list of "democratising" reforms is the need "radically to strengthen socialist legality and the legal order, so as to exclude the possibility of usurpation of power, to stand up effectively against bureaucracy and formalism, to establish guarantees for the constitutional rights and liberties of citizens, as well as the carrying out by them of obligations to society and the state".

He spoke of a new law in draft on religion, and of new laws on personal freedoms, the right to take officials to court for illegal acts, the rights of the mentally handicapped, punishment for those who try to suppress criticism, and also of action against thieves, slanderers, and hooligans. He clearly rejected the notion of allowing the creation of "opposition parties", to "prolonged applause". However, the most important passage in the present context was headed "The Formation of a Socialist Legal State" (the German *Rechtstaat* is a more accurate rendering of *pravovoye godudarstvo*). Criticising the existing system, its "multiplicity of prohibitions and petty regulation", he enunciated the principle that "all is allowed that the law does not forbid". He echoed Terebilov in stressing the need for judges to be genuinely independent, proposing their election for ten years by superior-level soviets. Using language that could have been written by Vaksberg, he spoke of the need for measures to prevent "lack of respect for the court, interference with its activities", and "the strictest adherence to such democratic judicial principles as a contest [*sostyazatelnost'*] and equality between the contending sides, openness, the exclusion of prejudice, of the accusatory deviation [i.e., the court's assumption that the prosecution is right], the full realization of the principle of the presumption of innocence".

Gorbachev put forward, as is known, far-reaching proposals for reforming the Supreme Soviet, the government, the institution of the presidency, and on the role of the Party, and of local soviets, plus a proposal for a constitutional court and a time limit on holding office. It is not the task of the present book to analyze or even to list these proposals, important though they undoubtedly are. For our present purpose, what is significant is the *way* they were proposed, and the response to them. Some of the proposals had been published previously as "theses" for the conference; others were new. They were put forward so that they could be discussed, and discussed they were. If there were some puzzling features, notably, affecting the role of the Party functionaries, this found its due expression in frank comments. Does one free the local Party secretary from everyday interference in the affairs of the local authority (the soviet) by making him a sort of *ex officio* chairman of that body? Can this release him for the more purely political tasks which the Party ought to be performing? At the centre, should the economic departments of the Central Committee apparatus be abolished (as Yeltsin proposed)? How is the function of selecting cadres, the entire *nomenklatura* system, to be reconciled with genuine elections? Yeltsin's critical remarks have been cited already. Others, like Usmanov, secretary of the Tatar *obkom*, expressed colleagues' doubts about combining the first secretaryship and the leadership of the soviet at local levels.

In the preconference discussion, too, the role of the Party functionary figured prominently, as did the relative powerlessness of the soviets at all levels. Indeed, the old slogan was deliberately revived: "All power to the Soviets"; or, to cite the title of an interview with a local Party secretary (A. Muranov) reported in *Moskovskie novosti* (26 June 1988), "Give power back to the people." The issues raised were not only the Party's domination, but also the domination within the Party of the functionary, the full-time official: "It is necessary that the Party organization be led not by its apparatus, but by the committee elected by the communists", with a sharp reduction in the size of the apparatus. The local soviets are powerless, asserted several authors and conference speakers, also because they have no independent sources of revenue, and because the economic enterprises located on their territory ignore them and are subordinate to distant ministries. Several Party officials have stated publicly that their "interference" is forced: without it nothing would get done. So we have official proposals to provide financial "teeth" to the local soviets at various levels by providing for them a share in the revenues of enterprises, with proposals for giving the local soviets some authority over them, though this at once raises the complex question of the powers of the economic ministries to which these enterprises are subordinated, an issue to be discussed in the next chapter. The ecological damage done, especially pollution of air and water by industry, is a matter of particular concern, and was raised by several speakers at the Party Conference.

In the discussions around the conference, much has been said about the undemocratic and authoritarian procedures of the Party itself, vis-à-vis its own members. An example: Felix Dymov (*Literaturnaya Rossiya*, 17 June 1988) speaks of Party "officials who rush past us in black 'Volgas', frequently receive apartments without regard to rules and waiting-lists, and usurp the right to express at Party forums the opinions of millions of communists". He asks: "How much money from the Party exchequer goes to pay the apparatus? How much to maintain official cars, garages, the *dachi* [villas] hidden from view and from criticism? How much is spent on special hospitals, sanatoria and rest-homes for the elect? . . . Why is there no published budget for the Party, the Komsomol, the trade unions? Maybe I am being naive, and until recently such questions were banned and even dangerous. But why in the twenty years of membership of the Party did no one report to me? . . . What organization should I have been in so that I, and the majority of its members, could approve the expenditures of the *raikom*, or *obkom*, not to speak of the CC [Central Committee]?" Openness would help get rid of rumours, such as that "the Party apparatus has distributed to it not only scarce goods but also gets them at reduced prices". This was before Gorbachev, speaking at the conference, spoke at length about "deformations within the Party itself", the need for democratisation of its procedures, including genuine elections to Party committees at all levels, with more candidates than there are vacancies, and so on.

A popular monthly, *Strana i mir* (No. 3, 1988), recently reproduced on successive pages a notice from the town of Bryansk announcing the issue of sugar rationing coupons (1.5 kilograms per head per month), and the lavish menu of the buffet restaurant of the Central Committee, which not only provides vast choices but has low prices (thus cake which costs 22 kopecks in an ordinary restaurant is here priced at 11 kopecks; the author adds sarcastically that "this is no doubt due to the superior quality of the cake in the workers' eating-house"). The menu is that of the general dining room of the employees of the Central Committee; "what the [party] secretaries eat we do not yet know".

In contrast, *Literaturnaya gazeta* (7 Sept. 1988) published an article about an *obkom* Party secretary, Braun, an ethnic German (whose father perished in the purges), who cited his salary as 550 roubles a month ("directors of state farms can expect to earn 700"). He stated that all special shops had been closed in his area.

One party or several? Formerly a taboo subject, this is now recognised as a question which can be asked, even if the media give to it but one answer. The following, from an interview with Muranov, is typical: "In the West among the reasons given for the slow development of Soviet society is the fact that there is only one party. It has been, so they say, in power all the time, hence 'stagnation'. Maybe we need an opposition party?" The reply was in the negative, with the view expressed that "the important thing is not a multiplicity of parties but the multiplicity of opinions".

It used to be regarded as a key element of "Soviet ideology" that no organizations be allowed that are not under Party control. Attempts to set up even unofficial discussion groups usually met with police intervention. Even during the Khrushchevian "thaw", participants in such a group in Leningrad found themselves in prison (see Boris Veil's *Osobo opasnyi*, published in the West in 1980). Here again, times have changed. There is even a law on unofficial organizations, a law whose interpretation is beset by ambiguities, but nonetheless the existence of such groups is recognised. To take one example which shows both the scale of change and its ambiguities, Boris Kagarlitsky served a prison sentence in Brezhnev's time for setting up an unauthorized (socialist) group. In 1986–88 he and his colleagues have met repeatedly, he has met visiting foreigners (including me) without hindrance, he has had articles published in the West (e.g., in *New Left Review* and the *Times Literary Supplement*), and his contribution to a discussion on today's problems was published by *EKO*, the excellent economic monthly published in Novosibirsk. However, his attempt in January 1988 to run a national conference ran into obstructions, and *Pravda* published a quite sharp attack on him. However, this has not led to any arrests, and he and his colleagues are continuing their activities under the banner of a sort of left-wing critique of and support for *perestroika*. As was noted in Chapter 4, unofficial organizations have been flourishing in the Baltic republics. There are a great many others, with or without a political view. One must again mention *Pamyat'*, with its Russian-nationalism and anti-Semitic outlook and numerous local branches, several times sharply criticised in the press and tolerated all the same. (Freedom of speech, one must remember, involves also freedom for undesirable speech.) The Party itself and the Komsomol have initiated or blessed what could be called semiofficial organizations: women's groups, various sorts of youth clubs, charitable institutions. The line now is to recognise, indeed to extol, the virtues of "socialist pluralism". Yes, the word "socialist" is intended to set limits. However, Gorbachev (as we have seen) used the word "pluralism" at the 19th Party Conference without the adjective. In a Party forum, he may have taken "socialist" for granted, but it was a delegate to the conference who, in *Moskovskie novosti* of 26 June 1988, urged "leasing out the greatest possible number of enterprises, factories, workshops and to lease land to the peasants for 50 to 100 year periods", which does require a redefinition of socialism (which I, as the author of *The Economics of Feasible Socialism*, of course welcome).

The Baltic republics present an immediate and urgent constitutional problem. The rising tide of national and nationalist consciousness has found its reflection in the media, as has already been pointed out in Chapter 5. Here I will confine myself to drawing attention to the paragraph of the Soviet Constitution which permits the union republics to secede. It was known in the past that anyone who actually raised such a question would be subject to instant arrest. Now, however, we have *glasnost'*, much talk of a legal order and of strict observation of the Constitution, and freedom to hold meetings and form unofficial organizations. Large demonstrations in Vilnius, Riga, and Tallin have taken place without interference, and have been reported in the press. The old flags of these once-independent nations have reappeared. As I write these lines, I read that Estonia is switching its clocks from Moscow to Finnish time, one hour back. Naturally, people are questioning the myth of their having voluntarily joined the union in 1939–40, and demonstrations are specifically linked with such anniversaries as the mass deportations of April 1941 or the Molotov-Ribbentrop pact of 1939. The (new) Party leadership has, so far, gone along with this movement. But how soon will the limits be reached? Will "secessionists" be allowed to stand for election to soviets?

*Moskovskie novosti* (21 Aug. 1988) recently provided a detailed account of a contested election for the post of first deputy of the executive of the city soviet of Alma Ata. There was a public announcement inviting applications, and fourteen applied. A selection committee interviewed them and reduced the number to five. Each then published his "programme for the development of Alma Ata" in the local evening paper, addressed meetings, and appeared on television. Two of the five candidates chose to withdraw before the actual election. It was pointed out that the low pay that went with the job discouraged most managers from applying. The remaining three were voted on in a secret ballot by the soviet deputies; one was elected by 244 votes against 30 and 21, respectively. The winner was in fact a *raikom* secretary, i.e., a Party official, but he was genuinely *elected*, insisted the authors of the article.

The question of official or unofficial (or tolerated) organizations becomes politically significant in the context also of Gorbachev's proposal to have a new Congress of people's deputies, which would elect a smaller full-time Supreme Soviet. This Congress would meet annually, and would include representatives of "Party, trade union, cooperative, youth, women's, war-veterans, scientific, creative and other organizations", which will be listed in the (new) Constitution. There is debate as to who should or should not be on this list and how they should be elected.

Unofficial trade unions caused the authorities much trouble in Poland. To head off such an outcome, Soviet trade unions are urged to carry out their "protective" function more effectively. Thus the secretary of the trade unions, Shalayev, admitted, "We have become too accustomed to the thought that in our society there are no reasons for social conflicts, for workers' agitation [*vystupleniya*] in these connections. . . . The working masses demand from us a more principled position" in defence of their rights. He also said that some party organs "exclude the very thought of the independence of trade union organizations. They consider it proper to interfere directly in trade union affairs, down to attempts to place in trade union organs those officials who were incapable or had disgraced themselves in their previous jobs." Felix Dymov, in his already-cited article, was ruder: "As the sad experience of the previous half-century has shown, they [the trade unions] failed to defend either the interests or the lives of millions."

This may be the place to mention an ironic and pointed article by G. Popov on "The Reform"—not Gorbachev's, but Alexander II's, the freeing of the serfs in 1861 (*EKO*, No. 1, 1987). The point of the article, which explores the ups and downs of that reform process (giving due credit to the tsar), is that if those whose job it is to draft and implement reform measures happen to belong to a class which could lose by these reforms, this causes problems. Indeed it does!

The question of how the leadership and functionaries are selected and promoted has been an important subject for debate and criticism, as we have seen. Academics have been theorising about what can be called the degeneration of elites. This brings us, not for the first time, to the same G. Popov, whose two review-articles in *Nauka i zhizn'* have already been cited. It will be recalled that he used Onisimov/Tevosyan to show that devoted and uncorrupted executants were the product of pre-Stalinist times, that the Stalinist

"Administrative system" could not generate such persons, and also that the creative independent scientist ("Zubr") is alien to it, though essential for its functioning.

There was also an article even more directly concerned with elite degeneration, by A. Efimov, in another popular science journal, *Znanie-sila* of January 1988. Efimov admits being inspired by the Popov review of Bek's book, his concept of the "Administrative system, in which the corpus of leadership—the *nomenklatura*—is formed in accordance with its laws of functioning". Efimov tries mathematical modeling of evolutions, physical and social. He cites the example of St. Francis of Asissi, whose Franciscan order soon abandoned poverty to "become bankers to the Catholic church". How did the aging ascetic monks get replaced? Monks who eat better live longer! Or, to change the image, "Maradona will be pursued as soon as the referee blows his whistle, and his leg will be broken sooner than a lower-class footballer".

In life sometimes the best, sometimes the worst, are eliminated first. Efimov then returns to Popov, citing his words: men like Ordzhonikidze, Tevosyan, "Onisimov", "brought into the System their faith in the Party, their strict discipline and total devotion to the task. And while such cadres continued to exist, it functioned." Theirs was the standard to which others aspired. However, "the axe of repression" in the thirties removed most of them, they "disappeared into labour camps". The military purges eliminated the most able and independent-minded soldiers. The replacements tended to be of a lower quality. Appointments were made by recommendation and co-option, and in Efimov's model "the elite group suffers from inevitable degradation".

Such factors as personal devotion play a key role. Efimov assumes in his model that in any group there are, at the start, both real elite elements and some "weeds", at first only a few. In competitive sport, despite the example of Maradona's leg, the "weeds" tend to be eliminated by the force of competition. Personal links, "devotion to the manager or the chairman of the sports federation" matter little. "G. Kasparov is a member of the Central Committee [of the Komsomol] because he is a champion", and not vice versa. An elite group can remain such if its leader is of exceptional ability, has good connections 'above', and can select his own staff; Efimov's examples are Yoffe, Tupolev, and Korolev (yet all three had serious troubles with Beria's police!). In wartime, sheer necessity led to the rise of talent and demotion of the stupid, but once war was over "personal loyalty" became again a dominant criterion, and degeneration again set in.

Efimov goes on to discuss a model of a selection process in which subunits "delegate" upwards on a competitive basis, as when football teams "delegate" their best players to the national team. He sees an analogy here "to the system of parliamentary representation, including the tradition in a number of countries of obligatory replacement [reselection?] of deputies. The principle in accordance to which the persons exercising power tend to be approved by those over whom power is exercised, and not [co-opted by] fellow power-holders, is not only effective but is also socially just."

Mathematical games theory, Efimov goes on, knows the distinction between "coalitions" and "cliques". For instance, using an analogy, "a family brigade is a coalition, a group of bootlickers around a boss debilitated by flattery is a clique". Personal loyalty played such a large role in the selection process, and in the complex informal links within the system, that the hierarchy, which is supposed to be a coalition, degenerated. "As a result the *nomenklatura*, ceasing to be an elite, becomes a clique. I will allow myself the following hypothesis: degenerating elite groups, completing their evolution, become highly stable cliques. Stability, as is known, is a characteristic of systems with negative feedback. Sociologists should check this hypothesis." Here he refers to Rybakov's *Deti Arbata*: Stalin feared and hated cliques, personal informal links. "A historical paradox: Stalin created the system as an instrument of personal power and then all his life fought against it and feared it." To repeat a quotation used earlier, "the axe of repression was directed not at persons but at their links with each other". Stalin's last act, in the face of what he believed to be the excessive influence of members of his Politbureau, was, at the 19th Party Congress, "to abolish the Politbureau itself! We never saw the final act of the tragedy, as the leader died." Efimov ends on an optimistic note. While urging more research by sociologists, economists, jurists, and mathematicians, he notes that "the formation of elite groups not subject to degradation is in principle possible", and that "this gives ground for hope".

This chapter has ranged far and wide in the general areas of politics, sociology, and law. There are many other things to explore. One relates to the social services, especially health and education. The other concerns women. Each could do with a chapter to itself, but that is not possible, although not because of any lack of appreciation of the importance of both topics. Again, the material and quotations are selected primarily to demonstrate the degree of frankness with which such matters are now discussed. It is only in this indirect way that I will be casting any light on the problems in these areas. It is also important to note, here as elsewhere, that there is some danger that a listing of deficiencies, now so openly discussed, will add up to a distorted picture. There are some positive achievements too.

Let us start with women. Again, it would be wrong to pretend that there was silence before *glasnost'*. A whole list of publications can be assembled in which criticism was levied at the excessive use of female labour in heavy unskilled work, particularly (but not solely) in agriculture, the "double burden" of full-time work and looking after the home, the lack of help from menfolk, the weary task of queuing for food, and so on. It was also obvious that women tended to predominate in the less-well-paid sectors of the economy, and in the lower ranks of the professions, and that they were almost totally absent from the high political ranks, though these points were seldom analysed together. Stress was laid instead on Russia's first woman astronaut, and on the very high proportion of women among graduates and in many professions, and of course on legal equality.

An important step taken under Gorbachev in 1986 was the creation of a network of "women's councils". There used to be women's departments (*zhenotdely*) in the twenties, but they were liquidated in the early thirties, and the myth was propagated that women had no specific problems or grievances. Whereas at the time of the revolution there were women prominent in left-wing politics (Vera Zasulich, Vera Figner, Alexandra Kollontai, Maria Spiridonova, to name the most prominent), politics had become an almost totally male preserve under Stalin, and this continued under his successors. The last female member of the Politbureau, E. Furtseva, was, to put it mildly, not a success (she was for a while minister of culture). As Gorbachev remarked, drawing attention to the unsatisfactory position of recent years, there were no women ministers in Moscow, and very few women in the upper ranks of the Party apparatus (a recent appointment to the Party secretariat was A. Biryukova, who became deputy premier in September 1988).

Women's problems began to be increasingly discussed in such journals as *Literaturnaya gazeta*. But perhaps the best way of highlighting the way the issues have gone public is to cite the forthright speech of the head of the Committee of Soviet Women, Z. Pukhova (*Pravda*, 2 July 1988). She pulled no punches. She began well, by saying that people called her committee one for "defence of women. From whom?" There is still much to correct. "A huge number of women are used in heavy physical unmechanized labour. Almost 3½ million work in conditions which fail to satisfy the norms and regulations of labour protection. . . . Prematurely aged are rural women, working from dawn to dusk without days off or vacations, deprived of elementary social and living conveniences and the needed medical help. These are facts, which cause pain and concern." She herself worked for thirty years in the textile industry, where 80 percent of the labour force is female, and conditions include "excessive noise, humidity, dust, constant strain, more night shifts than elsewhere. . . . One cannot be silent about the fact that with equal rights for women there is still inequality, in qualifications and so in pay." Furthermore, some aspects of economic reform hurt women with children, who do not easily fit into the brigade-contract system, since they may need extra time off or work fewer hours. "We have at present 4 million women working on night shifts. In the basic labour laws it is stated that night shift work for women is forbidden, save as a temporary measure in case of acute necessity. . . . Is it not time to demand that the law be observed? The fact that laws are broken is shown by the fact that tens of thousands of women apply to our committee to seek redress. They complain that women on maternity leave are sacked, that pregnant women are not transferred to light work, efforts are made not to employ women with small children." Women have many legal rights, but there is no effective defence against denial of these rights. Puhkova does not favour quotas for women (*raznaryadki*), but their number in senior positions is far too small, she insists, and has actually fallen. Apart from there being no women ministers at all at the union level, "quite recently out of the 15 ministers of social security in the republics there were ten women, now there are four". Out of the total number of provincial Party secretaries, 7 percent are women, though women form 29 percent of the Party membership.

Pukhova refers to some press articles which asserted that women lose out through exhaustion at home and at work, that children get neglected, divorce rates rise, and that consequently women should return to the home. No, most women would want to work even if there was an adequate family income. The problem lies elsewhere: "Women are weary of queues, of shortages of foodstuffs, of consumers' goods. Transport works badly, especially in large cities, so there is much strain in going to and from work. Little help is provided for the family by the service sector—it is too under-developed, there are far too few services, and for many they cost too much." She also asks for better treatment for the minority that stay at home. "They do not possess many rights which working women have—old age pensions, sick pay, etc." She also puts in a plea for soldiers' widows, "whose pensions are extremely small". (I have in no way distorted the tone or balance of her speech, which dwelt overwhelmingly on unsolved problems and real grievances.)

Articles have appeared, for instance in *Moskovskie novosti* (14 Aug. 1988), under such titles as "On the Question of the Woman Question" (by Svetlana Kaidash), asking why there is no encyclopaedia or cultural history of women's lives and achievements in Russia. Norway and Great Britain have them. "Quite recently the representatives of one women's organization used to assert that there was no woman question in the Soviet Union", yet "it turned out that problems were in fact vast". Kaidash refers to many of them. In the same issue, Galina Yerofeyeva deplores the lack of women in high political ranks, and contrasts this with the West, referring to the recent nomination of one woman, Novozhilova, to the post of ambassador to Switzerland. (Yerofeyeva wishes Novozhilova luck, though she came from a quite undiplomatic background—unspecified.) Feminist issues, so long hidden, are very much in the public eye.

Women's issues are the subject of a growing number of published studies. A sociological survey by E. Novikova and others appeared in *EKO*, No. 8, 1988. Included in it are attitudes toward marriage and divorce, commitment to work and family, and women's relations with their husbands and with work colleagues. The survey shows that a great many women feel overburdened and guilty of neglecting the home and the family, with a high level of worry (*trevozhnost'*). The "harmonious association of work, family and children" was found in 14 percent of women workers, and not at all among engineer-technical staff. The survey was followed by an article by T. Boldyreva devoted to work conditions: again, too much nightwork (nominally forbidden for women), far too much lifting of heavy weights, noise, vibration, and poor ventilation, causing numerous gynaecological troubles, especially among textile and chemical workers. The vast majority of women in factories are in the unskilled grades; very few reach high rank. Boldyreva points to the large proportion of women in the lowest-paid occupations (light industry, trade, health, education, culture): "The vast majority of poorly-paid workers, i.e., earning less than 100 roubles a month, are women." Women still do three times more housework than men, as was the situation fifty years ago. As for work, "in 'women's' sectors and industries new equipment is particularly slow to arrive, small-scale mechanization is neglected. Far too often the women are given monetary compensation for working in unhealthy conditions, instead of putting these conditions right."

Work conditions were the subject of a powerful critical piece in

*Pravda* (14 Sept. 1988) by Yu. Barulina, who works in the ZIL car factory and is a Hero of Socialist Labour. Again, the same complaints: in her capacity as vice-chairman of the Soviet Women's Committee, and in her own experience, she sees evidence of unhealthy conditions, "close to 3½ million women work in circumstances contrary to the laws on labour protection, amid dust and bad air, with excessive noise and vibration". Women in storerooms carry excessively heavy weights. Machinery is designed with no attention to the women who have to operate it. "I know that I am speaking of what we all long have known. But we were silent for so long, pretending that these problems did not exist." As for women in villages, they "work from dawn to dusk, without days off or holidays, often deprived of the most elementary amenities or qualified medical help". In towns, too, the legal rights even of pregnant women are ignored.

A remarkable article in *Ogonyok* (No. 33, 1988), by Andrei Popov, a doctor, tackles the issue of abortion: he cites an estimate that in the USSR there are 8 million abortions annually, 25 percent of the world's estimated total, "6–10 times higher than in developed capitalist countries". But the real figures are higher still, since the 8 million mentioned excludes abortions outside of the hospital system; the real total could be 50 percent or even 100 percent higher. "Taking into account the unhospitalized abortion, every year not every tenth but every fifth woman of childbearing age has an abortion." Furthermore, the methods are crude, in many instances without anaesthetic. Popov reminds us that in 1936 a law forbade abortions and in effect contraceptives became unobtainable. Abortions were legalized in 1956, but contraceptives remain scarce and inefficient. So "abortions are the basic method of family planning in our country, and in this respect our country is unique even on a world scale."

Finally, here is a sad letter, featured on page one of *Pravda*, 14 August 1988:

My name is Loskutova Galina Sviridovna, born 1947, secondary technical education, machine-minder working on pump-equipment at the Troitsk power station. Three-shift work, with a mobile free day. Fifteen years of such work has ruined my digestive organs, I suffer from insomnia. The children have grown up without me, as their mother is either at work or asleep after the night shift. I have no apartment, I live with my parents, I have no husband. I cannot now leave the power station—my health does not allow heavy work, and for light work there are plenty of other takers. For many years I asked to be transferred to day work, but it needs luck to get that. I cannot find winter footwear in the shops for my 12-year-old daughter, and I myself wear men's shoes I bought for 12 roubles. Food? I am saved by my garden-allotment and by the fact that my father derives advantages from being a war-veteran. Clothes? I sew my own, make-do-and-mend old garments, knit. Manicure and hairdressers are beyond reach. Leisure? Laundry, cleaning, cooking, washing up, repairs to the apartment. I have never been to a rest home. We have a leisure centre at work, but it is inconvenient for women who are shift-workers and have families.

So it would be wrong to call me a woman, though I am not a man either. Lads who started work after me have long ago been promoted, have become senior machine-minders, even if they were drunkards or had other such qualities. No one takes notice of women, no one promotes them.

I fear for my daughter. Is she too to suffer rudeness in shops, foul language in the street, coarseness in the hospital, and as for the abortion clinic. . . . It is hard to be a beast of burden at the factory and at home. So do something, so that at least our daughters will be women and mothers, and not machine-minders and tractor drivers.

Then—health. Evidence as to the unsatisfactory conditions was available before *glasnost'*, and was effectively used by such Western observers as Murray Feshbach and Christopher Davis. As in the case of much else that had gone wrong, what was lacking was a clear statement of the situation as a whole. Death rates had risen, expectancy of life fallen. Why? The appointment of a new and energetic minister, E. Chazov, signaled a new approach. He and others wrote a whole series of articles in 1986–88 drawing attention to the neglect and poor conditions of the health service. This was frankly referred to at the 27th Party Congress (in March 1986). Again, the most expedient way of showing the full effects of *glasnost'* is to cite Chazov's speech to the Party Conference, reported in *Pravda* (30 June 1988): "We were proud of our system of health care. Yet we were silent about the fact that in infant mortality we were fiftieth in the world, below Mauretania and Barbados. We were proud that we had more doctors and hospitals than in any other country, but were silent about the fact that in life expectancy we occupy the 32nd place in the world. . . . In Uzbekistan millions of roubles were diverted and stolen, while 46% of hospitals were in buildings without the most elementary sanitary-hygienic conditions." In Kazakhstan the then Party leadership spoke of "happiness and vast creativity", but there were over 60,000 stricken with tuberculosis, a "disease which we have too hastily declared to be liquidated in our country". No, Chazov insisted, the facts have not only just become known. They had been reported, some good resolutions were adopted, but then came the reply: "Yes, you are right, but today there are other more urgent state interests, and so it is necessary to wait. We waited. And inherited today a most grave [*tyazheleishuyu*] situation in health care, which will need more than one quinquennium to correct." He demanded a large, much-needed increase in funding. So serious has been the underfunding that, according to his calculations, the share of gross national product devoted to health puts the USSR "in the middle of the seventies" out of 126 countries of the world. He urged a sharp increase in imports of medical drugs. There is a grave shortage still of essential equipment, such as operating tables. Furthermore, because of poor hygiene in the meat and dairy industries and lack of pure water, "1,700,000 people every year in our country suffer from acute intestinal disease". One can hardly be franker and more open than that!

A series of decrees and decisions are intended to improve the educational system. In this connection the press has printed many criticisms of old-fashioned teaching methods, the discouragement of initiative and originality among both teachers and pupils, as well as the poor pay of the teaching profession. One delegate to the 19th Party Conference, a woman named O. Zakharova, from Yakutsk, mentioned, as an important obstacle to *perestroika*, "the absence of independent thought. For decades we were taught in school, in the Komsomol, at work, to live by the principle of blind obedience to the administrative and superior organs, to 'know your place', and 'not to wash dirty linen in public'."

Again, the speech of the minister, Yagodin, to this conference summarizes past errors and omissions with the openness that characterised most of the speeches: "In our country half the schools have no central heating, running water or drains. A quarter of all schoolchildren use the school in two shifts, some in three. . . . In respect to the number of students [in higher education], per 10,000 inhabitants we have in the past ten years slid down from 9th place to the 23rd. Why?" Shortage of money is one reason. Also a prolonged "undervaluation of intellectual labour . . . , formalism, chasing after percentages, authoritarian methods of teaching and upbringing". In common with other countries, the USSR faces the problem of training the nonacademic stream to become skilled workers, good craftsmen: "We must not send [to such training schools] pedagogical no-goods, deprived children. In a socialist country, is this the way to recruit the new members of the working class? This is wrong, immoral, we must stop this! [applause]." Yagodin explained that they were compelled to abandon the history examination "because we could not place the pupil or the teacher in a defensible position on this ideological subject". Next year the subject will be restored. On the national-language question, he agreed with the Ukrainian delegate Oleinik (cited above) that the national language should be equal in status to Russian, that textbooks on all subjects should be available in both languages, that each nation's history, culture, and language must be properly taught and studied. "There is no more important problem today than this."

Supporting Chazov, he stated that 53 percent of pupils are not fully fit, and there should be more opportunities for physical culture. He then ended by asking that education be "liberated", that teachers be allowed to experiment. Each school should have a council, elected by secret ballot, with some representatives of senior pupils and local enterprises, with power to dismiss or prevent dismissal of the headmaster and teachers, and to regulate the school's budget.

A final remark is appropriate. The Soviet media and the Party itself have raised or uncovered many problems, social and political. But the USSR is most certainly not alone in having such problems. Funding the health service is a hot issue in Great Britain, and here too there are complaints of shortage of textbooks, which cannot be taken home as they are needed at school. Or to take another subject altogether: we, too, have parents who push for special advantages for their children; we, too, have a variety of partly hidden business "perks". Nor do we all have proper democratic procedures in political parties. In fact, on the very day I am writing these lines, *The Times* (22 July 1988) reports from Atlanta, Georgia, that "the man from Russian television just managed to keep a straight face as he explained to the Moscow evening news that stage-managed unity prevented the voicing of any dissent at this American [Democratic] party rally". (!)

*Glasnost'* has given us, and, more important, the Soviet people, a much clearer view of what is wrong with their society, what needs to be put right by the Gorbachev "revolution" (it is he who frequently uses this word). A recognition of the negative aspects of reality is certainly no guarantee that they will be put right. It is, however, a precondition for making the attempt.

After this chapter was completed, I noticed in *Argumenty i fakty*, No. 37, 1988, an article by V. Pavlyuchenko which gave details of party functionaries' salaries. Thus the first secretary of the Belorussian republic is paid 700 roubles a month, the second secretary 620, a *raikom* (district) secretary 340, a party "instructor" 270 (urban) or 200 (rural). The average income of a *kolkhoz* chairman in Belorussia he gives as 600. (It seems that my university pension is roughly double the salary of the first secretary, at the official rate of exchange. No wonder "privileges" are so important!)

# CHAPTER 8

# Economic Problems and Issues

Economic issues lie at the heart of *perestroika*. Some Western observers believed that economic reform would be possible only if there were no political reform; the latter was thought to be out of the question. They pointed to Hungary, where the economic reform of 1968 was not accompanied by political upheavals, and contrasted it with Czechoslovakia, where the economic reform proposed by Ota Šik and his colleagues was halted by the Soviet invasion, the latter being due to the political reforms which had been envisaged in the "Prague Spring". And this also in 1968.

However, others argued that economic reform could not even begin to get off the ground in the USSR without being accompanied by major political changes, that without these it would run into the sand—indeed, it may yet do so anyway, as a number of Soviet critics have been pointing out. Gorbachev certainly sees *perestroika* as involving politics as well as economics. And it must be pointed out that the Soviet Union cannot invade itself.

In this connection, it is significant that a round-table discussion headed "Is Economic Reform Possible without *Perestroika* in Politics?" should be the main feature of *Voprosy ekonomiki*, No. 6, 1988. So there is a considerable overlap here with the previous chapter. One contributor to the discussion, K. Mikulsky, stressed the need to drop obsolete ideas on the link between economics and politics, which tended "to counterpose political requirements to effective management, saw politics as a means of combating "commercial', i.e., economically sound, approaches to the solution of economic tasks", though of course political power remains important, indeed essential, in carrying through the economic reform. At which point S. Valentei expressed the fear that "the [necessary] use of harsh methods to break the resistance of the bureaucracy would simultaneously form the basis for the creation of a new bureaucratic structure". Mikulsky in reply expressed the hope that, once coercion has been used to introduce the reform, "the governing stratum will change".

E. Ambartsumov followed up with the following statements. "I think that right now it will be impossible to proceed directly to a fully democratic society, since we have never had one. It is difficult to envisage such a transition without passing through a certain 'authoritarian' stage, but not of the Stalinist despotic type, but one consciously oriented towards democratization. . . . The social basis for decisive action from above, in my view, cannot be provided by the existing administrative apparatus, the bureaucracy, which is objectively interested in preserving the existing position. It seems we need a new middle class. . . . We must not confuse the role of the *intelligentsia*, of specialists, which are to be the nucleus of the new middle class, with the bureaucracy."

He then went on to some more fundamental observations: "We often hear that our principal misfortune is that we now have not state socialism but departmental [or sectoral, *vedomstvennyi*] socialism. This is so. But departmental socialism emerged out of state socialism precisely because, contrary to Marxism and to the experience of developed countries, the very relationship between state and society was stood on its head. Our socialism became statified. So that every new step always begins with the creation of a state-bureaucratic structure, which ensures its low effectiveness and lack of confidence among citizens. Our real misfortune lies in the fact that we have not developed a civil society. On the contrary, its first manifestations were suppressed." He welcomed the recent emergence of nonformal groups, when they put forward ideas which help to "liquidate the 'deficiencies' [*defitsit*] of Party leadership". He urges the abandonment of such terms as "democratic centralism" in relation to a reformed economy. "The misfortune of our society is excessive regulation. Of course some will say that without it there will be chaos. I think that a degree of deregulation of dynamic processes is preferable to the stagnation we had, which, incidentally, did not exclude chaos and led to monstrous waste of the social product." The danger, the harm, comes "not from political decisions as such, but from ideological decisions, when ideology, acquiring political force, dictates the laws of movement of the economy and drives it into the marshes".

He was followed by B. Rakitsky, who also spoke of the necessary role of politics: "How, in conditions of social revolution, can one avoid intensification of relations between classes and social groups?

The point is to pass from arbitrariness to a legal order [rule of law]."
He criticised the new law on the enterprise for making the election of
management subject to approval of superior authority. He then
turned to freedom, as distinct from rights and duties. "Freedom
implies the right to use your initiative when no one asks you to. This
is not a right, not an obligation, it is freedom. Well, the category of
freedom, of the right to act, does not exist in Soviet law."

So economic reform raises fundamental questions of political
economy in its widest sense, including the economic *and* political
roles of the Party. S. Dzarasov spells this out: "In my view, we must
first of all alter the relationship of Party and state leadership, of
Party leadership and soviet power. At present these functions are
merged. The Party does not so much lead as exercise power, which it
must not do. According to Lenin's conception all power belongs to
the people, in the form of its deputies who were freely elected. This
we do not have. Firstly, we have no free elections. . . . Secondly,
legal enactments are adopted by Party organs, and the soviets merely
formally confirm them." Yet people still speak of "the raising of the
role of Party leadership. . . . The Party has concentrated in its own
hands the function of rule [administration], removing the working
people from the exercise of power." So now we have a "command-
bureaucratic system of government. It has become a brake on our
development. We must change it. How? First of all by returning
power to the people." Decisions must be taken "without being first
adopted by the Party's organs".

S. Tolstikov spoke of a major problem. "*Perestroika* is being
carried through as a 'revolution from above', when the masses are
conscious of and understand the need for radical change, but the
deformed conditions in which they are placed lead to the nonconfor-
mity of current and short-term interests of a sizable part of the
population with the strategic aims of *perestroika*."

The discussions ranged far and wide, emphasising two things.
One is the very intimate link between economic reform and new
ways of thinking on politics, law, and sociology. The other is that
formerly unmentionable problem areas are now open to free debate
within the broad confines of *glasnost'*. *Voprosy ekonomiki* has a
new editor, none other than G. Popov, whose ideas have been
quoted repeatedly in earlier chapters.

Popov promised a livelier *Voprosy ekonomiki* in his "editorial" in
No. 7: "The years of stagnation had serious effects on the development of theory. Scholastics, fruitless cleverness, were combined with
shameless apologetics for any measures taken by the leadership,
with praising them as if they were grandiose theoretical achieve-

ments." Instead of relevant theory, one had "orthodox [*pravover-nyi*] interpretations of quotations from the classics of Marxist-Leninism. . . . There was no decisive breakthrough in the elaboration of a contemporary model of socialism. . . . Yet after Lenin, not to speak of Marx and Engels, there were huge changes in the real world." He set out an ambitious programme of discussions on a long list of major issues, not forgetting ecology and nationality problems. There is to be a "round table" devoted to Bukharin. The experience of other socialist countries will be critically studied ("overcoming the tendency to gentle approval of all that they do").

The same issue contained a lively debate on the draft of a textbook on political economy. Thus, it is now proposed to present contemporary "monopoly-capitalism" as a mature stage, with earlier forms as immature. Where, asked Dzarasov, does this leave Lenin's theory of imperialism? Either capitalism is dying, in which case it is incapable of carrying through scientific-technical revolution, which it has, or it is so capable, and then it is not dying. V. Musatov asked: What is the answer to a student who wants to know whether foreign capital in joint enterprises "will exploit our labour-power and create surplus values on our territory"? He also suggested that capitalism *was* dying in Lenin's time, just as in those days one died of double pneumonia, but penicillin changed all that. (What was capitalism's penicillin?) A. Sergeyev put a fundamental question: "It is known that Marx and Engels held that socialism and commodity production were not only contradictory but incompatible. Lenin too took this view. Even today no one has the 'theoretical effrontery' to assert that Lenin was the creator of the theory of commodity production [i.e., markets] under socialism. Was the theory of Marx, Engels, and Lenin about socialism wrong, or was their theory on commodity production wrong? Or are we wrong in interpreting what Marx, Engels, and Lenin say about the nature of commodity production?" R. Belousov pointed to a question, frequently put: "Do we now have socialism or do we not? Under Stalin? Under Brezhnev?" L. Abalkin spoke about "the necessity for a complete reassessment of many of our concepts regarding socialism".

Critique of the "classics" was taken further in a facsinating discussion based upon Engels's *Anti-Dühring*, which fills twenty-three pages of *Voprosy ekonomiki* (No. 10, 1988). Popov and others argued that Marx and Engels were men of their time, capable of error, that in particular they—and also Lenin and Kautsky before 1918—did envisage a future socialist economy on the lines of a single factory or office, and that this did have centralizing implications. Engels's view on the absence of a market (commodity-

money relations) under socialism must be seen as mistaken. There
was also Lenin's parallel with the postal service—though one participant pointed out that the postal authorities do not dictate the contents of letters! The question was put explicitly: Can Engels, Marx,
and Lenin be blamed for the creation of the "administrative-
command system"? Economic thought must free itself from dogmatism. "Engels was wrong in linking the fate of commodity production with the ownership of means of production by society",
argued B. Rakitsky, but he then reminded the meeting that it could be
argued that Soviet society does not own the means of production.
Lenin did say that "our power is on behalf of the people, not by the
people". Rakitsky went on: "I do not think that we live in socialism.
We live in a barracklike deformation of socialism, our society is not
yet socialist. Our society is so arranged that the means of production
belong not to society but to the caste that manages (them) in society's
name". In his concluding remarks, G. Popov was sharply critical of
several of Engels's formulations: "Engels said nothing about the
achievement of anything by the human will, and indeed the concept
of the free individual is not adequately present in the work we are
discussing. . . . As I already said, in *Anti-Dühring* there is no reflection of all the complexities of the transition period, there is not even a
view of socialism as a stage". There is nothing in Engels's concepts
about "the mainsprings of development", or of innovation. An
incorrect view of capitalism, derived from Engels, gave insufficient
emphasis on personal freedom, which is linked with capitalism and
the market for labour and with democracy. This led to an incorrect
view of fascism in the thirties, seen as a form corresponding to the
nature of capitalism. Engels's implied centralist model of a socialist
economy omits all discussion of *who* is to allocate labour and other
resources, who plans, and by what mechanism. (These are the sort of
questions I raised in my own book, *The Economics of Feasible
Socialism*, and such arguments would have been unpublishable in
the USSR even as recently as 1985.)

Before returning to the discussions concerning remedies to existing ills, and obstacles to change, let us look at what is being said
about the ills themselves. As has already been stressed in earlier
chapters, quite severe criticisms of particular malfunctions appeared
repeatedly in the Soviet press long before Gorbachev and *glasnost'*.
My own books, and those of my colleagues in several Western
countries, could quote dozens if not hundreds of instances of
irrationality, waste, and distortion generated by the system. But
whereas we could say that it was the *system* that generated them, our
Soviet counterparts could not—at least not in published work.

Aganbegyan and Zaslavskaya wrote memoranda, some of which were leaked to the West. In one of these, Zaslavskaya pointed out that it had been no one's task to elaborate a reform model. The top leadership, even Brezhnev, could speak of the need for a radical change "in an age of scientific-technical revolution", but conservative forces were much too strong, until after Gorbachev's accession.

A milestone in published criticism was N. Shmelev's article "Avansy i dolgi" (*Novyi mir*, No. 6, 1987). A few extracts will give the reader the flavour of this piece. "The condition of our economy satisfies no one. Its two central deficiencies—the monopoly of the producers under conditions of shortage and the lack of interest of enterprises in scientific and technical progress—are surely clear to all." Marx, Engels, and Lenin had only the vaguest notions about "how a socialist economy should function not in emergency but in normal conditions". Shmelev was among the first to praise NEP, to say that its abandonment was a disaster:

> We are still dominated by the conception that the existing system of economic and property relations is the embodiment of Marxism-Leninism in practice, fully consonant with the nature of socialism as a social formation. . . .
>
> Marx and Engels elaborated the theoretical bases of revolution, showed its objective inevitability, but as for what shape the economy would take after victory, on this they only had guesses [*dogadki*]. . . . They left us virtually nothing which could be considered as practical advice about the methods of reaching the aims [of socialism]. The prerevolutionary works of Lenin were also in the main devoted purely to politics . . . , and not to what will have to be done to organize a full-blooded economic life after the revolution. Thus the revolution caught us without a thought-out or complete economic theory of socialism. . . .
>
> It is essential to realize that the cause of our difficulties is not only or not solely due to the heavy burden of military expenditures and the very expensive global responsibilities of our country. If we expended them correctly, even the remaining resources would be sufficient for maintaining a balanced and technically progressive economy and for satisfying the traditionally modest needs of our population. However, prolonged attempts to break up the objective laws of economic life, to suppress the age-long natural stimuli for human labour, brought about results quite different from what was intended. Today we have an economy characterised by shortage, imbalances, in many respects unmanageable, and, if we were to be honest, an economy almost unplannable. . . . We have one of the lowest levels of labour productivity of any industrial nation, especially in agriculture and in construction, since through the years of stagnation the working masses have reached a state of almost total disinterestedness in freely-committed and honest labour. . . .
>
> Apathy, indifference, thieving . . . have become mass phenomena, with

at the same time aggressive envy toward high earners. There have appeared signs of a sort of physical degradation of a sizable part of our population, through drunkenness and idleness. Finally, there is a lack of belief in the officially announced objectives and purposes, in the very possibility of a more rational economic and social organization of life.

. . .

Clearly all this cannot be swiftly overcome—years, maybe generations, will be needed.

Shmelev went on to express concern about the "half-heartedness and indecisiveness" of reform measures so far taken or envisaged. Some fear anarchy, but "the attempt to achieve 100 percent control over all and everything causes such confusion [*stikhiya*] and uncontrollability that anarchy would seem like order". He denounced abuses and campaigns against private activities in agriculture (of which more in a moment), with such phrases as "things should be given their proper names: stupidity is stupidity, incompetence is incompetence, today's Stalinism is today's Stalinism". He called for radical measures to deal with the economic ministries, and for order in monetary and fiscal affairs. He also pointed to the need for some unemployment, a precondition, in his view, for flexibility and for labour discipline. Interestingly, Gorbachev made this last point the one exception to his general agreement with the tenor of Shmelev's article.

This piece set the tone for subsequent discussions. Shmelev returned to the charge in a joint article with V. Popov in *Znamya* (No. 5, 1988). This was one of several analyses of the causes of *defitsit*, persistent shortages of so many items, both producers' goods and consumers' goods. The authors showed that this is inherent in the centralised planning system, a *zakonomernost'* ("lawlike regularity"), since the system generates shortages. Of course in theory its plans in physical units are supposed to balance, but the total number of products, fully disaggregated, they estimate at 25 million, so in practice errors and imbalances are inevitable, and are not due solely to human stupidity. Faced with supply uncertainty and with stress on plan fulfillment, enterprises naturally avoid "relatively unprofitable and troublesome items, especially if they do not greatly help to clock-up *val*" (gross value of output), hence, shortages of such things as "buttons, toilet paper, clothes pegs, peppermints, mops, thermometers". Hence, overapplication for inputs. Hence, the tendency to make one's own components, forgings, castings—i.e., self-supply. Some 8 million people are engaged in repairing machinery, more than are engaged in producing it. "Repairs to tractors exceed their initial cost 5 to 7 times."

Shmelev and Popov cited cases where, in order to fulfill the repair plan, farms are ordered to send for repair equipment that does not need it: "Repair becomes an end in itself." They cited a case in which zinc was sent for scrap to avoid a fine for nonfulfillment of the scrap plan, though the zinc was of good quality! "Self-supply" was also denounced at the 19th Party Conference in the course of a very colourful speech by Kabaidze: "Everyone accepts the cretinism that each enterprise makes its own components. If we cannot cope with nuts, bolts and screws, the devil knows what sort of *perestroika* we will have!" (*Pravda*, 1 July 1988).

Many link the notorious *dolgostroi* ("long-build", construction delays due to the excessive number of investment projects) with the powers of departments, ministries, and localities. Several authors point in this connection to the *weakness* of centralisation, the excessive powers of the ministries. Thus E. Gaidar (*Kommunist*, No. 2, 1988) pointed out that the effort to cut back the excessive number of construction projects actually under way by 40 percent resulted in the end in a reduction by 2 percent, since "it proved impossible to overcome departmentalist and localist resistance". Selyunin (*Novyi mir*, No. 5, 1988) also referred to loss of control: "The American economy is more centrally managed today than is ours." B. Bogachev, writing in *Voprosy ekonomiki* (No. 5, 1988), vigorously attacks the behaviour pattern of the ministries, who ruthlessly exploit their monopoly position and seek to increase the value of output and turnover and exercise pressure on "their" enterprises. They neglect infrastructure, ignore consumer requirements, fail to supply spare parts, "inflate" output even of raw materials by "heavy admixtures (water, gravel, earth)". One has "sectoral corporations, uniting in common interest everyone from the minister to the worker. All are in their own way interested in the same thing: concealment of reserves, obtaining additional resources, a reduction or formalisation of evaluation criteria, claims to successes, genuine or fictional, needed or not needed, real or purely statistical." He added: "Whatever the evaluation criteria may be, there will always be found a means of satisfying them without any adequate and useful outcome or even contrary to social utility." Far from being centralized, "the economy is torn apart into feudal departmental princedoms [*udely*]", and they actually appeal to the principles of *perestroika* and to antibureaucratic slogans to protect them from urgently necessary central intervention. Gaidar in his article cited many examples of "departmentalist" wastefulness, especially in investments: "We produce 6.4 times more tractors, 16 times more combine-harvesters than the USA. . . . To produce as many combines as were immobilized through technical breakdown [in the USSR] would take American industry 70 years." The huge T-330 tractor is being rejected by farms, yet the ministry orders that more be produced, and plans a huge new tractor factory at Elabuga. Meanwhile, investment in much more vital sectors lags behind. "The hard-surface road network of our country, covering a sixth of the world's land surface, is equaled by that of Japan. India has overtaken us in the construction of motorways." (!!)

Much is being written about the financial situation, "inflation" being no longer a word confined to capitalism. Shmelev in his first article drew attention to the level of "frustrated" savings, of "holes in the budget, inflationary methods of financing, such as the inclusion in budget of revenues from unsold products, which may in fact never find a customer, the granting of credits which take the form of nonreturnable grants—agriculture alone has hopeless debts which approach 100 milliard roubles." E. Gaidar also drew attention to the gaps in the budget; so, in his speech to the 19th Party Conference, did Gorbachev. The problem has been complicated by the combined effects of the cut in vodka production and sales and the fall in world prices of oil. The latter had a double effect, reducing the budget's "take" from foreign trade and reducing the imports and sales of consumers' goods. However, so strong has been the tradition of claiming that the budget is in surplus, that the minister of finance would not admit to a deficit; the statistics he presented in his budget speech in 1987 were *not* an example of *glasnost'* in action. He was bound to do better next time! The more so as *Kommunist* (No. 11, 1988) published an article by K. Kagalovsky which not only spoke of "fictional revenues which create the appearance of there being no deficit", but mentioned "money emission" by Gosbank as a source of revenue, estimating the real budget deficit in 1986 as 15–17 percent of total revenue.

The minister finally admitted in his budget speech to an anticipated deficit of 35 milliard roubles for 1989. However, in a striking article in *Kommunist* (No. 17, 1988), E. Gaidar and O. Latsis pointed to another revenue figure, 63.4 milliard roubles, described as "resources of the state's loan fund" (*ssudnogo fonda*), which, say the authors, has the same source, i.e., advances from the State Bank. Together they amount to close to 100 milliard roubles, which represents over 11 percent of the gross national product (GNP). American deficits, which so worry everyone, represent (they point out) a much smaller percentage. They sound the alarm. The truth had been hidden by the "simple method of exaggerating budget revenues." They cite the commissar of finance of the early twenties,

G. Sokolnikov, who proposed to erect a large banner to the effect that "Money emission is the opium of the national economy". They take the opportunity to draw attention yet again to the huge and misspent investments in agriculture, especially those wasted on "melioration".

Since we are discussing *glasnost'*, it is worth stressing in how many instances published articles and speeches not only advocate policies independently, but actually criticise the official line, even when Gorbachev has given it his backing. Examples include the following. Popov and Shmelev, in their above-cited article, strongly criticise the policy of instructing industrial enterprises to run auxiliary farms and heavy-industry enterprises to make consumers' goods as sidelines ("locomotive works that produce lemon-squeezers"). N. Shmelev (*Novyi mir*, No. 4, 1988) attacks the campaign to reduce vodka sales because it encourages the distillation of *samogon*. Far better to sell more, legally, at lower prices! He also advocates negotiating a large loan to finance the imports of consumers' goods, so that citizens will feel that *perestroika* benefits them. This they cannot feel now.

Indeed, they cannot. Speaking to the 19th Party Congress, a worker, V. Yarin, of Nizhni Tagil, said: "The workers ask, where is *perestroika*? Food supply was bad, it is still bad, and now they have introduced ration-coupons for sugar. There was no meat, there is no meat. Industrial consumer goods seemed to have vanished." The same speaker also had much to say about pollution, which is particularly bad in Nizhni Tagil.

Turning now to the reform process in general, dissatisfaction with its pace and its results is virtually universal. No one pretends that progress has been rapid or satisfactory. Concern is expressed at the survival of the "traditional" centralised methods in a slight disguise. Thus, to cite a few examples among a great many, L. Abalkin wrote in *Moskovskie novosti* (26 June 1988) under the title "Uneasy Start of the Reform", on the eve of the 19th Party Conference: "And if we are to speak of real economic successes, of growth indicators, of the situation in the market, in the shops, then, alas, very little has been achieved. . . . Why should things have suddenly got better? Have we in fact brought into action all the levers, factors, potential [of the reform]? Several laws and a package of decrees have been adopted, a number of documents accepted. But it is naive to expect that decrees and declarations can alter real life. We have begun to alter the real economic relations not two or three years but only a few months ago. Furthermore there is so far no complete [overall] system of management which could produce results." Abalkin raised the question of the damage done to the reform by the continued insistence on carrying out the current five-year plan, adopted before the reform: "Some put the point quite sharply: either the five-year plan or the reform. This is an important question. If we are to be serious about *perestroika* and technical progress, then we must abandon the stress on volume indicators . . . , thousands and tens of thousands of indicators passed down from Gosplan, the ministries and other organs to enterprises. We cling to this, and it ties us hand and foot."

Abalkin, who is director of the Institute of Economics, also spoke at the conference itself, and there too he said: "It must be stressed with total clarity that no radical transformation of our economy has occurred, that it has not emerged from the condition of stagnation." He went on: "The changes in the structure of social production, between groups A and B [producers' goods and consumers' goods], between accumulation and consumption, proceeded in a direction quite contrary to that determined by the 27th Party Congress. The state of the consumer market has worsened. Particularly serious is the situation in the sphere of scientific-technical progress, where our arrears, compared with world levels, are increasing and becoming alarming." He returned to the theme of the five-year plan targets, which aimed at "simultaneously achieving quantitative growth and qualitative transformation. From a scientific point of view these tasks are incompatible. . . . It was necessary to choose: either quantity or quality. In view of our traditions and experience it is obvious to what we gave preference."

He joined others in condemning the tendency to include nearly all productive capacity within the ambit of "state orders" (*goszakazy*), thereby preserving the old system of ministerial domination. Of this Gorbachev also spoke at the conference when he said: "And it is utterly impermissible when, through *goszakazy*, enterprises are compelled to produce goods which are not in demand. They do this just so as to ensure the notorious *val* [gross-output target]. How many among us serve faithfully His Majesty the *val*. Is it necessary to prove that this totally contradicts the sense of the reform, it is tantamount to retaining the old system of management, which brought our economy to a dead-end." Another delegate, G. Zagainov, director of a branch of the Aerodynamics Institute, said that "we see a repainting of the façade, while retaining the dictate of the planned *goszakaz*. . . . Our economy is now in a contradictory state. On the one hand we have started to introduce economic methods of self-regulation of the economy, on the other we fulfill the five-year plan, born in the old system and orientated toward gross-output indicators. . . . It is necessary decisively to block the way to His Majesty the *val* and the cost-inducing mechanism, the waste of our natural resources." He then criticised Abalkin: from the director of the Institute of Economics "we had a right to expect to hear a developed constructive programme of action", not just criticism. He then went on to touch a fundamental point: "Egor Kuzmich Ligachev, in his speech at Togliatti, while supporting *perestroika*, also expressed fears about alien ideas . . . about the unacceptability of the untrammelled market [*rynochnoi stikhii*] of the West. But the market, as an effective feedback mechanism in the economy, is a most ancient invention. For many years we based our economy on direct regulation, without effective feedback. . . . This inevitably leads to distortions." He asked that Ligachev should speak more definitely about these questions.

The replacement of Ligachev by V. Medvedev as chief of ideology clears the ground for the reformers. As may be seen from Medvedev's article in *Kommunist* (No. 17, 1988), he is more positive about the market, though he cites Western critics ("A. Nove and W. Leontief") in support of the view that some decisions require to remain centralized. It has been announced that *goszakaz* is to cover a much smaller share of output in 1989, though it is too soon to see whether this will actually be the case.

The relative roles of plan and market have been debated with increasing frankness, and (understandably) controversy has erupted. A full survey of the argument on this one theme could fill a great many pages. Thus, Fedorov had argued both for leasing land to peasants for up to 100 years and also for leasing "the maximum number" of factories, too. "Why should there be state property for the production of toothbrushes?" The word for "competition" (*konkurentsiya*) used to be confined to descriptions of capitalism, the correct word in the USSR itself being *sorevnovaniye* ("emulation"), as when enterprises or dairymaids seek to be the first to fulfill plans or to increase milk production. Now *konkurentsiya* is "in", with both senior political figures and economists extolling its virtues as a means of improving quality and rewarding the satisfaction of demand. The very notion of "trade in means of production"—i.e., giving the manager choice as to his suppliers (instead of having them designated by the supply plan)—*implies* competition, between suppliers, and this is official policy (though still in an early stage of implementation). The law on cooperatives adopted in June 1988, and the speech by premier Ryzhkov introducing it, makes many references to the need for cooperatives to compete with each other and with state enterprises in the provision of a wide range of goods and services.

There are unsettled questions, too, on prices, concerning both the basis on which they should be fixed and whether they should be fixed at all. Fears are expressed about possible monopolistic abuses, and about the effects of excess demand and shortage. A particularly difficult problem is what to do about the astronomic food subsidies and rents, the latter unaltered (per square metre) for well over fifty years. Gorbachev has several times spoken of the need to take action to raise prices and charges, with compensatory wage increases so that the low-paid would not suffer. Zaslavskaya has written on this theme in *Kommunist*. However, this step would be unpopular, and letters opposing this (much-needed) measure have been published in many journals.

A wide range of views on the market has been published too. G. Lisichkin, in *Druzhba narodov* (No. 1, 1988), argues strongly "for", though he also stresses the existence of objectives (e.g., ecology, beauty, leisure) which are not to be subjected to market criteria. A very different approach is that of M. Antonov, writing in *Oktyabr'* (No. 8, 1987): he writes of "cavalrymen" and "merchants", and perhaps we should translate this as "cavaliers" and "roundheads". The "cavalrymen" are neo-Stalinists, who wish to resolve the problems of inefficiency and indiscipline by harsh measures. They are, fortunately, in retreat, notes Antonov. But he is not happy with the "merchants". For them financial results are everything, they would tolerate unemployment, take no responsibility for finding jobs for the redundant. Both the cavalrymen and the merchants have in common the disregard of the interests and aspirations of ordinary working people. Antonov's positive programme looks to cooperatives as a solution, though it is not clear how he would apply it to large-scale industry.

The phrase "cavalrymen and merchants" was in fact coined by Anatoli Strelyany, in *Znamya*, No. 6, 1986, in the course of a most eloquent denunciation of the inefficiencies of the centralized planning system with an equally eloquent plea for radical market-type reform. He developed his ideas further in his book, *Sennaya Likhoradka* ["Hay Fever"], published in 1988. It is worth quoting from this, as his language is indeed colourful:

Planning for "the achieved level", invented by the cavalrymen, is the most unnatural and harmful of any imaginable or unimaginable arrangements which social Man ever did, does, or could undertake. As a matter of principle it blocks changes in the nature and structure of production and thereby dooms economic life to stagnation. It makes impossible any deep-going zonal specialization in agriculture, and so in areas where for centuries there was good pasture they sow wheat decade after decade,

and vice versa. It renders impossible timely structural changes in industry, and so it is with the greatest difficulty that there appear new sectors
and new products, and technical evolution (not to speak of revolution)
moves with soul-shattering creaks. All this, which the cavalrymen call
genuinely socialist planning, renders useless any creative or businesslike
persons in the administrative, design, and construction spheres, which is
why one finds in key positions so many sterile weeds. All that has been
achieved could only occur through some kind of hidden or open (and
more or less belated) departures from the spirit or the letter (of regulations). . . . The cost-based price system invented by the cavalrymen
renders acceptable, justified, and inevitable any expenditures of materials, fuel and labour for the production of anything, and so we have the
heaviest tractors and combines in the world, the greatest amount of metal
shavings, the most "empty" fertilizers, the blackest smoke, the widest
and deepest quarries, the worst roads and storehouses . . . [and so on for
several pages (p. 588ff)].

Shmelev, Popov, and Lisichkin are criticised by Boris Kagarlitsky,
the Moscow "left-wing" semidissident, in the piece he wrote for
*New Left Review* (No. 169, May-June 1988). While recognising the
need for market-type reforms, he represents a view concerned with
the domination of technocrats, the neglect of the low-paid,
unemployment, and price rises. He seems to be less than fair to his
opponents, whom he accuses of ignoring "social provision". Thus,
Shmelev specifically states that it is in his view essential that "the
weak, the old, the deprived, should not lose from *perestroika*"
(*Novyi mir*, No. 4, 1988). The same point has been made repeatedly
by Zaslavskaya in connection with the proposal to increase food
prices, and by Gorbachev too.

The point here is not to say who is wrong, but merely to point to
the openness of the debate. Kagarlitsky has contributed to published
discussions in the USSR, for example, in *EKO*.

Particularly sharp comments have been made about agriculture.
Shmelev's second article (*Novyi mir*, No. 4, 1988) roundly asserts
that "the crisis-situation in our agriculture is evident to all", and this
is due not to lack of investment, which has been ample: "They in
fact yielded nothing. The crisis in our village is due to over five
decades of the triumph of coercion over common sense. . . . Few can
now doubt that the basic reason for the deplorable condition of our
agriculture, its stagnant state, lies in the undivided power which the
administrative stratum has acquired during these decades over
everything in the village." Yes, there have been steps in the direction
of small-group contract, family contract, and leasing, but still "it is
essential to take all possible measures against administrative arbi-

trariness in the village". It would do no harm publicly to punish those local officials who continue to throttle family contract, leasing of land, private plots, rural crafts, the sale of private and kolkhoz produce in local or distant markets. The people must see that in the struggle that is now taking place, "Moscow has the power over the local feudal princelings [*udel'nykh knyazkov*]".

Much has been written about the essentially phoney "cooperative" nature of *kolkhozy*: "They never were real cooperatives. That is our misfortune, the basic reason for the emergence and durability of the food problem. . . . They are subject to orders from above about the structures of sown area, livestock numbers and so on." (L. Nikoforov, in *Voprosy ekonomiki*, No. 3, 1988). One could fill a sizable book with quotations, from Gorbachev down to *kolkhoz* chairmen, all protesting about constant interference from Party and state officials, and from the agroindustrial complex (*Agroprom*) bureaucracy, in the everyday affairs of farms. This in turn has deplorable effects on the (sound and sensible) policy of breaking up the huge *kolkhozy* and *sovkhozy* into smaller units which act as autonomous subcontractors, organize their own work, and are paid by results. These are in many cases family units, and leasing to families has also been authorized, as well as the creation of small and genuine cooperatives (with the *kolkhoz* and *sovkhoz* preserved as a sort of federation of cooperatives). However, as A. Emelyanov pointed out (in *Voprosy ekonomiki*, No. 6, 1988, in the round-table discussion mentioned earlier) "The collective contract [*podryad*] to which so much significance is attached will not function unless we smash the mechanism at higher levels. For how can the contract unit be genuinely in charge [*khozyainom*] when this is not the case with the *kolkhozy* or *sovkhozy* as a whole [of which they are a part]? If *kolkhozy* and *sovkhozy* are compelled by orders from above to adopt a given structure of the sown area or the numbers of livestock, then the management is compelled to pass these orders—which are, by the way, forbidden by official documents and legal provisions— down to the contract subunits."

So, not for the first time, we encounter the problem that centrally decided reform measures are frustrated by intermediate levels of authority. The same complaint is heard repeatedly about industrial enterprises: regardless of the new law on the enterprise, they are given compulsory output targets (now disguised under the appellation *goszakaz*, state orders), the material allocation system continues to exist, profits are arbitrarily removed by the ministry, and so on.

But to return to agriculture—critical material on this subject is overwhelming in sheer volume. A few examples only can be cited here. Many bear on the alienation of the peasantry from the land, their indifference, summed up in a saying quoted by S. Vikulov in *Pravda* (4 Feb. 1987): "In the old days the peasants reasoned: why should we work, we will not be paid. Now they reason: why should we work, we will be paid anyway!"

In an earlier chapter, I cited the criticism directed even at Lenin himself for his view of the "petty-bourgeois" peasantry. I will here cite two more instances of what not so long ago would have been seen as unutterable heresies. First is a statement made by Svyatoslav Fedorov, delegate to the 19th Party Conference, writing in *Moskovskie novosti* (26 June 1988, i.e., on the very eve of that conference):

> I think that the most important thing in economic *perestroika* [should be] the handing over, on lease-and-contract, of the maximum number of factories and workshops [!!], the granting of land to the peasants on leases of 50 to 100 years, not just 5 years, as is now done. . . . Not just to the individual, to the family. . . . The land needs to be restored. . . . And this can be done by one who knows that in 50 years' time he and his children will have good land, and not a desert. . . . Those who govern [*unpraviteli*] publicly proclaim their love for the people but their real beliefs are quite different: everybody is lazy, everybody steals, no one wants to work. Hence the numerous institutions of inspectors and checkers, sloganmongers and organizers. People steal because they do not consider the property theirs. People do not steal their own. When there is a lease, a market, a cooperative, individual labour, attitudes change, there will be order to a degree which no inspector could dream of.

Second is a letter from a former peasant, a young man who moved to town, published in *Selskaya molodezh* (December 1987):

> It seems to me that some do not understand the situation that has arisen in agriculture. . . . Millions of people have abandoned their villages and gone to town, where they live in hostels . . . , wallowing in sorrow and in drink. Those who remain in the villages are in a still worse state. The land is no longer theirs. They are not peasants any more, they are just *batraki* [landless labourers]. Where is it known for a *batrak* to work well on someone else's land and wish to have children? What for? So they too should be *batraki*? What is the consequence of the fact that today the land is controlled not by those who work on it but by officials, bureaucrats? Our agriculture is three to five times behind America's. I consider that the granting of land [to the peasants] is the most vital and immediate task. It would be as significant as were in its time the abolition of serfdom and the agrarian revolution. One must save the peasants from final degradation

and rural officialdom from nervous and mental breakdown, or else they will fall victim to the most clumsy, chaotic and senseless agricultural policy. Whence the panic fear to resemble capitalism? Did not Marx say that private property was to be transcended, not forbidden?

A very few years ago, if such a letter were printed, both the author and the editor stood a good chance of making an involuntary journey to Siberia. This is *glasnost'* indeed. The reader must be struck by the similarity of the arguments of this young ex-peasant and Svyatoslav Fedorov, cited above. Fedorov's background is quite different: he is the director of the famous optical microsurgery outfit. Both men raise the issue of property, and one could cite a number of other authors who stress the alienation of the producer under conditions which some describe as a "perversion" of the idea of people's or social property.

The other factor which stimulates out-migration of villagers is the low standard of living. No longer does this take the form of low pay: on average this compares reasonably with urban labour (though there is desperate labour shortage in Siberia, where pay in the cities and oil-bearing districts is much higher). Rather, it is the conditions of life, and to some extent also of work: as was mentioned by Pukhova in her speech to the 19th Party Conference, many peasant women "work from dawn to dusk with no days off". (I noted some criticisms of the practice of a "spreadover" from 5 a.m. to 9 p.m. for milkmaids in an article I wrote in 1952! Still it goes on!) Some authors have spoken of a marriage problem, the problem being that girls are fed up with the prospects of rural life, with virtually every mechanized or skilled job being for males, and move to town, causing young men to wish to follow them. The lack of elementary amenities and the poor medical services, mud, and educational gaps (few rural schools teach any foreign language, without which access to higher education is not possible) are all the subject of repeated public comment, and find reflection in decisions and resolutions designed to put things right. The task is a huge one, and is not helped by the reluctance of the state's construction enterprises to carry out work in rural areas.

The practice of issuing orders to farm management, apart from its effect on responsibility and on morale, is also blamed for high cost, inefficiency, and loss of production. Thus in the view of V. Tikhonov (*Argumenty i fakty*, No. 51, 1987), "even with the existing backward material-technical base, our agriculture only produces three quarters of what it could" because of the imposition of a production pattern unsuitable to local conditions. On top of this there are heavy losses: "Crops rot because of lack of storage space and processing capacity. The weight of livestock is lost when it is kept without fodder at slaughterhouses. . . . So in addition at least another quarter of what is harvested is lost on the very long journey from the field to the consumer." He also strongly criticised "gigantomania". Vast livestock complexes, which several critics have called "palaces for cows", have also been denounced by V. Belov in his *Novyi mir* article; they were erected by order, often against protests by farm management. To cite Tikhonov, "We build a complex for 2000 head, and keep the cows indoors the year round, because tor so large a number there is no pasture. The cost per cow exceeds that of a well-equipped one-room apartment." D. Yakova (*Voprosy ekonomiki*, No. 2, 1988) pointed out that huge sums have been devoted to "these extremely ineffective" complexes, which "frequently are a kind of monument to uneconomic management". Belov complained that the manure is largely wasted, or, worse, washed down by rain into rivers, thus polluting them. In his speech to the Party Conference, F. Morgun, in charge of the new committee on ecology, quoted appalling figures: "In the non-black earth zone, 60% of manure is washed into water. In 1965 53 million tons of manure remained unused, in 1985—115 million tons." Total losses of organic fetilizer in the country as a whole are "astronomic". The very large expenditure on "melioration", conducted by the Ministry of Water Resources (*Minvodkhoz*) at the budget's expense, have been denounced repeatedly, by Tikhonov, by Gaidar (*Kommunist*, No. 2, 1988), by Nuikin (*Novyi mir*, No. 2, 1988), by several speakers at the 19th Party Conference. Can it really continue calmly to spend huge sums to so little purpose? If so, *glasnost'* is an ineffective weapon.

On the question of family farming there is clearly a wide-ranging debate. While a number of articles welcome the reappearance of the *fermer*, and while in some areas the family farm is making headway, others are plainly dubious. L. Nikiforov, in a discussion reported in *Voprosy ekonomiki* (No. 2, 1988), supported the *semeinyi podryad* (family contract), but considers that "it is wrong to regard it as a return to peasant smallholdings . . . , as a form which should replace *kolkhozy* and *sovkhozy*". G. Chubukov, in the same discussion, stated that "if it is to take a form similar to Western farms, I believe that for socialism this is inacceptable". He expressed serious doubts: "The introduction of leasing will lead not to the strengthening of *kolkhozy* and *sovkhozy*, as has been said here, but rather to their liquidation", whereas G. Shmelev was willing to welcome their liquidation, their replacement by (small and genuine) cooperatives.

V. Gorbanev, director of a *sovkhoz*, favoured small-group contract, since this "returns the [peasant] to the land, gives him the opportunity to think for himself and plan his own work". Nikiforov added: "People want to get out from under the bureaucratic system which does not organize but destroys." A Party official from Estonia mentioned the reluctance of some farm managers to sign contracts with family groups, because they would then be responsible for contractual obligations which they could not carry out—e.g., because they could not obtain the necessary supplies. Then there is the question of small-scale mechanization, which is seriously lacking. Speakers also referred to "social-ideological doubts": many see such autonomous groups as nonsocialist, as making too much money, even as *kulaks*. A report on what has been achieved in Chinese agriculture was discussed. Nikiforov stressed the big difference: "Of course, if we adopt what has been done in China, then nothing but generalized chaos would result." The debate continues.

There have been some vigorous attacks, in *Literaturnaya gazeta* and in the literary monthlies, against the measures taken by local authorities to obstruct the private sector. In *Voprosy ekonomiki* (No. 6, 1987) there were some truly astonishing reports about punishment meted out for growing tomatoes and early vegetables in greenhouses and under plastic sheeting: "axes and even bulldozers" were used to destroy them, the area of the allotment was arbitrarily reduced. *Literaturnaya gazeta* wrote about *kriminalnyi pomidor* ("criminal tomatoes"), describing the vigorous steps taken by the local authorities to prevent private tomatoes from reaching the market.

Bitter remarks abound concerning the so-called *neperspektivnye derevni*, "futureless villages", a policy which must surely bring to mind what Ceausescu is now doing in Romania. Thus, according to Belov and other sources, tens of thousands of small villages in northwest Russia ceased to exist; it was planned to reduce the number of villages in all of the "non-black-earth region" from 140,000 to 29,000. Belov calls this "a crime". The motive could only be bureaucratic convenience. The damage done to peasant life, the stimulus to out-migration, has been widely commented on, and is much criticised for the blow it struck both at agriculture and at Russian rural life and national tradition. G. Gorodetsky, in *Literaturnaya Rossiya* (17 June 1988), refers to "abandoned and forgotten Russian villages . . . a mine placed under *perestroika*, of our ever-suffering agriculture, exhausted by *diktat*". At the Party Conference (1 July 1988) V. Starodubtsev, of peasant origin, said: "We remember how we worked for absolutely nothing, we had no vacations or days off, no pensions. . . . The peasants gave their all to our people and our state." So he appeals "to the working class and the intelligentsia: how long before this debt is repaid?" When will living conditions in villages improve? Plans exist, but they take time.

One could go on. I hope that the point is clear: *glasnost'* has illuminated the many dark corners of agriculture and rural life. It has also shown that, despite the legitimation of new and radical ideas on reform—and the adoption of some far-reaching decrees, especially on cooperatives—changes come slowly, are meeting resistance, and the would-be reformers are by no means agreed about what the changes should be. Gorbachev, speaking to the 19th Party Conference, referred to "the food problem, this being the most painful [*bolevaya*] and the most urgent problem in our society. There is some improvement, but this cannot satisfy us. . . . We have neither the moral nor the political right to tolerate a prolonged delay in solving the food problem."

An example, of wider relevance, of the way things are debated today may be cited from the speech to the 19th Party Conference by G. Arbatov, the director of the Institute for the Study of USA and Canada, and known to many Western observers as a defender of official policies: "Can we forget how passionately many responsible officials, members of the commission under the then premier Tikhonov, denounced in violent language any attempts to revive economic methods of control, lost their tempers at anything which reminded them of a market, of the experience of Hungary, China, Yugoslavia? And if we had proposed then the idea of family contract, cooperatives, individual enterprise, they would have had a heart attack." This was in the context of criticising Abalkin's relative gloom about lack of progress. Arbatov was stressing in his speech the "unchaining" of economic thought.

Abalkin was interviewed at length in *Sovetskaya Rossiya* (27 July 1988), where he made a stout defence of cooperative enterprise, criticised excessive restrictions and taxation of their activities, and also stressed the harm done by the continued emphasis on quantitative plan targets and their imposition by higher organs upon state enterprises. He also claimed that economics, despite some errors and omissions, has succeeded in devising a sound reform programme, which "significantly differs from that of Gosplan and, in our view, is more progressive". "Today," he said, "one can speak of the state planning and management organs having fallen behind in applying the conclusions of [economic] science."

This produced a vigorous counterblast from M. Antonov (*Sovetskaya Rossiya*, 7 Aug. 1988). Why, he asked, is Abalkin so optimistic? Economists spend too much time on mathematical models, substituting "dry and artificial economic categories" for real life. They speak, for instance, of relating wages to labour productivity, but, for example, on the railways it is measured in ton-kilometres, and so its pursuit can cause waste rather than economy. The recommended emphasis on financial results can produce deforestation, pollution, regional distortions, and neglect of infrastructure. "It is naive to leave it all to economic levers, and the rouble will do all the rest." And what about the theory of political economy of socialism, which, in Abalkin's own admission, remain poorly developed? What of nonmonetary motivation for work? "We need now not the mathematical equations of economists, but a programme to save the country, recovery of ruined land, a clean-up of poisoned rivers, the replanting of excessively over-cut forests, the ensuring of the technological, economic, and political independence of our country, the extirpation of cultural and spiritual wildness [*odichaniye*] of wide strata of the people, the *intelligentsia* too, not excluding those in academic life."

This was the same Antonov who had written in *Oktyabr'* about "cavalrymen" and "merchants". Western correspondents linked this article both with Nina Andreyeva's now notorious outburst, and with the speech made in Gorky by E. Ligachev, printed in *Izvestiya* (7 Aug. 1988), in which he criticised those who wished to introduce Western-style market economy. Evidently the debate is still in full swing, at all levels.

P. Bunich, chairman of one of the Academy's committees on reform, interviewed by *Argumenty i fakty* (No. 25, 1988), agreed that the reform process has had little effect: "The main brake is applied by the central economic organs, by Gosplan." They distort decisions of the Central Committee, while appearing to agree with them. Many enterprises have the right to engage in foreign trade, but exchange rate manipulations have eliminated the incentive: "for example, suppose a good is sold abroad for 200 dollars and the analogous domestic price is 100 roubles, the firm receives a price of 100 roubles. We now have 3000 exchange rates! These are called 'differential exchange coefficients'. The object of each of them is to adapt the export proceeds to the internal price! This destroys the whole idea of the [foreign-trade] reform."

A few more examples to illustrate *glasnost'* may be cited. The second secretary of the Leningrad *obkom*, A. Fateyev, speaking at the Party Conference, said: "It is now becoming clear that [economic reform] is encountering the tough conservatism of the sectoral principle of administration. Many ask: what is preventing us from achieving more, will the present reform suffer the fate of previous reforms? We must plainly state that such fears are not groundless." Then V. Platonov, Party secretary in the Chelyabinsk tractor factory, stated: "We are worried about the weakening of economic links . . . , of contractual discipline. There is uncertainty. We restrict administrative measures, without yet having created economic ones." (He also poured some cold water on the possible role of cooperatives.) The ministries continue, despite everything, to take away the bulk of profits, said N. Emelina, director of a knitwear factory, while E. Primakov pointed out that, owing to shortage and administered allocation of means of production, retained profits frequently cannot be spent. He also criticised the anti-vodka campaign: "In fact the state liquor monopoly has been undercut, there is now a shortage of sugar, an increase in its use to make *samogon* [hooch] is evidence that drunkenness has not greatly declined. Meanwhile toxic poisoning has risen. I do not mention the political costs, which are also large." Shmelev (*Novyi mir*, No. 4, 1988) estimated that in the early eighties one-third of sales of liquor was by illegal *samogon* producers, but that now it may be two-thirds. Then, speaking to the Party Conference, A. Melnikov, a car factory foreman, said: "What worries me? Again we have a gap between words and deeds, as in days not long gone by."

New ideas that previously would have been considered heretical are being put forward. Thus N. Shmelev (*Novyi mir*, No. 6, 1987) criticised "the prejudice" against stocks and shares (bonds) as a means of "mobilizing the resources of our citizens and of our enterprises", to invest them. He repeated this argument in *Novyi mir*, No. 4, 1988. The whole question of a capital market is thus opened. Indeed, *Pravda* (30 May 1988) featured an article titled "A *Sovkhoz* Issues Bonds [*aktsii*]", these being purchased by over 200 of the *sovkhoz* employees, to the tune of 262,000 roubles, on which they received dividends. The issuing of shares (*aktsii*) is strongly advocated by L. Grigoria in *Moskovskie novosti* (21 Aug. 1988). Similar proposals have been aired for *kolkhozy*. This is not yet a mass phenomenon by any means, but it is an important innovation.

Also out in the open is the advocacy of currency reform, of making the rouble convertible. This is put forward in various ways. Thus, *Literaturnaya gazeta* (26 Aug. 1987) printed an article by V. Soloukhin, the author, in which he complained that book circulation is restricted by shortage of paper; when British book publishers expect to sell many copies they can import paper, whereas their Soviet counterparts cannot use (domestic) roubles to buy anything abroad. Another article in *Literaturnaya gazeta* (by L. Pochivalov,

26 Aug. 1986) was titled "We, Abroad", and spoke of the shame felt by Soviet visitors to foreign countries, with their tiny ration of foreign currency and the worthless roubles. Criticism has also been directed against *Beryozka* shops in the USSR, which accept only convertible currency and stimulate black-market dealings. Convertibility has been urged by G. Lisichkin (*Druzhba narodov*, No. 1, 1988), and N. Shmelev (*Novyi mir*, No. 6, 1987) urged direct links between internal- and world-market prices and convertibility of the rouble. He denounced the "so-called transferable rouble", which he calls "a stillborn child, long ago a mere unit of account, fulfilling none of the functions of money". Shmelev also urged the creation of "free economic zones" to attract foreign capital.

Critical material abounds on internal trade, on prices (delay and uncertainty about the principles of price reform), on the chronic crisis on the railways, on trade unions, on the quality of consumers' goods, on frustration of management and obstacles to innovation, the black ("shadow") economy—one could fill this whole book with telling quotations, illustrating *glasnost'* many times over. A devastating account of neglect of track maintenance, in pursuit of plants in ton-kilometres and increases in "labour productivity", points to a sharp rise in train crashes as a consequence (*Pravda*, 3 Aug. 1988). A major article in *Pravda* by Daniil Granin, the author of the novel *Zubr*, provides a sample of the reaction of noneconomists to the discussions. "Today we hear reproaches: 'Much talk, no results!' What results? The simplest everyday ones. Queues continue to wait, as before. For food, basic food, not delicatessen. For housing. People are tired of waiting, tired of promises, of delays. One cannot today just wave these complaints aside as idle chatter and point to statistics of the growth of consumption, etc. Shops are empty, the market is undersupplied. Things have become really bad with medical drugs. Ecological conditions in a number of regions are catastrophic. All this was said at the [Party] conference. We have reached a dangerous stage; continued disappointments would affect the practical implementation of *perestroika*." Urgent reconsideration is needed of prestige projects, including the Leningrad dam, foreign aid, space research. "Finally we might reduce the period of military service, providing additional millions of young hands to cope with our economic needs. I cannot judge in greater detail, since we the citizens have no means of knowing how our money is spent on defence, the cosmos and some other items."

This brings me to the subject of statistics, their availability and reliability. As mentioned earlier, the systematic publication of economic statistics was resumed in 1956 after a long interval.

However, in the late Brezhnev years some figures began to disappear: thus foreign trade data were severely pruned, grain harvests became secret, as did infant mortality. Under Gorbachev the last two reappeared, but there were still gaps, and economists frequently and publicly complained about the inadequate statistical "ration" with which they had to work. Defence expenditure was an evident example: the published figure is likely to have been exceeded as much as fivefold, which, naturally, puts into question the validity of other budgetary figures, since presumably very large military items are hidden in them. It has been publicly admitted, in interviews with foreign correspondents, that the real figure *is* higher (Marshal Akhromeyev has said so), but as yet no figure has been published—though it may be at any time.

Are Soviet physical-output data reliable? Most Western analysts accept them, though with reservations. There are *pripiski* (padding of production figures), but also some concealment (e.g., to sell illegally in the black market). In any case, the published figures represent what the Soviet statisticians themselves work with. Volume and price indices are a different story. To the credit of Soviet economists, a number of them did succeed in expressing their doubts publicly: Krasovsky, Faltsman, Valtukh, Sverdlik, and Khanin have in various ways written about disguised price rises and misleading volume indices. I presented a paper (to the Manchester Statistical Society) in 1983 with the title "Has Soviet Growth Ceased?" using Soviet sources to show that growth had fallen to close to zero at that time, that official figures understated the fall in growth rates. The fact that these were stagnation years is now admitted.

Typically, it was a literary journal that published the first general (as distinct from partial) challenge to the official data: in *Novyi mir* (No. 3, 1987) there appeared an article by Khanin and Selyunin entitled "*Lukavaya tsifra*" ("Cunning Figures"). It was a species of time-bomb. The authors pointed out that the official indices, if chained, show that Soviet national income grew 90-fold from 1928 to 1986. In their considered view, the real figure was between 6- and 7-fold. This is not the place to discuss the validity of the methodology developed by Khanin, which he had already set out in an earlier work. For the first time the official figures for both pre- and post-war years were directly challenged, and an alternative proposed. This was surely the largest downward amendment in growth rates known to recorded history! For 1928–41 Khanin showed a rise in national income of 50 percent, against the official figure of 5.5 times. The calculations were challenged, but the challengers did not defend the official data.

Khanin's calculations, showing growth rates very far below official levels, were given the *cachet* of being published by the Party's own organ, *Kommunist* (No. 17, 1988). Clearly the new Statistics committee will have to do some major recalculations of its own.

Some devastating criticisms of official statistics were published in *EKO* (No. 12, 1988) by the Leningrad economist A. Illarionov. The official long term growth rates are nonsensical: were they correct, the USSR's per capita GNP would now be 2.8 times higher than that of the United States. If the statistical annual is to be believed, the USSR reached 67 percent of the U.S. national income in every year from 1975 to 1984, but this "fell" to 66 percent in 1985–86 and to 64 percent in 1987—despite allegedly higher growth rates—so that "Achilles, though running faster than the tortoise, falls ever further behind". The national income growth figures in current and "unchanged" prices are in blatant contradiction—even with the official price index—and so "by publishing mythical growth tempos, the central statistical department continues to conceal the truth about economic stagnation". The USSR is falling further behind.

> Of the five largest economic centres of the world—USA, EEC, USSR, Japan, and China—our country has the lowest growth rates, in fact close to zero. We are in a dramatic situation, which can have catastrophic consequences. Yet, because of prolonged, systematic statistical falsification, our society is still not fully aware of the seriousness of the situation.

While official data imply that Soviet per-capita national income is 57 percent of U.S. levels, Illarionov's calculations suggest that 44 percent would be nearer the truth. However, this too overstates the real level of economic development. Housing space per-capita is one third of U.S. levels. In the number of cars per thousand inhabitants the USSR is far behind Hungary and even Mexico. Grain harvest yields are among the lowest in the world, behind even Turkey, Pakistan, Brazil, and Mexico. ". . . [O]ur agriculture has reached a state of total paralysis". Consumption of paper per capita is a small fraction of the countries of Western Europe, less even than Mexico and Chile. There are far fewer telephones per head than in Portugal and Yugoslavia. Per-capita consumption of goods and services the author puts at 30 percent of U.S. levels, well below the 44 percent mentioned earlier, because of a lower share of consumption and a higher share of military expenditures. So "we are at best a semi-developed country", in the same category as "Spain, Ireland, Venezuela, Greece, Uruguay, Argentina, Portugal, Chile, and Brazil".

Other critics are equally forthright. Thus, in *EKO* (No. 9, 1988), V. Dmitriev states that "one has the impression that the State Committee on Statistics is capable of anything to prevent us from knowing the truth", e.g., about living costs and real incomes. The data on family budgets, consumption of specific products, and savings bank deposits are unreliable and contradictory; the sampling methods dubious and never disclosed. Health statistics are still very incomplete, and many disagreeable social facts remain hidden. O. Zamkov in *EKO* (No. 11, 1988) asks "from whom and why do we conceal"? He lists a large number of inexcusable and continuing omissions. How can economists analyse the real situation when there are no published data on intersector flows? "Maybe we feared that our opponents would calculate how much military hardware we produced". He joins others (for example V. Frolov in *Ogonyok*, No. 43, 1988) in attacking the secrecy surrounding the military budget. He added:

> Would such publication subvert our defence capacity? . . . How can we evaluate the real potential of our economy without knowing the magnitude of the defence burden? What part (the best part) of our resources has been devoted to this sphere? If you enter a race and you have a ball and chain on your leg, you should not be indifferent to its weight.

Earlier, O. Bogomolov, a senior economist, published in *Literaturnaya gazeta* (16 Sept. 1987) his or his institute's calculations as to the rise in the urban cost of living: according to him, it "more that doubled since the late fifties". Let us say that this gives an increase of close to 100 percent in the period 1960–86. The retail price index published in the statistical annual shows a rise in the same period of less than 10 percent. Since average money wages rose by 120 percent in those years (no one disputes *these* figures), this would imply not a doubling of real wages in 26 years but a rise by some 20 percent, much less than 1 percent per annum. In the same issue of the same journal, and in many other issues too, A. Rubinov cited numerous examples of rises in prices—often taking the form of the disappearance of a cheap model, its replacement by a "new" and much dearer one, and openly mocked the official index. Some of the Soviet recomputations have been showing lower growth rates than those calculated by the CIA and some Western scholars.

Why, some readers might think, have I quoted so much from literary journals? What about the economic and statistical publications? I suspect the answer here lies not only in censorship or timidity: there are grave methodological problems in recalculating the "correct" figures. Khanin's methods are rough, as he himself freely admits. This is not just a question of the index number problem. It is a matter of comparing unlike with unlike; new products appear and there are changes of model, and this under conditions in which management has a material interest in increasing prices and, in order to evade price controls, has to deny that it has done so. The central statisticians have not got a "correct" figure which they are concealing from us.

There is a sizable Western literature on this whole subject, stretching back many years. Involved in it is a theoretical point of practical significance, relating to the appropriate theory of value. As such Soviet economists as Petrakov and Borozdin (e.g., in *Voprosy ekonomiki*, No. 12, 1987) have been pointing out, a crudely understood labour theory of value assigns value and price to a commodity on the basis of cost, this being a measure of the effort required to produce it. But it is plainly nonsense to assume that two baskets of goods which share only the characteristic of requiring the same effort to produce have the same "value", if by this is meant value-in-use. In a market economy effort and result are brought together (imperfectly, no doubt) by the process of purchase and sale, the market: a good which costs more than the customer is prepared to pay will not sell at its full cost price. In the USSR, for reasons familiar to students of the subject, there is frequently no choice, and official prices have been cost-based for fifty years and more (though some have been subsidized). The point in the present context is that the use of such prices distorts comparisons over time and between countries. The interest of many managers in avoiding economy in inputs, so as to fulfill plans in value of turnover, also has its statistical effects, when avoidable waste counts as "output"—hence, the reformers' insistence on devising a "cost-limiting" mechanism, on which much is written.

It is also worth mentioning one significant step forward. It may surprise some readers that such a step represents a bold innovation. This was the publication in *EKO* by V. Orlov of an article comparing the five-year *plans* with the *outcomes*. Western analysts have been doing this ever since there were five-year plans. Not a single such table had been published in the Soviet Union, to my knowledge, until this number of *EKO* (No. 11, 1987). Orlov naturally drew attention to the frequency with which physical-output plans were not fulfilled.

A subsequent article (*EKO*, No. 8, 1988) by Orlov is titled "Illusion and Reality of Economic Information". Here he points to falsification of statistics in the thirties, giving numerous examples relating to national income, agricultural output, real wages, and monetary circulation. He goes on to the gaps and distortions of more recent statistical publications: thus, "close to half of the reported rise in produced national income in 1986 was due to hidden increases in prices". He also joined in the pressure to fill another gap in the statistics. To cite his words: "For a long time official documents distorted the real level of the state's defence expenditures. The published data served purely propagandist purposes and did not reflect the real burden of these expenditures. Only in 1987 was it stated that the budgetary allocations for defence cover only a part of the expenditures." Sh. Sverdlik (*EKO*, No. 12, 1988) complains that "*glasnost'*" has not yet touched data on money circulation and fiscal and credit policy.

Another welcome innovation is the appearance (in *Ekonomicheskaya gazeta*, No. 10, 1988) of price data on free markets, an average for 21 cities for January of that year. Here are some of the figures (per kilo):

|          | official price | free price |
|----------|:--------------:|:----------:|
| potatoes | 0.10 | 0.71 |
| cabbage  | 0.20 | 0.71 |
| onions   | 0.50 | 0.63 |
| beets    | 0.15 | 0.83 |
| carrots  | 0.15 | 0.70 |
| tomatoes | 2.00 | 5.61 |
| beef     | 2.00 | 5.01 |
| pork     | 2.10 | 4.59 |
| butter   | 3.60 | 8.16 |

The inadequacies of the state trading network, the unfair distribution of such scarce commodities as meat among towns and regions, and the toleration of endless queues (which help to explain the high free-market prices) are vigorously discussed in many papers (e.g., *Pravda*, 3 Aug. 1988; *Sovetskaya Rossiya*, 7 Aug. 1988).

Repressed or disguised inflation is now quite extensively discussed. Apart from such calculations as Khanin's and Bogomolov's, already cited, there are some recent articles seeking to measure "concealed price rises" in machinery and equipment, supplementing earlier calculations by Fal'tsman, for example, by A. Kornev (*Voprosy ekonomiki*, No. 6, 1988), which show a rise of 25 percent in the five years 1981–85, contrary to the official index, which showed a drop. Very high estimates have also been published in respect of concealed rises in costs of construction. This puts in question the validity of investment statistics, which, misleadingly, show a rise in "volume".

Agricultural statistics are questioned for other reasons. Bogachev (*Voprosy ekonomiki*, No. 5, 1988) speaks of statistical inflation "through a reduction of the usable content of the crop: of dry clean grain in the 'bunker-harvest', of sugar in the sugar-beet, of starch in the potatoes, of fibre in the raw cotton. . . . It would be interesting to calculate how much soil is transported to town attached to various root crops." The reference to "bunker-harvest" relates to the fact that grain crops are measured in bunker weight, not in "barn yield", and impurities are thus included. This is all apart from postharvest losses, which Gorbachev himself put at close to 20 percent of grain, and many sources give much higher estimates for vegetables. So in these instances the physical-output data are misleading. To take another example: "A quarter of the [mineral] fertilizers produced simply do not reach the users" (*Moscow News*, No. 34, 1987, quoting V. Pavlov).

L. Ivanov (*Literaturnaya gazeta*, 11 May 1988) estimates the difference between bunker weight and the real barn yield of grain at 25 percent, sometimes more; it is essential that the authorities stop fooling themselves with "inflated statistics". If in 1987 there really were 211 million tons of grain harvested, there would have been no need to import any. Ivanov casts doubt also on milk statistics. The milk yields of private cows he considers to be deliberately under-estimated, because "to show a higher percentage produced in the private sector cannot be considered desirable".

One other gap in published statistics deserves a mention: several authors refer to widespread overtime working, especially by women (this was also referred to at the Party Conference by Emelina). Yet the published data on hours worked suggest that there is hardly any overtime at all. Is it unreported, and so unpaid? More information is needed. There is also far too little information about wages and salaries: What is the average pay of women, of directors of enter-prises, of ministers?

One further "offence" against *glasnost'*: the national income data on 1985 and 1986 were mysteriously inconsistent, with no expla-nation (so far) vouchsafed. As pointed out by Western scholars (P. Hanson, J. Vanous), national income in current prices supposedly grew less than the volume of national income in "comparable prices", which is plainly unbelievable, since even the distorted official data show a rise in prices. The explanation, beyond doubt, is that vodka production and sales were omitted from the volume index so as to give a less unfavourable picture. It is no coincidence that the statistical report on 1987 presented for the first time a figure for the growth of the gross national product in its Western or U.N.

definition. This gave a higher growth rate than the Soviet "national income" (net material product), for several reasons: the inclusion of services, the exclusion of turnover tax (which is the major part of the "value" of vodka), and a different treatment of revenues from foreign trade.

There is wide-ranging and reasonably free debate about the whole basis of economic reform, the role in it of the market, the plan, the price mechanism. Opinions vary widely, among economists and among the leadership. Ligachev clearly shares with some of the less radical economists the view that the market should be limited. I have already cited the arguments of Antonov in *Oktyabr'* about "cavalrymen" and "merchants"; on the opposite flank is G. Lisichkin, notably his article in *Druzhba narodov* (No. 1, 1988), in which he argues vigorously against the widespread view that the pursuit of personal material well-being, acquisitiveness, is "bad". Though he does agree that acquisitiveness can go too far, and that the market is not a cure-all (quoting West German economists in support), his fire is directed at "antimarket economists who foam at the mouth to prove that socialism and the law of value are incompatible". No one, in any country, least of all in Thatcherite Britain, can confidently assert that we have found the appropriate balance between public and private, state and society, market and plan. Such works as O. Williamson's *Markets and Hierarchies* remind us that large hierarchically structured corporations exist here, too, with their own bureaucracies. This is not the place to discuss the pros and cons, only to note that they are being freely debated in the Soviet Union. While no one is advocating, or would be allowed to advocate, "capitalism", much can be and is being said which a few years ago would have seemed outrageous.

As for the reform, there is almost a consensus that it has barely begun, that it has as yet produced no significant results, that its success remains problematical. Things might indeed get worse before they get better. But will people be patient that long, when *glasnost'* gives them unprecedented opportunity to protest?

Finally, Selyunin, in *Znamya* (No. 7, 1988) under the headline "Deep Reform or the Bureaucracy's Revenge", criticises the whole reform strategy, Aganbegyan's alleged stress on growth-acceleration instead of on drastic structural change in the pattern of production. Far too small a part of the national income is devoted to consumption, far too much is spent on heavy industry. The share of investment is 1.7 times what it is in America and 1.5 times that of Western Europe, but its effectiveness is half. It is wrong to expand machinery production when many machines lack personnel to operate them. The share of consumption is low even in official statisticians; it is lower still if price distortions are allowed for. There are 350,000 construction (investment) projects now being undertaken, which is ridiculous. Meanwhile, there is serious excess purchasing power. Reform measures so far taken have changed little, "the old planning system has been preserved", complete with the old prices, material allocation, and commands. The price "reform" of 1990 or 1991 may well be along traditional lines and therefore ineffective. Ministries are still charged with ensuring the production of needed items, and so their power over enterprises is unaltered and looks like it is staying that way—and so on.

Commenting, G. Popov, O. Latsis, and N. Shmelev, all three leading reform-ideologists, very largely agree with Selyunin's picture of lack of progress, with some differences of detail. Thus, Popov points out that "the situation is highly contradictory. The necessary major structural changes require an end to the arbitrary interference of the centre. However, the necessity of speedily overcoming the lags points to the need for the centre to act vigorously. In my view this is the main objective contradiction in our economic *perestroika*." (He could have added that this is so in politics, too: reform can come only from above, yet its purpose should be to limit the power of the centre.) Investments too often depend on the relative power and influence of specific sectors and ministries, which stands in the way of structural change and leads to waste. Latsis defends Aganbegyan, saying that he would probably agree with most of Selyunin's analysis. He, too, cited instances of ridiculously ineffective investments, as illustrations of the "ministerial disease", and pointed to inflationary pressures. Shmelev agrees that the "law on the enterprise" has no effect, that ministries retain power, that the current five-year plan and its growth targets should have been abandoned, that the share of accumulation, if correctly calculated, could well be as high as 40 percent and so is too high, too ineffectively utilized. He raises directly—for the first time in the present context, I believe— "our real possibilities of improving the lives of our population at the expense of reducing the army and defence expenditures, the system of state security" (i.e., the KGB). He concludes: "It is sad, my dear comrades. When will we finally return to simple common sense?"

Similar frank critical assessments of the lack of progress of reform appeared in *EKO*, No. 8, 1988. G. Grenbek criticised the law on the enterprise, pointed out that the depreciation allowances are insufficient to finance replacement because of the sharp rise in prices of machinery and equipment. Ministries continue to exercise power because they remain reponsible for output, which means that they issue detailed orders to enterprises. "Even if by 1990 we do elaborate a theory of a price system, actually to introduce it will require not a year but maybe a whole quinquennium. So we will be drafting a new plan without prices, and will be fulfilling it in transitional prices (the old ones will be no more, the new ones will not yet be fixed or confirmed by practice)." Enterprise managers still have few rights, and are in any case unprepared for the role assigned for them by the reform. Grenbek cited a manager: "I and my fellow Heroes of Socialist Labour are lucky individuals. We happened to be Heroes, others happen to be in jail. This is the sad truth." S. Zverev, a specialist on light industry, was even more scathing. He pointed out that plans are nowhere near being fulfilled. Quality remains poor. The volume of output has in fact fallen, when allowance is made for price increases. Supplies are unreliable; thus, the chemical industry is uninterested in supplying dyestuffs, and Zverev recommends that light industry should set up its own chemical plants. Machinery is also of poor quality, and they should make their own machinery too. ("The saving of the drowning shall be the task of the drowning.") B. Prilepsky states that the supply system remains as it was: "It is impossible today to get any raw materials through wholesale trade. It is intended to channel only 3% of materials through wholesale trade, but even they are hidden behind a high and unclimbable wall of instructions."

One notes the rapid growth of articles about the real economic problems of socialist countries by not only Soviet authors, but also of discussions of Soviet reforms by, for example, Czech authors (e.g., B. Urban and Z. Sula, in *EKO*, No. 8, 1988—"The Risks of Perestroika"—and L. Rusmich, in *Voprosy ekonomiki*, No. 8, 1988). *Voprosy ekonomiki* (No. 8, 1988) contains two articles on Chinese reform by Chinese scholars (Lo Yunchan and Li Chuifa), and a detailed analysis of small-scale enterprise in Hungary written jointly by a Soviet and a Czech scholar. Finally, *EKO*, No. 9, 1988, contains an article of mine, titled "The Limits of Full Khozras-chyot". *Glasnost'*, indeed!

If some readers of this chapter come to feel that the picture is *too* dark, that the economy cannot be in such grave disorder, I can only reply that the picture being painted by a large number of Soviet critics is indeed very dark. It is possible that they, and Gorbachev, too, are exaggerating the scale of the problems as part of their campaign to push through the reforms they deem necessary. Be that as it may, there is clearly a crisis of confidence in the planning system, a sense of crisis that is widely shared, though there is considerable disagreement, as we have seen, as to the remedies.

Thus, in the conservative-leaning *Nash sovremennik* (No. 12, 1987), A. Ochkin not only opposed the proposed increase in food prices, which would lead to a price-wage spiral, but attacked N. Shmelev for his advocacy of "competition, free markets, unemployment, and profit maximization".

We are far indeed from the days when any and every reform promulgated by the leadership was unanimously cheered by a well-drilled choir! So much the better for that.

As this chapter goes to press, many Soviet reforming economists are expressing both gloom and alarm: Gaidar (*Kommunist*, No. 2, 1989), Abalkin (*Komsomolskaya pravda*, 8 February 1989), Aganbegyan (*Pravda*, 6 February 1989), Latsis (*Literaturnaya gazeta*, 25 January 1989), G. Popor (*Smena*, 10 January 1989), Lisichkin (*Izvestiya*, 25 January 1989), and N. Shmelev (*Znamya*, No. 1, 1989), to cite some examples. Inflationary pressures, the huge budget deficit, shortages, delays in capital construction, the survival of imposed gross-output targets, the persistence of heavy losses and large-scale waste, and the still very slow development of cooperative enterprise and family farming are all pointed to. The old spending habits persist, and economy is not rewarded. The crisis could become acute if remedial measures are not taken soon.

# CHAPTER 9

# Conclusion: Now What?

Three quotations to begin with:

> Conflicts are possible, and the outcome is difficult to predict. For the second time in this century there has arisen a curious sort of "dual power" [*dvoevlastiye*], in which neither side is ready for a decisive advance and awaits its hour. (Nuikin, *Novyi mir*, No. 1, 1988)

> In our country there really has arisen a revolutionary situation. The "rulers" can no longer rule and the "ruled" no longer wish to live in the old way. (N. Shmelev, *Novyi mir*, No. 4, 1988)

> We face changes not less revolutionary [than the shift from war-communism to NEP]—the workpeople do not wish to live in the old way, the administrative apparatus can no longer govern in the old way. ((N. Selyunin, *Novyi mir*, No. 5, 1988)

The *dvoevlastiye* in the first quotation refers to the period in 1917 when power was shared between the provisional government and the Petrograd soviet. Both the following quotations paraphrase Lenin's well-known definition of the revolutionary situation, and apply it to today's USSR—an unheard-of presumption!

The Novosibirsk journal *EKO* examined various alternative scenarios and used the animal kingdom to illustrate them (a summary was reprinted in *Moskovskie novosti*, 29 Nov. 1987):

> (a) *The "ostrich" scenario:* "The slogan of a revolutionary *perestroika* is seen as left-wing extremism, a break with the principles of socialism." Conservative—keep things as they are.
> (b) *The fox scenario:* Yes, something has to change, but not too radically. "Foxes" propose a large number of minor reforms, to "improve performance while changing nothing", or nothing fundamental.

(c)  *The bear scenario:* Deal with disorders "with iron claws". Many of
the older generation consider that present ills, openly spoken about for
the first time, are new. "There was no disorder under Stalin."

(d)  *The scenario of the separatist technocrat:* "Give us authority, the
right to buy and sell, and problems will vanish." This, according to V.
Bykov, deputy-editor of *EKO*, is the attitude "of a certain part of
economic managers and of their ideologists from among the academics".
It could lead to neglect of general political-social problems *and* of the
interests and rights of subordinates.

Bykov pointed out that all four scenarios suffer from one built-in
defect: "They ignore the concerns of working people, their aims lie
outside of their concerns: privilege, increased power, the solution of
purely technological or purely economic tasks, the fulfillment of
national ambitions." He went on: "*Perestroika* is a social revolution. It is carried out on the initiative of the ruling party. As in any
party, there are some more progressive elements, fully sharing and
actively supporting the leadership's new course, but also cadres of
the old type, who dislike *perestroika* and are silently sabotaging it."

He ended as follows: "The revolution has no precise scenario. The
essential is to ensure that the initiative of renovation should come
down from the topmost level of government to the lowest levels and
become the personal interest of millions. . . . From foreign journalists we often hear the question: 'So what are you intending to create
as a result of *perestroika*? Communism?' The answer, it seems to
me, is simple: no, we are ever so far from that! We intend to restore
the better features of socialism, its humanity, the exercise of power
by the people, dynamism, love of peace, to bring society to the
condition when it can make a new start on the long and difficult road
to happiness. . . . It is often written and said that there are no
alternatives to *perestroika*. I think that there are. Suppose we
stumble, make errors, delay, or unthinkingly move too fast, then an
impatient and oh-so-familiar hand will try to shift the historical
clock onto one of the four scenario-variants—or may even invent a
sixth one."

There is among the reformers no certainty of success. The
opponents of change are strong indeed. To cite Shmelev yet again:
"Who will break our economic leaders, especially at higher levels, of
their feudal psychology, caste-like self-conceit, assurance of survival, of 'God-given' right to command, to be above the law and above
criticism?" All the evidence points to a political struggle, in which no
one stands up *against perestroika*, but in which there are quite basic
disagreements both about means and about ends. *Literaturnaya
gazeta* on 30 September 1987 published an article by V. Drozd,

under the title "Will Their Time Return?" "They" are the *apparatchiki* who speak of *perestroika* but continue to cling to old ways and to established privileges. An *obkom* secretary demanded that *raikom* secretaries stand to attention in his presence. So they in turn sought compensation for their humiliation: "Yes, I could be stood to attention and a fist waved at me, but I ride in a black limousine and the rules of the road (and not only of the road) do not apply to me. Yes, I could at any time be punished like a small boy. Yes, I live by the well-known principle—you are the boss, I am a fool—but I have the right to enter any shop by the back door and my wife does not stand in a queue. ... I once dared, in a meeting of writers, to say roughly the following: the Minister of Trade should have a high salary, as his work is responsible and very difficult, but his family should get food in normal shops and stand in the normal queues, and only then would the queues be shorter and trade will be better run. Some leading comrades reacted quite sharply, accusing me even of anti-Soviet ideas." He went on to criticise excessive privileges, citing some colourful examples. He ended: "So can their time return? Yes it can, if we continue to talk of *perestroika* rather than actually doing it, if we run on the spot without taking real and decisive steps toward democratization and renewal of our lives. ... Our society has two ways forward: either the further development of democracy or a vigorous 'tightening of the screws'." The victory is not yet won.

Fine words there are in plenty. It was good to read Daniil Granin (a full page, *Pravda*, 5 Aug. 1988) on "How to make of soviets not the adjuncts of Party organs but real masters? ... I was at one time a deputy of the Leningrad soviet, but I could do practically nothing. ... Today things are much the same, I need not repeat what the press says about this. Our political system has long ago petrified, for decades we have 99.9% votes 'for', with these same polling booths for secret ballots into which no human foot has stepped." Faced with Gorbachev's proposal to combine the role of (local) Party secretary with the chairmanship of the (local) soviet, Granin's first reaction was: "The soviets have no real power, so adding this post to that of Party secretary will add nothing to his power. One cannot transfer that which does not exist." But he now sees that this is a means of giving some power to the soviet. He welcomed the reality of discussions, complete with proposed amendments and votes against, at the 19th Party Conference. He advocated equal rights, in jobs and promotion, for non-Party people. "Except for appointments to the Party-political apparatus membership of the Party should confer no advantages." He denounced long-ingrained habits of officialdom, the "boorish attitude to people, the lies told".

Ivan Vasiliev, in *Pravda* (11 June 1988), under the heading "Remove the Iron Press of Authoritarianism", asked: "How can we progress when the System is still untouched. It is as it always was. ... It does not like openness, opposes *glasnost'*, is lazy and frequently simply incapable of independent thought. In such a situation it is not easy to break out of the general environment and to turn a *nomenklatura* functionary into a revolutionary", or for a Party secretary "to part with the concept of being all-powerful". A key element, which recurs in many articles and speeches, is that the functionaries "see themselves not as empowered by their collective but as representatives of higher organs in their collective". Full-time officials, be they of the party, or of a local soviet, or of trade unions, or in agricultural administration, should cease being commanders and turn into executive officers responsible to their respective subunits or members.

Less than clear is the future of the *nomenklatura* system itself. For years its very existence was not allowed to be mentioned. Now its nature, power, and privileges are in the arena of discussion. But can the Party, will the Party, let go its grip on "the selection and distribution of cadres"? How can it be reconciled with genuine elections and competitive selection, in and out of the Party? Is even a limited degree of real democratization compatible with a one-party state? This question too is in the public eye; I do not know the answer.

Has *perestroika* the necessary "teeth"? As Postnikov put it in his speech to the party conference, addressing Gorbachev: "Mikhail Sergeyevich, *perestroika* is a revolution. You say we should act calmly, humanely. But if it is a revolution, it cannot be implemented by such methods." It is all very well to talk of democratization, but is there a majority now for necessary change? Are not the people more conservative than today's leadership? Archie Brown, acute observer of the Soviet scene, summarized the attitude of some reformers to democratization with words attributed to St. Augustine: "Lord, give me chastity and continence, but not yet." For the time being, whatever fine words there are about democratization, this is a "revolution *from above*", or else it will bog down. And because some of those "above" are less than revolutionary, it may bog down anyway. The more so because of the formidable purely practical problems, particularly evident in the process of economic reform. The centralized planning system, with production tasks and material allocation decided by Gosplan, Gossnab, ministries, needs to be converted into a fundamentally new system, with a much larger role for the market. But where are the institutions, the information flows, the required price mechanism, the personnel trained to manage in new ways, able to find customers and suppliers independently, and all this under conditions of chronic shortage and structural imbalances? Even if everyone were agreed on just what needed to be done, even if there were a fully elaborated and internally consistent reform model, it would be a formidable task to make the change, with every possibility of initially making things worse before they get better. Soviet reformers are painfully aware of all of this.

*Glasnost'* has made limited progress also in international relations, which are not, as such, our subject. Change is at last noticeable in the reporting of the politics of communist-ruled countries. True, very little indeed is said about Ceausescu's (appalling) policies and the worsening relations between Romania and Hungary. But the real situation in Poland is discussed. There is intense interest in and much published on economic reform and economic problems in Hungary and China, with achievements and difficulties presented in a reasonably balanced way, as are the problems of much of the Third World. The West, too, is being presented in less stridently propagandistic tones. Even the tragic events in Northern Ireland have been given serious treatment, without the usual assumption that the withdrawl of British troops would solve everything (in *Sovetskaya Rossiya*, 27 July 1988). Gefter has been able to suggest in print that not only the West is responsible for the Cold War, asking, "Why were people afraid of us?" He quoted a propagandist of many years ago: *Dogonim—pobedim; peregonim—unichtozhim"* ("When we catch up, we win; when we overtake, we destroy"), and added that Khrushchev was reflecting that tradition when he tactlessly used the phrase "We will bury you". He implied that this is a thing of the past, but again one must recall the title of his article: "Stalin Died Yesterday".

A. Latynina (*Novyi mir*, No. 8, 1988) also takes up the question of expansionist ideology, citing an article by the American scholar Carl Sagan which was printed in *Ogonyok* (No. 11, 1988): Americans, wrote Sagan, see Soviet communism as "poverty, backwardness, Gulag, . . . the cruel suppression of the human spirit and a desire for world conquest. . . . Even now on your coins your national symbol covers the whole world." Arbatov had ironically remarked that the half-moon on the Turkish flag does not imply a claim by Turkey on the moon, but this does not satisfy Latynina: "The very origin of the symbol is linked with the conception of an inevitable world revolution." She cited a world-revolutionary poem by Pavel Kogan, and went on: "Not only for professor Sagan do such appeals seem to be proof of the scale of our ideological claims, which turn into territorial claims", including, in the eyes of Sagan and others, the Soviet presence in Afghanistan. This is a myth, but one paid for in blood and which has contributed to the Cold War.

Latynina links this whole subject with a controversial article by S. Kunyaev which appeared in the (Russian-nationalist) *Molodaya gvardiya* (No. 8, 1987). That author offended two "targets". One was connected with his assertion that only pure Russians could be real patriots. The other was his criticism of prewar and wartime poets who expressed the ideology of the Third International. Both led to indignant attacks on the author. Yet, while deploring the nationalism, Latynina can see that he did hit the second target. These doubtless idealistic young people, who believed in a world soviet republic, were rendered obsolete by the *patriotic* war. It is not their internationalist, communist values, but those human values represented by Bulgakov, Pasternak, Mandelshtam, and Akhmatova which live on. Latynina appeals for a common ground of discussion for those who "cannot justify the death from hunger of millions of peasants, the destruction of the village, the terror, the destruction of our own culture, by reference to the superior objectives of industrialization, which, were it not for genocidal actions, could well have been better achieved". She finds it necessary, in this connection, to rescue and extol the words "liberal" and "liberalism", for so long excoriated. "Historically in our country liberalism lost. The people preferred the idea of social justice to that of individual freedom. . . . But now, when we have seen the inadequacy of the idea of social justice and equality if unaccompanied by the idea of personal freedom, when we are elaborating the principles of freedom of conscience and human rights, liberal ideas are fruitful."

The way foreign policy issues are treated in history textbooks was queried in *Voprosy istorii* (No. 9, 1988), by V. Vozgin and G. Kovalenko, who quoted a typical passage: "Whether defending or advancing, Russia as a whole waged wars that were just and inevitable. If the country were to live and develop, then it had to throw away the scabbard and prove with the sword its right to life and growth. These wars were in a definite sense people's wars, with the constant and active participation of the armed formes of the nation and of the cossacks." They ask: Is this acceptable? Meanwhile, "Marx's work on secret diplomacy in the 18th century is still unpublished". Should one not examine critically Peter's policy on the Baltic lands, later policies toward Poland? (Yes indeed! One also needs a more critical look at Stalin's foreign policies—Khrushchev's, too.)

We also noted earlier that Volkogonov questioned the wisdom of the Nazi-Soviet friendship pact, and "Ernst Henry" denounced Stalin's part in facilitating Hitler's rise to power. However, serious critical discussion of Soviet foreign policy, past and present, is yet to come. For example, the invasion of Czechoslovakia in 1968 is still almost a taboo subject.

There is now a wider availability of foreign newspapers in the Soviet Union, and broadcasts to Russia from abroad are no longer jammed. Also, Soviet visitors have spoken on (for example) the BBC's Russian service. One motive for bringing life and controversy into the Soviet media lies in the fact that so many were getting their news from foreign broadcasts. The Chernobyl disaster, and the futile efforts made to conceal its magnitude (from Moscow, too) acted as a catalyst. Foreign specialists are quoted, interviewed, even invited to write articles for Soviet periodicals. Soviet academics may now answer letters and can accept invitations. More managers are beginning to travel, as part of a long overdue and welcome reform in foreign-trade procedures—though there are still complaints about limits being placed upon export-orientated enterprise by obsolete regulations.

Let us turn to the question: Now what? Where is it all going? Will it last? Many years ago the former British ambassador, Sir William Hayter, wrote: "The Soviet rulers believe, and history provides little evidence to contradict this belief, that Russia can only be governed as an isolated autocracy" (*The Times*, 9 Sept. 1973). Brezhnev would certainly have agreed. His shade is doubtless deeply disturbed, wherever it/he now is: the basics of Soviet power are being undermined, *glasnost'* is a dangerous folly, party control is endangered, all kinds of dissidents are being let loose on an unprepared people, foreign ideological penetration spreads apace, disaster threatens.

Such a view must surely be shared by a number of the surviving members of Brezhnev's Politbureau, possibly by some who are not yet pensioned off. Just as surely, the old Western cold-warrior Kremlin-watchers must be in disarray. Pluralism (albeit "socialist")? Elections with choice of candidates? Unofficial organizations? Spontaneous demonstrations, even strikes? Genuine debates in the Party? Release of (nearly) all political prisoners? A constitutional court? A legal order? One way to preserve the established stereotypes is to pretend that this is all a fraud, a pretence designed to fool credulous Westerners. I hope that the evidence presented here—and it is a small fraction of what is available—will convince all but the most blinkered reader that *glasnost'* is real. That is *not* to say that the promises of *perestroika* have been fulfilled, that there already is a legal order, that all prisoners of conscience have been released (Burlatsky and his committee are publicly urging that they should be), that "refuseniks" have all got exit visas, that real elections are the rule, or that there is full freedom of the press (and in this respect the provinces are far behind Moscow). No. All Soviet reformers agree that there is a long way to go, that there are many obstacles, that counterattacks from "conservatives" are not only possible but actually happening. Tatiana Zaslavskaya, in a conversation with me, said that there is bound to be opposition, and the fact that there is, that sparks are flying, is evidence that serious reform *is* being attempted. The "cold-warrior" interpretation excluded even the possibility of the attempt. The system could not, according to that view, produce a Gorbachev. In fact, judging from remarks quoted in Chapter 7, it very nearly didn't—it was a close-run thing.

What sort of society do the reformers have as a goal? I am not sure that they know, and certainly there is no clearly defined model, economic or political. The views of Bykov, quoted above, are much clearer about what is *not* wanted ("ostrich", "fox", "bear", "technocrat") than about what is. The idea is to let the people choose, guided by reform-minded leaders, with greater freedom, legal guarantees, a (limited) free market, with the Party still ruling, but in a quite different way, within the law and through elected institutions, with a much freer press and intellectual life. Is all this a viable mixture? Is the economic reform package which is emerging implementable? (No one pretends that it has been already implemented.) Many questions, and few answers, yet, which can be made with confidence.

Much can go wrong. There is an interval, dangerous for an author, between sending a manuscript to the printer and its final emergence. So much is happening. Two dangers lurk in the near future, in my opinion. One is an outburst of nationalism, this time (unlike the quarrel between the Azeris and the Armenians) directed at Moscow control. Just where this might happen is a matter of guesswork. Also, the Russian nationalism around *Pamyat'* could get out of hand. The other is a riot by some large group of workers as a consequence of a too-rigid imposition of financial discipline, which could result in wage cuts, especially if these coincide with the long-delayed rise in retail prices of basic foodstuffs. If such things were to happen, there could be a political crisis, perhaps involving the position of Gorbachev himself, and so of *glasnost'*. This seems to me unlikely. But Gorbachev may have to make some compromises, and these may compromise some part of the reform process. Anyhow, this is a book about *glasnost'*, and I do not have to speculate about the outcome of the reforms.

What new revelations will the next months bring? Some items are already on the agenda. The 1988 examination in history has been cancelled, and a new textbook will have to appear, if only as a stopgap. Soon the principal remaining "white patches" will have to be filled. How many were arrested, shot, detained in Gulag? How many peasants died in 1930–33? What were Soviet losses in killed and wounded in the war? What were the real demographic data in the thirties and in the first postwar years? The process of rehabilitating victims and canceling false legal verdicts will go on. (Zinoviev and Kamenev were finally reported cleared of *all* their "crimes"; *Pravda*, 5 Aug. 1988.) Presumably, we will soon hear that the other well-known trials—of the mensheviks, of the "Industrial party", the "Shakhty" trial—were the frauds that they were. We may at any time hear more about what really happened at the 17th Party Congress, and about the Kirov murder. There is a proposal for the posthumous expulsion of Stalin from the party, which is as logical as (though less probable than) the postumous readmission to the Party of Bukharin, which really has happened! We may see, by contrast, the granting of a petition (referred to by D. Granin in his above-cited article) to strip Leningrad University of the name of Zhdanov, which it bears, perhaps at the same time as the repudiation of the infamous "cultural" decrees of 1946–48 with which he was associated and which formally have yet to be repealed (in fact both of these things happened almost simultaneously in October 1988). A monument to Stalin's victims will surely now be designed. Where should it be located? (One correspondent pointed out that his victims resided all over the USSR, so there should be one in every town!) Maybe Gorky will again be Nizhni Novgorod, and Kalinin will turn back into Tver. Guilt for the Katyn massacre may well be admitted, and blamed on Stalin and Beria. It could be pointed out that Soviet officer-victims were far more numerous than were the Poles.

The next statistical annual, the first to be put out by the reorganized Statistics Committee, should publish many new figures, including data on crime (now partially appearing), accidents, diseases, more details on labour, wages, overtime, crop losses, the budget deficit, and—surely due very soon—the real levels of military expenditure.

Nationality problems will be further illuminated following the Central Committee plenum devoted to the subject, with a debate on the powers of national republics under a revised Constitution. The draft Constitution was published in October 1988 and is being debated in the press as I write these lines. Gorbachev has become president. The votes on this issue in the Supreme Soviet were unanimous in the old style, but at its subsequent meeting a number of deputies did vote against government proposals, notably against one which regulated public meetings and demonstrations. Thus, an important precedent was set: votes against are legitimate at last. We should learn more about real public opinion from the new institute headed by Zaslavskaya. A new law on religion will probably be discussed and promulgated, authorizing charitable works and some limited opportunities for religious education, if only in the home.

In agriculture, the "agroindustrial complex" bureaucracy must surely be drastically trimmed, its powers and staff surely cut, and the policy of creating small cooperatives and family units pressed forward, with still more publicity devoted to exposing the obstruction of these measures. We might also see a further substantial reduction in the functions and staffing of industrial ministries. But the process of economic reform is slow and is likely to remain so, given all the difficulties involved.

Is the process already irreversible? It is too soon to tell, but I would have thought that in matters connected with culture and history the genie is truly out of the bottle, and maybe the bottle has been thrown away. Only within a disaster scenario, justifying a state of emergency, can one see a future for the neo-Stalinist "bears" or "cavalrymen". Such a scenario cannot be excluded, given all the uncertainties surrounding political and economic change, and the unpredictable effects of being able to speak freely and to organize unofficial groups and protests. There is, after all, a lot to protest about.

It is too much to expect the transformation of the USSR into a Western-style democracy. I would go along with Archie Brown's definition: "a more enlightened authoritarian regime . . . in which some elements of pluralism are to be found". At a recent conference I attended, a Soviet scholar said, "We live in an enlightened dictatorship, in which enlightenment is in short supply." It remains a one-party state, and no one is about to abolish the KGB. In his speech to the 19th Party Conference, M. Ulyanov expressed a widespread feeling when he stressed how much depends on Gorbachev personally. This was not at all a form of flattery, at a conference where paeans of praise for the leader were conspicuously absent. It was a widely felt recognition that both *glasnost'* and *perestroika* would not have got off the ground at all had Gorbachev not won the leadership in April 1985, and that the process of change might stall if he were, for any reason, to vanish. His vision of a more civilized and more open society is one which we should welcome.

Finally, I would like to repeat a point made in the Preface: it is possible that some readers will draw the wrong conclusion from this book. It might appear to them to be a long catalogue of crimes, suffering, inefficiencies, illegalities, abuses, falsifications, errors, and omissions, and as such a compendium for the use of anti-Soviet propagandists. This is not so. My object is to draw attention to the truly dramatic transformation wrought by and reflected in *glasnost'*, the openness and honesty with which painful issues of past and present are being publicly discussed. It is not "anti-Soviet" to say that millions of peasants died in the famine of 1933, or that most senior officers were shot on the eve of the war, or that many laws are not observed and that the health service is in a mess. These are facts. It was the suppression of these facts that reflected badly on the Soviet leadership and media, and conversely it reflects well on them that they are speaking out about matters formerly hidden from view. Indeed, some readers may make a contrary complaint: that I have provided too favourable a picture by my stress on the extent of *glasnost'*. There is thus the possibility of displeasing everybody, the pro and the anti. It is a fact that Soviet intellectual life, the media, literature, public and published discourse, have become transformed in ways which seemed unthinkable a few years ago. It is also a fact, potentially a disturbing one, that, to cite Martin Walker of the *Guardian*, writing in *Marxism Today* (June 1988) "the folk doing well out of Gorbachev's *perestroika* are the chattering classes, never terribly popular with the lads on the shop floor. All this *glasnost'* is exciting and fulfilling for the intellectuals, the media, the film-makers, and novelists and playwrights and rock musicians . . . and get-rich-quick coop enterprises." This he contrasts with "the worried Soviet worker facing a three-hour queue to buy a bottle of vodka, with a hole in [his] pay-packet, an empty larder and the prospect of being redeployed to another and possibly worse job". Gorbachev is well aware that the masses must be brought into the process of *perestroika*, that they must identify with it. I will end with the words with which Martin Walker ended his article: "The unpredictable has returned to public life. Real politics have revived in the Soviet Union. The effect is exhilarating." The result is unforecastable.

The old ideological reference points are disintegrating before our eyes. A Soviet philosopher at a recent conference spoke of a collapse of a whole weltanschauung (*mirovozrenie*) at a speed unique in history. And as I send this text to the press *Novyi mir* publishes a truly fundamental critique by Igor Klyamkin, who is quoted at length in Chapter 3. He calls for an "ideological *perestroika*", a complete reassessment of the entire system of social values, in the direction of "individual self-development". He openly and explicitly criticises Lenin for giving the party and its unity priority over democracy. The article is accompanied by an editorial note distancing itself from the author. No doubt there will be a reply. The essential point is that the open debate is now concerned with the very essence, the fundamentals, of the Soviet system—this for the first time in living memory. What kind of society did they have, and where are they now? Where are they going? One has a feeling that no one quite knows. Does this matter? After all, where are *we* going? In the Soviet Union it does matter, since the legitimacy of party rule rests upon its role of leading the people towards a goal. What is urgently called for is a redefinition of what that goal is.

Meanwhile, in *Neva*, No. 1, 1989, S. Andreyev speaks of the danger that "*perestroika* will end in failure" and that "we may miss the last real chance of putting things right without having recourse to a regime similar to a military dictatorship". Change, in his view, is being sabotaged by the new ruling class, which controls the economy and has interpenetrated with the party apparatus. He urges the creation of a new political force, since, in his words, "it is the party leadership which has brought the country to economic crisis and moral decline". He sharply criticises the recently adopted constitutional changes. Which is further proof, if proof is needed, that *glasnost'* has gone far beyond improving communications between government and people. But where will it all end? Let us hold our breath and see.

# Appendix: A Guide to Soviet Publications

Below are some particulars of the newspapers and periodicals cited in this book. These are, needless to say, only a very small part of the total number published in the USSR.

## Dailies

*Pravda*: organ of the Central Committee of the Party
*Sovetskaya Rossiya*: as above, but primarily covering the Russian federation (RSFSR)
*Izvestiya*: government and Supreme Soviet organ (*Nedelya*—weekly supplement)
*Komsomolskaya Pravda*: communist youth daily (*Sobesednik*—weekly supplement)

## Weeklies

*Literaturnaya gazeta*: literary and social-political organ of the Writers' Union
*Ogonyok*: illustrated popular weekly
*Kommunist* (fortnightly): Party theoretical journal
*Literaturnaya Rossiya*: organ of the Writers' Union of RSFSR.
*Moskovskie novostie*: Russian version of foreign-language paper from Novosti press agency
*Argumenty i fakty* (All-Union "Knowledge" Society)

## "Thick Literary Monthlies"

*Regarded as bold and progressive*

*Novyi mir* (Moscow)
*Druzhba narodov* (Moscow)
*Oktyabr'* (Moscow)
*Znamya* (Moscow)
*Yunost'* (Moscow)

*Regarded as nationalist-conservative*

*Molodaya guardiya* (Moscow)
*Nash sovremennik* (Moscow)

*Provincial*

*Neva* (Leningrad)*
*Don* (Rostov)
*Daugava* (Riga)*
*Zvezda* (Leningrad)
* *Also regarded as bold and progressive*

## Academic Journals

*Voprosy ekonomiki* (Institute of Economics)
EKO (*Ekonomika i organizatsiya promyshlennogo proizvodstva*) (Siberian
Academy, Novosibirsk)
*Mirovaya ekonomika i mezhdunarodnye otnosheniya* (Institute of World
Economics and Politics)
*Voprosy istorii* (Institute of History)
*Voprosy istorii UPSS* (Institute of Marxism-Leninism)
*Sovetskoe gosudarstvo i pravo* (Institute of State and Law)

## Popular Science and Current Affairs

*Nauka i zhizn* (All-Union "Knowledge" Society)
*Knizhnoe obozreniye* (organ of state publishing houses)
*Rabochii klass i sovremennyi mir* (Institute of World Labour Movement)

# Index